Linda McCullough-Thew left school at the age of 14 to work in the village store which she described in her first book, *Pit Village and the Store* (Pluto Press, 1985). In 1942 she joined the ATS in which she worked on anti-aircraft radar – 'Ack-ack'. She subsequently transferred to the Army Education Corps and it is these experiences which form the basis for this book. When she left the army at the end of the Second World War she took a teachers' training course in Newcastle. After a career teaching in a number of schools and counselling, Linda McCullough-Thew turned to full-time writing. Her work has been broadcast, she has written short stories, wrote the script for and appeared in the film of her first book and is at present engaged on a full-length novel. This is her second book.

Linda McCullough Thew

From Store to War

Pluto Press
LONDON

First published in 1987 by Pluto Press,
11-21 Northdown St, London N1 9BN

Copyright © Linda McCullough Thew, 1987

British Library Cataloguing in Publication Data
McCullough Thew, Linda
From store to war.
   1. Coal miners — England — Northumberland   2. Northumber
land — Social life and customs
   I. Title
   942.8'8082   DA670.N8
ISBN 0-7453-0251-3

Set in 10/12 Plantin by AKM Associates (UK) Ltd,
Ajmal House, Hayes Road, Southall, London
Printed and bound in Great Britain by Billing & Sons Ltd,
Hylton Road, Worcester

To all those who served on
Ack-ack
during the Second World War
particularly
The GL wallahs of 625 Battery
and
to the Education bods
who ushered in the peace

Contents

Preface

Most of us have, at some time, been in a situation something similar to this.

It is a small gathering of friends. The general conversation has turned on 'sleep'. With regard to this topic, the world, it seems, is divided into two groups: those who can sleep undisturbed through an earthquake and those who lie awake sleepless till the pale grey dawn begins to make its presence obvious, when they fall into a light doze only to be wakened by the uproar three miles away occasioned by a bird fluttering its wings. The world is so arranged that a member of one group is married to a member of another. Such a couple are Mr and Mrs A.

'One morning about three years ago,' says Mrs A, 'I had just dozed off when I heard a noise. John was still snoring his head off so I got up and went to the window and had a look and there, at the bottom of the garden, was a pullman carriage on its side. I ....'

'Just a minute,' puts in B. 'Was that rail crash when the X ran into the Y? Because if it was, that happened ten years ago.'

'No,' says C. 'The XY rail crash happened before that. You're thinking of the WZ crash.'

'Just a minute,' says D, 'I'll tell you exactly. I keep a dairy. I'll just go upstairs and find out.'

In the discussion about the date, Mrs A's story of exactly what it felt like to be awakened by a noise and finding out that a twisted and tortured wreck with its resultant mass of terrified, injured and dying lay at the bottom of her garden, is lost. For her purpose the date was immaterial. All that was necessary was that it was light enough for her to see. Nor, as she helped in the immediate aftermath, was it necessary for her to discover exactly who she helped or who directed her actions.

Thus it is, that in this book, I have been deliberately vague about most of my postings. For those who like the facts, I am sure that somewhere in the War Office, there are detailed records of the movements of 625 Battery and other batteries in 184 Regiment.

Similarly, I have been reluctant to supply the names of everyone with whom I came in contact. Partly, this is because I have forgotten. Often, I can hear a voice and recognise a face, but I cannot supply the name. More frequently I have merely wished to protect the individual.

The book is an account of my memories and experiences supported by note-books, letters and scraps of paper that have lain gathering dust for upwards of forty years. That most of these are still extant is due mostly to my mother, Margaret Summers. Like me, she was a hoarder and could not bear to throw anything out, not even the most forlorn scrap of paper.

I should also like to thank Joyce Madden for the information she gave me regarding her first husband , Billy Tippins.

My thanks are also due to Joan Summers, who laboured long over a red-hot typewriter that my illegible scrawl be turned into legible typescript in the original manuscript, and to Margaret Brett, who coped womanfully with the edited version, dealing with cuts and inserts so that the surgery did not show.

Lastly, my grateful thanks go to my husband, Bill Thew, and my son Malcolm McCullough for their invaluable help with the illustrations.

Linda McCullough-Thew
19 February 1985

1.Crisis

'Well. How do you feel now that there isn't going to be a war?

'Well – I—.' For a moment I was nonplussed as I tried to focus my attention in the speaker. In truth, I had hardly been aware of the Munich Crisis. I was, at the time, going through a crisis of my own – what would now be called a common-or-garden adolescent identity crisis. It had so concentrated my thoughts and occupied the forefront of my mind that everything else was out of focus and blurred.

'I – I'm glad, of course,' I stammered out.

This personally confused and unhappy time is almost impossible to describe because words themselves are so ambiguous. Put briefly, what I was trying to do was to bring myself to that state of life to which, it seemed, I had been called. I ought to be thinking of 'getting myself' a decent lad and be turning my thoughts towards settling down and bringing up a family. There were two young men, canny lads, who 'wanted to be serious', but I could not bring myself to go out with either, even on a friendly basis.

I was angry with myself because I felt this way. As far as I knew none of my other friends had any doubts or qualms. I was no different from hundreds of others who had to follow a course marked out for them. Most young lads were destined for the pits, especially if their fathers worked there. Of these, some followed the only occupation they had ever wanted. Others went because they had no other choice. There were some parents, however, whose ambition it was *not* to allow their sons to go down the pit, and they made great personal sacrifice to see that their hopes were realized.

The options open to most girls were equally narrow.

This personal crisis was made easier in some ways by the fact that I lived such a structured life. From Monday to Saturday I worked in a busy shop. But my evenings and Sundays were free. It was then that this resevoir of repressed energy would begin to boil and bubble and I felt so close to bursting that I had to have some release.

And so I walked . Or ran. I concentrated on using my body to the point where the physical conflict equalled the mental conflict: helped by walking along familiar, almost deserted roads, I seemed to be able to think more clearly. Actually I hardly skimmed the surface as far as thinking went. I had neither the skill nor the knowledge to do more. I pined for the unattainable, not knowing what this was; an ideal, but what kind of ideal? I had been brought up to please, at school, at home, at work. Sometimes, I found that when I had done nothing but try to please, I was being told off. Yet, when I felt anger, I could not express it. It seemed to me that men and boys growing up could say what they liked and get angry without cause and be wooed back into an agreeable frame of mind, a state of affairs somehow denied me. Thus I ran or walked till all the rebellion seemed to have been quelled within me, and the state of mind to which I had brought myself appeared to coincide with the outward appearance I presented to my restricted world. I still didn't feel I was cut out for what appeared to lie ahead but no escape seemed possible, so, again and again, I determined to conform and not to behave in this stupid fashion. My upbringing demanded nothing else. We were reared to an appreciation of duty with no suggestion at all that we had any rights. We must always put others before ourselves: it was sinful to question this doctrine. We had no concept of our real selves.

One telling incident happened about this time. One night, as I prepared to go out, my mother asked, 'Where are you off to?'

'A walk,' I said. 'I'll not be long.'

'By yourself?'

'Yes.'

'Your father came home yesterday and he was a bit upset. More than a bit. Somebody had collared him at the pit and said, "I saw your daughter out walking by herself round by the Dene. What's the matter with her? Can she not get herself a mate [friend]?" You know what your father's like. It upset him.'

'I just like walking quick. I'm a quick walker. Everybody else dawdles when they go for a walk. As if tomorrow would do. And none of my friends like walking as much as I do. If you say, "Let's go for a walk," they think you mean up and down the street to look at the shops and see who you can meet.'

'Yes. I told him it was nothing to worry about. But you know what he's like.'

I did not wish to cause my father any further upset so I told my mother I wouldn't walk round there again.

What I then had to look for was somewhere to walk where it seemed I had a purpose. To this end I tried walking up one row and down another, but here there was no privacy. I was hemmed in by the houses themselves on the one side and the coal-houses, netties and washhouses on the other. Also, standing and smoking a reflective pipe, leaning the while on the bottom part of the stable door or simply leaning on the fence to observe a section of the world go by, was a popular pastime in the rows.

And so I looked for another refuge and found it, under my nose so to speak, in bed. I had stopped being afraid of the dark; now it was a comforting friend. Lying in bed shut off from the rest of the world I was cocooned and safe, mistress of my own thoughts and dreams. The danger was that this became a reality and the reality was a dream world to be got through.

I soon did realize, however, that the 'peace in our time' was illusory. At home my mother was building up a stock of sugar and of tinned goods, though we hardly ever ate of the latter. My parents owned a house in Dene View. The tenants decided to move out and return to Scotland, whence they'd come. My father and mother decided to move in. My mother was convinced war was not far away and this was one of the rainy days against which they had saved. The house in Dene View was, therefore, fitted out with new furniture, carpets and curtains.

The government were also sure that war was not very far away and they mounted a campaign to increase the ranks of those in civil defence. I was one among the thousands who responded. I attended a course of lectures and passed an examination in Air Raid Precautions(ARP), so my certificate tells me. I was awarded my ARP badge and encouraged to take a course in elementary first aid.

I did so. I and countless others. We filled the classes to overflowing. There were insufficient splints, bandages, etc. to go round so that we had to take turns at the practical work. When the course was over, we were told there would be an oral examination. We were to go into the exam room in pairs and we would each be asked two questions. I was paired off with a woman of large proportions. She was a thoroughly capable woman, domestically speaking, but the thought of having to take an examination reduced her to a quivering mass.

'I never slept a wink. Not a wink since I heard about this exam,' she said. ' Before I came out he gave me a right stiff glass of whisky. "Get that down you," he said. I took it but I'm in such state it hadn't a chance. D'ye mind, hinny, if he asks me first? I'm shaking like a jelly.'

I would have said a blancmange. She had more substance than a jelly. However, I agreed that she should go first and presently our turn came and we were called in.

The examiner was a pit deputy on night shift and Pressed For Time was what he was.

'I'm first,' said my partner, wiping the perspiration from her forehead.

'Right,' said the examiner. 'Now, I'm going two ask you two questions. Are you ready? Right? What do they call the very fine tubes that bring the blood to the skin?'

She put her hands to her temples. 'Just a minute. Just a minute,' she said. 'Hold on. I've got it. I've got it. Gardens. Something to do with gardens. Caterpillars.' And she sat back with her eyes closed exhausted after all this exertion.

'Aye,' he said drawing his breath in. 'Near enough. Capillaries. Now for the second question. How would you treat a burnt finger?'

She opened her eyes as her answer came out in a rush. 'Roll it in a mat. Have I passed?'

The examiner looked down at the book in his hand and considered the matter briefly. 'Aye.' he said at last. 'You have,' and then he looked at me and said, ' and you have an' all.'

Looking at my certificate I realize that I was credited merely with having attended a course of instruction at the Ashington branch of the St John's Ambulance Association and was qualified to render 'first aid to the injured'.

2. At War

'I'll tell you what it is, Arch. Mark my words. Listen now. As soon as war is declared they'll be straight over here and we'll all be bombed to smithereens. I don't care what they say. Them Germans know all about Ashington pits. They've been here. They've seen them for themselves. They'll be over here. Mark my words. We'll be the first to get it and no make game.'

Glum silence greeted this decisive speech. Only the clock on the sideboard carried on doggedly doing its job. The rest of us just sat there, my father, my mother and I at the table where the remains of supper still stood. The speaker, a workmate of my father's who had just 'dropped in' on his way from the pit, stood near the door. Having delivered his speech he straightened up, looked at the ceiling and put the hand that had sawed the air to give emphasis to his words back into his pocket.

The last news bulletin on the wireless had brought us no more comfort, no further ray of hope, than had the previous one, or the one before that. Our interest now was restricted to news bulletins. The time between one bulletin and the next was filled in with records and Sandy Mcpherson at the theatre organ. We were further hemmed in by the blackout put up that night for the first time – at first so near to total that restrictions had to be relaxed.

It was Friday night. It had been busier than ever at the shop. The stock of put-up sugar which, under normal circumstances, would have filled the sugar fixtures and seen us through Saturday and into next week, was gone. The fixtures were also looking bare of certain tinned goods. The boss, Mr Joe Dunn, had summed up the situation and marked off the amount of sugar and so on that could be sold the following day. We had stayed behind to bring this stock forward and to fill a number of two-pound bags of sugar. Only one to a customer, the Boss had decreed, and 'when them four fixtures have gone – we're out of sugar.'

'I hear,' said my father's friend, still poised for leaving but obviously without any serious intention of actually going, 'the Terriers [Territorials] are moving out of the drill hall.'

'I think I'll have a walk down,' I said getting up, and went to put on my coat. So changed were circumstances that no one remarked on the lateness of the hour or the fact that I wanted to go out at all.

Outside there was nothing but unrelieved darkness. No warm friendly glows from back-end windows, no shafts of light from opened doors. The heavily shaded street lamps did no more than emphasize the darkness.

I knew all about troops leaving for the front and the send-off they were given. I knew all about the Great War. The war to end all wars. And here we were on the brink of starting this insanity all over again. I knew about the awfulness of trench warfare. I'd seen pictures on the screen.

A depressing drizzle began to fall as I groped my way to the drill hall. Here there were no numbers of people lining the road to wave the brave troops off.

In spite of the black-out regulations, the drill hall door was open and a shaft of light illuminated part of the pavement and the dispirited heavy drizzle. A man and a boy watched a waiting truck being loaded at intervals. They stood independent of each other outside the shaft of light . I also stood by myself outside the lightened area. It was all right for the Terrriers to break the regulations in this emergency, but we had no such exemption.

From time to time a soldier came out and put a bundle in the waiting truck. Less frequently a sergeant came into the lighted opening and issued a command. I couldn't distinguish the words. I don't really think the command was necessary. I think that he was merely emphasizing the gravity of the occasion and the fact that he was in charge.

Presently, I moved away and made for home through the main street now black and shuttered and seemingly deserted. I paused near the Presbyterian church, which, like the Salvation Army barracks and the Methodist church, was near the pavement. But, for what I had in mind, this was cheating and I knew it. I was Church of England.

At the store corner opposite the church I stopped. Overhead the night sky had been pierced by search-light beams. I watched their jerky, stiff-legged dance taking a little comfort from the light although it shed no radiance. Suddenly and silently the beams shut off and everything was blacker and bleaker than before. Alone, I could put the moment off no longer.

The church looked haunting enough on a normal night when, at least, there was a street lamp to draw the passer-by away from thoughts of what lay beyond in the silent churchyard. Bereft of this warm glow there was only now the bulk of the church and the slight dripping of the dark, mournful trees.

I forced myself to enter the gates of the church and walk up the gravel path, the crunching of my footsteps sounding like the tread of an unseen traveller rather than of my quaking self.

It wasn't just the fanciful terror of the night that filled me with jittery trepidation, nor my lack of courage. My embarrassment for what I was about to do filled me with a reluctance to go any further. I was about to speak aloud to God of my deepest feelings – and this was difficult. There was something in it of self-reproach. These intimate things were not to be expressed aloud even to God. The prayers we said aloud every week, or even every day, were the well-known accepted ones in a familiar framework rendered worn and comfortable by constant use.

I reached the church door and groped for the ring handle. I forced myself to breathe regularly. I tried turning the handle but very lightly, ignoring the fact that it needed a firm heavy movement to lift the bar at all and I persuaded myself the building was locked. I put two hands on the ring and closed my eyes and tried to ward off the blackness closing in on me; the tombstones and the ghostly night creeping nearer.

Please God, I prayed, *don't let there be a war. If there's no war. I promise I will get myself a decent lad and get married and look after him and the house and have a family and look after them. I won't grumble or feel sorry for myself any more. Only, please God, no war. Please. Please. No war. Amen.*

I stood still for a few moments and then made myself walk back, puny, arrogant, mortal that I was. As if a holocaust could be stayed because of a ludicrous bargain put forward by one insignificant, inconsequential morsel of humanity! And yet, how many such simple prayers born of sincerity were being wafted heavenward then and throughout the next 36 hours.

Saturday was no less busy than we'd anticipated. The sugar had 'run out' by dinner-time. That didn't actually mean we hadn't any. There was a reserve stock (less than usual) in the warehouse and in a back-shop fixture there were still some two-pound bags.

We counter-hands had suddenly become important. With the sugar gone we were flattered, appealed to, told sad tales of why there was no sugar in the house and subjected to red-faced declarations of misplaced loyalty when we stuck to the fact that there was no sugar. Sometimes the vehement declaration that we were out of sugar preceded the remark, 'But I'll tell you what we do have, the washing soda you wanted,' and in mutual understanding a parcel wrapped in rough brown paper would be handed over. 'Under-the-counter' trading and rationing had been anticipated by many months. Needlessly, as it turned out. Our stock was replenished in full and there was no real shortage for the remainder of the year.

On Sunday morning I went to church, sitting in the elevated choir-stalls. Before the service started a contingent of Territorials marched smartly in and sat at the back. The service began and after a while the door opened and there was a little whispered conversation, after which the verger took his wand and walked slowly up the main aisle towards the vicar, Mr Samuel Davidson. We were in the middle of responses. The vicar stopped chanting and we stopped responding and every eye followed the verger. He acknowledged the cross before he spoke to Mr Davidson. The conversation over, the verger returned from whence he came and the vicar stood in the centre of the chancel steps.

'It grieves me to have to tell you all,' he said in his soft, intimate voice, 'that we are now at war with Germany.'

In common with the remainder of the congregation, I'm sure, I tried to put down the lump in my throat and keep the tears from my eyes. When Mr Davidson had finished speaking, the officer in charge of the Territorials got up smartly. His men followed suit and they marched out of the church.

'I think,' said the vicar as the door closed behind the last soldier, 'we'd better all go to our homes. May God bless you all.'

The organist, Mr George Turnbull, having a feeling for the

occasion, played the chord for 'O God, our help in ages past' and we stood up and sang with all the fervour we could manage before we left the church.

Once outside, everyone quickly dispersed. I hadn't gone far when the alert sounded. It was even as had been said. The war had just started and we were about to be bombed out of existence. It didn't seem right that I should simply go home and wait for it to happen. I was a member of the ARP with a first aid certificate to boot. I must be needed somewhere. But where? I turned back and saw a man coming out of a nearby house in a purposeful hurry.

'Where should we go?' I called as I ran up to him.

'You can please your bloody self where you go, hinny,' he said. 'I'm off to the White House.' [A working man's club]

Before I got home the all-clear had sounded.

When my father came home he said, 'I've a message for you from Major Richards. You haven't got to do anything this afternoon. No filling sandbags or anything like that. You've to be at Wansbeck School at five o'clock and have your tea first.'

I was completely taken aback by this news. Major Richards was the Woodhorn Colliery manager, as well as a senior officer in the ARP. I think God got in touch with him. That he even knew I existed came as a shock.

'Why? What do I have to do?' I asked when I found my tongue.

'I don't know. I've told you as much as I know. I must say I was surprised but you don't ask questions of Major Richards, or at least I don't.'

It was a glorious hot afternoon. Like all the others who had no specific task that day I walked slowly up and down the main street. Later I presented myself at Wansbeck School.

'Ah, yes,' said the Great Man, 'we are having two meetings here to enrol more people for civil defence. Women first, then men. I'm going to talk to them first to tell them of the sort of things they can still do. Then I'll have them come out in single file to tell us what they're volunteering for.'

I had never felt so important in the whole of my life. Somewhere on the sidelines were a group of officials of one sort and another. To this group came Dr Bruce of whom, in my childhood, I'd seen a fair bit because of the smallpox. He came over to me and putting out his hand he cradled my chin with it.

'Ah, Linda,' he said in his gentle Scot's voice, 'you're too young. You're too young to get yourself as involved as this. Give us old ones a chance. You'll get your chance. This war's going to last a long time and it'll see us out. Bide your time and get out and about and enjoy yourself now.'

We already had a sizeable ARP service in Ashington. Today's exercise was intended to recruit those people who, hitherto, were not involved.

Briefly Major Richards spoke of the work of the ARP and its various branches, fire-watchers, wardens, roof-spotters, etc. The women came forward and I took their names and addresses, developing a sort of shorthand that could be filled in later as I went along. The process was repeated for the men volunteers. When they had all given their names and gone, coffee appeared for the Major, Dr Bruce and Mrs Thain, the principal woman present. I, in the meantime, tidied up my sheets of paper and finally gave them to Major Richards together with his silver pencil. Major Richards, Mrs Thain and Dr Bruce then left for Hirst where they were due to do the whole operation over again. My services were no longer needed.

I should have left for home then, having no idea what else to do, except that a woman came forward and said they were making tea. I followed her to what had been someone's office but was now the nerve centre of the Ashington ARP. There were several women sitting around and one man.

They nodded (respectfully, I thought) as I came in. One seat was vacant – the one behind the desk. I took it. Dr Bruce and Major Richards between them placed me on a pedestal, the height of which made me feel giddy and which prevented me from speaking unless I absolutely had to, in case I put my foot in it and gave away what a fraud I really was.

The time was then about half-past eight. Putting out the tea and drinking it took up a certain amount of time and after that we sat looking at each other.

I wondered if this meant we were all, we here in this room, to be paid for our services. I had heard about people at the pit having to take two jobs in the last war. I wondered what we were supposed to do next. Just sit here and wait for the war to actually start? We sat on. And on and on. Nine o'clock. Half-past nine. A quarter to ten. Gosh I was hungry.

'D'ye think,' one woman began, looking in my direction. Everyone became suddenly alert and looked at her and she seemed to falter. 'I only thought,' she went on lamely, 'if nothing is likely to happen I might slip home and make a few sandwiches. Even if anything did happen I'd be soon back. I don't live far. We could have some tea with them. . .' she tailed off.

'It's . . . it's . . . a . . . marvellous idea, I think,' I said cautiously. 'If anything happens we can . . . er . . . hold the fort . . . er . . . so to speak . . . till you get back.'

Suddenly the place was alive with purposeful activity. A man (the caretaker as it turned out) went outside and came back to give it as his opinion that we could take the risk. When they came, we ate the sandwiches saying over and over how good they were and what a good idea it had been. When everything was eaten or cleared away we relapsed again into silence.

Eleven o'clock. Half-past eleven. At quarter to twelve there was a sound of determined purposeful footsteps. The door opened and Mrs Thain stood there thin, aghast, ten feet tall.

'WHAT,' she demanded, ' IS ALL THIS? What on earth are you lot doing here? Do you intend to sit here like dummies for the rest of the war? Get out. Off you go. Such nonsense!'

Like small children caught with our hands in the dog's dinner we scuttled off without looking at each other.

A week after, on Monday morning when I went into work, one of the apprentices came up to me and said, 'Gordon Patton is a relative of yours, is he not?'

Gordon Patton was an extremely nice lad, tall, the middle boy in a family of three. He had just missed going into the militia for which he was glad; he had a burning ambition to enter the police force.

'Only sort of ,' I answered. 'In a distant way. A relative of mine is married to a relative of his but it's not something he wants to acknowledge because I . . .'

'Not now he'll not,' said the apprentice who, I could now see, was bursting with news. 'He's been killed.'

I looked at him open-mouthed and wide-eyed.

'No,' I said finally, shaking my head.

'Yesterday. He was coming through Pegswood on his motorbike in the blackout following the white line in the middle of the road and a lorry was coming the other way and *he* was following the white line an' all. He's in an awful state, the lorry driver. Never saw him he said. Made mincemeat of him before he knew. But Gordon was still conscious. It took a bit of time, but they got him to hospital and managed to get hold of his dad. He was still conscious when the Old Man got there.

"I've made a right job of it this time, Dad," he said. Never spoke again, poor bugger. John Wheatley had the same blood group so they got hold of him and he gave some of his blood. Gordon might have got over it but he'd broken his leg among other things and gas gangrene set in so they took his leg off but it was too much for him. They tell me his father walked up and down outside their house before he could go in and bring himself to tell Gordon's mam. It's a bloody shame. He was a real canny lad. A bit stuck-up, but canny with it.'

Gordon Patton. The first casualty. A bomb had fallen on at least one house in the first week of the war after all.

3. The Phoney War

The weather continued fine and warm and, after a short time, the cinemas and dance halls which had closed when war was declared were in business again.

There were several dance halls in Ashington, of which the Arcade and the Princess Ballroom were the two principal. The latter was the most ornate. It was called after the then Princess Elizabeth and there was a delightful full-length picture of her as a child painted on one wall. One of the restrictions issued after the dance halls opened up again was that no long dresses were to be worn. (In the event of an air raid, long evening dresses would hamper a speedy dash to the air-raid shelters. They would also be unsuitable garb for those who happened to be on duty. When the sirens went, they would have to dash from the dance hall to their posts.)

And so the Phoney War continued.

There was no shortage of food for Christmas and no shortage of gifts to be bought. Rationing began and ration books and coupons became my province as far as the grocery was concerned.

After New Year a bitter winter set in. It was so cold that, on one occasion, when a bucket of warm water had been taken outside to wash down a car, the water froze before the task was completed.

During this time I continued in my duties as an ambulance driver for the ARP. It was a career distinguished only by its complete lack of distinction. Mercifully, I was never called upon to drive one of the coal wagons. In the early days of the war, these had to be emptied during an air raid and brought to the ARP post where they were redesignated 'ambulances' to be driven by ARP drivers.

Before long we were each allocated a car that had been loaned for the duration. Mine was an old black Ford. There was a change in policy too. Instead of the cars remaining in the school playground during air raid, we were instructed to disperse to given points where, if we were needed, a messenger would come to acquaint us of the fact. I turned out for every alert that sounded out of shop hours. My pitch was just outside the Store Killing Shop (The slaughter-house) and eerie was what it was. It had the wide metal roll-type doors (which rattled in sympathy with the guns) before which I faced, the park railings and trees on my right and the end of Wansbeck Store houses on my left.

Most raids took place in the hours of darkness. Ashington never had a raid as such but we were called out whenever the coast or Newcastle was being bombed. There, at my post, often in total darkness and often cold, I sat gazing at the searchlights and the occasional flashes and being grateful for the Ack-ack (anti-aircraft) pounding away defending with all their might this particular corner of our vast empire.

Only once was I called into action. A land-mine had dropped at Lynemouth and thither I was sent. I was asked to take a man to the eye hospital in Newcastle. He had an enormous pad over one eye and a very satisfactory pristine bandage holding it in place. Thank goodness his other eye was all right. The rest of his face was pitted with little splinters of wood. It seems he had been blown from wherever he was when the mine went off on to a garden and had landed on a door.

I was given the address of the hospital. It didn't convey an awful lot to me as, apart from passing my driving test, I'd only been in Newcastle six times to date, and then my interest had centred on the shops, the Stoll and the Empire.

The patient sat on the passenger seat.

'Are you all right?' I asked as we moved off.

'Fine, hinny, fine.'

'Are you in any pain or discomfort?'

'No, pet, no. I'm right as rain. Don't worry yourself about me.'

'Can you see at all?'

'I can see everything there is to see in this blackout. There's nothing wrong with this eye.'

'Do you know much about Newcastle?'

'Canny bit.'

'Do you know where we're going?'

'The eye hospital.'

'Do know where it is?'

'Aye. I think so.'

'Do you mind telling me? I know the way to Newcastle, but after that I'm finished. I didn't even know they had an eye hospital.'

'Oh, yes. Oh, yes. Yes. They've got an eye hospital.'

By this time we'd bumped our way past the appurtenances of the other services that had been summoned to the scene and were out on the open road.

'No, you needn't drive canny for me,' said the patient, whom I'll call Jim. 'I'm not that bad.'

'This is just about as fast as she'll go ,' I said. 'She's not in her first youth.'

'Well. There's nothing spoiling,' Jim returned agreeably.

He spoke prematurely. As we travelled, all did not seem to be well. To date, as far as I know, this was the longest journey that car had undertaken since it came under the aegis of the ARP. I stopped and lifted the bonnet and stepped back smartly as I was greeted with a burst of hot, angry, hissing steam.

Jim made to get out of the car.

'Sit still,' I said. 'Please. Remember you are the patient. You might be a lot worse than you think you are. I've been losing water. I've got a leaky radiator. All I have to do is get some water from somewhere and fill her up.'

The shadow of a cottage loomed not far away and thither I went and knocked on the door. No answer. I knocked louder. An upstairs window opened and a voice screamed, 'Get away. Get away this minute. I'll shoot. I'll shoot with gun. Bang. Bang.'

'I only want—' I tried.

'Go away.' The screams rose higher. 'I'll shoot. Go away. Bang. Bang. Shoot. Go away.'

I retreated into the shadows and walked away a litle bit. When I heard the window go up I stopped and went quietly back and fished about. There was an outside tap and among some rubbish I found. an old tin kettle which I seized. Taking it to the tap, I turned the water on. A stream of ice went down my front. The kettle had at least two holes.

Keeping one hand over the biggest hole I scuttled back to the car.

'What was all that in aid of?' asked Jim as I got as much water into the radiator as I could.

'Stupid idiot. He thought I was a German parachutist. I ask you. Do I look like a nun?' (German parachutists were at that point supposed to come down dressed as nuns.)

'Not at the moment,' he said.

'He was going to shoot me, so he said, but how he was going to do it with a broomstick I don't know.'

I made two more trips and decided to keep the kettle just in case. Finally, we jerked off and hardly had I begun to gather speed (a relative term) when the door dropped off.

I stopped the car, retrieved the door, let down the window and attempted to drive the car with one hand and hang on to the door with the other. It nearly took my arm off. Finally, I parked the door in the back seat.

Dawn was already breaking as we negotiated the streets of Newcastle. It was daylight when we finally fetched up at the hospital. Jim got out of the car and shook hands with me.

'Thanks,' he said. 'I'm grateful.'

I didn't think it politic to ask him what he was grateful for.

I got home to find everyone knew more about the night's events than I did. Any adventure I had to recount was anaemic by comparison. I went up to bed to recover my wasting strength.

Not only did I turn out for alerts, in common with everyone else I did my stint at the post in the evenings and at weekends.

At that time in Ashington, there was a group of men and women who were supposed to live it up. They were a 'fast set', in the vernacular of the day. They were probably no more than young people in their middle to late twenties who, being single, had sufficient money and freedom to please themselves what they did in the field of enjoyment. Certainly they were out of my ken, being older and much more sophisticated than I.

One Sunday before the end of the Phoney War, in the early evening shortly before I was due to come off duty, two of their number arrived to see me. It appeared the officers of an RAF station had given them an invitation to visit their mess. They had managed to get hold of a car but they had no driver. They had heard I could drive. Would I go with them to drive the car?

I was able to say quite firmly that I couldn't possibly because I was on duty where I would have to stay till 11 p.m.

'Oh, no, you haven't,' said the man who'd just come in to relieve me. 'You can go now. I'm here. Now just get yourself away and enjoy yourself. Let your back hair down for a change.'

Driving a strange car filled with people I didn't know, intent on spending an evening drinking, was just about as far away from enjoyment as I could get at that moment.

'Well,' I said lamely, 'it's not that only. When I said eleven o'clock I'd forgotten for the moment that I was ending my duty, not beginning it. That being the case, I'll have to get back home now. I'm expected and I promised my mother faithfully to give her a hand tonight.'

'There's no one in,' they said. 'We went there first. A woman who came out to see what we wanted said your brother's up at Nicholson's and your mother and father have gone out. She thinks they've gone to the Hyslops. They looked as if they were going that way, and she says if they have they'll not be back till supper-time at the earliest. She told us you were here and once you got home, you'd likely stay in.'

'Yes . . . but . . . yes . . . but . . . yes. But even if they're out they'll

26

be back by ten o'clock. And I've got to be home by then otherwise I'm in trouble. They won't know where I am. When they don't know where I am I've got to be in by 10.'

'Then there's no problem,' they said. 'We'll be back long before ten. The sooner we get away, the sooner we'll get back. So it's up to you.'

'I don't know what you're hesitating for,' said the man who had come to relieve me. 'Some folks don't know their luck. Here you are, got a chance to enjoy yourself handed on a plate and you turn it down.'

I went. They were all very pleasant and agreeable and said how kind it was of me to give up my Sunday night, but they understood I'd had nothing else to do. The man next to me knew the way and although the car was strange I managed not too badly.

We got to the air force base and the officers who'd given the invitation were ferreted out. I got the feeling they were a little taken aback but they quickly recovered and made us welcome. I was given a drink in the mess after which I faded into one of the tables.

After a while the grin on my face became wearisome and difficult to maintain. As everyone had forgotten I was there I let the grin go and just sat there while the laughter became louder and louder and the time ticked by and I grew more and more uneasy. I realized we weren't going to be home by 10 o'clock. Indeed, we weren't going to be away by 10 o'clock and my discomfort became acute, but there was nothing I could do but sit.

Suddenly, I realized I was being spoken to. So relieved was I that I was aware only of the interest and concern of the person speaking and I blurted out, 'Yes, I am a bit uneasy. We were supposed to be back in Ashington by ten. My folks will be worried. Not only that, I'm getting worried about the car. I drove it here in daylight. Now it's dark and I don't even know how to put the lights on. I've never driven it before.'

'First things first, Cinderella,' he said. 'I'll see that a message is sent to your home if you can tell me how to get in touch.'

My father, who with two others shared a permanent duty at the colliery telephone exchange, was not due to start till 6 in the morning. However the exchange, like every other area of the colliery, had a messenger, a young lad 14 or 15 years of age whose job it was to be a dogsbody and do the instant bidding of his superiors. He would take a message. So I gave the colliery number and asked if a message could be sent to my parents to say that I was with a Miss Y and I would be home late but they were not to worry.

Thereafter we went outside and together we looked the car over identifying all its working parts. Finally, I got into the driving seat and drove around the camp in company with my mentor, to test whether or not I was in complete command of the vehicle.

'And now,' said my companion, 'let us see if we can speak to someone who will remind the revellers we all have beds to go to.'

While we hung around waiting for the others to sort themselves out my friend, whom I shall call Jeremy Browne, said,

'Is the telephone number you gave me the one where you can be contacted?'

'No,' I said, 'that's my father's.'

'Do you have access to a telephone?'

They were all ready to go by this time. Not wanting to give any explanations, I gave the shop number.

Fortunately, Jeremy and I had gone carefully over the route till I should reach a known road. On the journey back the stops we had to make were frequent, as first one and then another wanted to make contact with the bushes.

It was 1.35 a.m. when I finally got home. In the living-room my father was sitting at one side of the fire place, my mother at the other. In spite of the lively fire, the temperature had dropped to well below freezing.

I had not taken into consideration that my well-meant message had to be passed on by four people before it reached its destination. Each link in the chain would stamp a little bit of his personality on the content before it was passed on. In any case, the messenger himself would have been enough. Regardless of the type of 14-year-old he is beforehand, the mantle of messenger invariably results in a perky, cheeky stripling guaranteed to annoy as soon as he opens his mouth.

On this occasion the urchin concerned had rattled the sneck, opened the door in the darkened scullery and shouted, 'Are you there, Arch?' and without waiting to be formally acknowledged or admitted had gone on: 'The dowter's just been on the phone. She's havin' the time of her life up at one o' them aerodromes. Erw! She's among the Brylcreem boys, doncher knerw. She's with Y's dowter and that lot. She says she'll be late. Ye'll be lucky if ye see her before the morrow.'

'How long,' asked my father as soon as I got in the room, 'have you known that crowd?'

'I don't know them.'

'You must. Traipsing over the countryside ...' and so it went on.

It was difficult, if not impossible, to describe what had actually happened or that, in any case, the people concerned had done no more than just laugh and have a good time. Nothing untoward had happened.

It was only when I was finally tucked into bed and on the verge of sleep that I suddenly became alert. The young man, the officer who had been so helpful, had worn wings above his breast pocket. He was a pilot. So wrapped up in my own concerns was I that I had not realized the eminence of the person who had come to my aid. It was most unlikely I'd hear from him again. On the whole, it was just as well. What a fool he must have thought me.

Monday evenings I usually stayed in. However, it was the birthday of a friend of mine and she had asked me and two others to go home with her to tea to mark the occasion. She lived at Lynemouth.

The temperature had not risen notably. As I left home to go back to the shop at lunch-time I said, 'I can't be late back tonight. Half-past nine at the latest. The last bus leaves at nine o'clock. Just leave the ironing and I'll do it when I get back.'

After tea at my friend's house , we decided to contact the Ouija board to find out what was going on and what was in store for us. We laid out the letters on a polished table and sat around solemnly concentrating, one finger each placed on the upturned tumbler. Suddenly the glass began a frenzied circling of the table and we had difficulty in keeping up with it.

'Have you got a message?' we intoned in its direction repeatedly until finally it spelled out: 'Yes.'

'Who for?'

A lot of guesswork was needed because the glass wasn't all that good a speller, but it was remarkable the information we gleaned.

By the time we'd each had a go at asking questions and working out the answers it was after 9 o'clock and supper was on the table.

With much laughter and chatter we walked home.

It was 1 a.m. when I got in. My father had gone to bed. Without a word my mother got up to join him.

The ironing had all been done.

I decided I'd have to wait till Thursday night to do what I could to smooth things over, because I had to go out on Tuesday evening (again this was unusual) and I went out on Wednesday evenings as a matter of course.

On Thursday the shop was packed and everyone was scuttling around serving or putting up orders. The Boss surveyed his minions from the top of his little fight of steps. The telephone rang and he went in to answer it. 'It's for you , Leenor,' he shouted down the shop.

I went forward somewhat dazed. This was the first time I'd ever been called to the phone since I'd started. The Boss didn't do any pretending not to listen. He sat in his swivel chair staring at me and the telephone. As the office was only the width of his roll-top desk and the length of the depth of the desk plus the space needed to open the door, I was almost on top of him.

'Yes,' I said nervously as I picked up the ear piece.

'Linda? Jeremy here. You got home safely on Sunday, I take it?'

'Yes.'

'Sorry. You'll have to speak up a bit. I can't hear you.'

'Yes.'

'Good. Are you free tonight, and if so, may I have the pleasure of your company?'

'Yes.'

'Yes, you're free, or yes I may have the pleasure of your company, or hopefully, both?'

'Both.'

'Good. Where and when?'

'What?'

'Where shall I meet you and at what time?' In this fraught situation it was remarkable that I could think at all.

'Seven o'clock. The Queen's Morpeth. Do you know it?' I said in a rush.

'Now it's my turn. Yes. When the roll is called up yonder hostelry I'll be there.'

'Yes.'

'Is that all you have to say?'

'Yes.'

'See you tonight then.'

'Yes.' I put the phone down.

'Have you got yourself a lad then?' asked the Boss.

I couldn't possibly explain the situation.

'No.' I said. 'No. I had a bit of trouble with the ARP car on Sunday and that chap helped me to put it right. He was just ringing to see if everything was all right now.'

'Didn't sound like that to me,' said the Boss. 'It sounded like you're going out drinking with a lad. I didn't know you drank. I just hope you're not going to get yourself into trouble. I wouldn't like that to happen to you. Think on. Now you'd better get yourself back to the counter. You've wasted enough time.'

This 'not getting myself into trouble' was a euphemism for 'now just be careful' which was a euphemism for 'now be canny what you're doing' which was a euphemism for. . .

The word 'sex', when it was used, which was rarely, was equated with gender. The words 'sexual intercourse' had no real acceptable form for the simple reason that no mention of it *was* acceptable in society. That is not to say the subject never came up (no pun intended). If it did it was spoken by implication, expressive nods, silences or euphemisms in a low voice that young ears might not hear. The expressive four-letter word was extremely vulgar and was only used when being vulgar was the object. I was so naïve, not to say downright ignorant, that I did not realize till about a year before I left the store that when one young lad/man asked another, 'Been ower lately?' he was referring to his sexual activities, although I was dimly alerted when one or the other of the single lads said, 'I was oot wi' a tart las' night,' and the question automatically followed: 'Did you get ower?'

This word 'tart' was not a derogatory term. It was a shortened form of 'sweetheart' and often referred to any unmarried girl although there was a sort of hierarchy as far as courting (gan oot wi') was concerned. A girl started off as 'a lass', became 'the tart', finally 'the wife', 'wor lass' or simply 'hor'.

Like the British Constitution, standards of behaviour between young people were not written down but, also like the British Constitution, somehow without our actually ever having been told, some inescapable facts filtered through. Nice girls didn't.

The term 'a nice girl' was by no means disparaging. As far as I know, all the girls I knew aspired to be nice girls – myself included. Decent lads respected you and didn't ask. However, it was recognized that lads being lads, their passion might get the better of them when they might 'try'. It was then the responsibility of the girl to refuse, or at least see that they didn't 'go all the way'. If you 'gave in' the lad thence forward didn't respect you. It also had to be borne in mind that, generally speaking, 'all lads were after *one* thing'. So that, all in all, any sexual or erotic feelings *had* to be subordinated to the possible consequences (both to oneself and to others) of giving way to this intense, erotic feeling.

When engaged couples found they had to move the wedding date forward they were looked upon with indulgence. They had 'jumped the gun'. They weren't the first and they wouldn't be the last. In spite of this understanding it did not deter certain interested parties from saying when a baby was born 'D'ye say so? When were they married again? Aye. Well. Yes. July, August, September, October. I thought there was a *something*!'

When a girl was found to be pregnant and she had no steady lad, her distress was very great indeed. It was not unknown for a father to 'take the pit belt' to the girl in this unfortunate condition before going to see the lad's family. When a girl became pregnant, there was only one outcome. The couple had to get married. His parents were no less insistant on that than hers. He'd 'had his fun' and now he had 'to pay for it'. He had been 'caught'.

In my own case the restraints were very great. I had no desire whatever to ensnare anyone into matrimony and I had even less desire to cause any pain or anxiety to my parents and my family. Also, I had been in the store long enough to see what happened to some marriages. Some young couples hardly ever went out together after they were married – he went about with his father and their mates. She stayed at home or went to her mother's. That sort of marriage didn't appeal to me. Then there were the individual cases

32

I knew. The girl who made it to university when, suddenly, without prior warning, her parents were sent for. She had given birth to a baby. Somehow she had kept this information to herself, just as, afterwards, she would not disclose the name of the child's father. Her career was over before it started. The family 'stuck by' her but the shame they all felt was acute. They felt they couldn't hold their heads up. The child was brought up to think of its grandmother as its mother and its mother as its sister. They persisted in keeping up this pretence even in the knowledge that everyone else knew the true state of affairs. As for the girl, she was buried under a weight of obligation. Having no money of her own, she was without status of any kind and domestically speaking, she was at everyone's beck and call.

Young love has a fragile beauty all its own. The whole being throbs with intense feeling: the yearning to be with the beloved; the trembling exquisite delight of physical closeness; the shutting out of the rest of the world. To each successive generation it comes anew. Each girl, each young man feeling the passion and the tenderness, is convinced this is the first time in the history of the world that it has ever happened. What can the ageing remnants of an earlier generation possibly know of the ecstasy that fills them (the young) now?

But the older generation does know. And they know the pitfalls. And so they advise. Or try to.

The Boss felt he was quite within his rights to listen to our conversation and to comment as he did. He had obviously not heard Jeremy's voice or he would have realized immediately he didn't come from Ashington or anywhere round about, and this in itself would be cause for concern. Without a doubt he would consider I was 'being tekking a len on' (taking a loan of) and he would have told me so.

The question 'Hev ye getten yorsell a lad yet?' was frequently asked of any unattached young woman between the ages of 17 and the right side of 30. The older she was, the more necessary and important it was for her to repair any omission. After 30 the poor woman was obviously 'on the shelf'.

I went back to the counter in a daze for two reasons. First I couldn't understand why Jeremy had telephoned; there were girls far more exciting than I he could have had a casual relationship with. I was glad I'd thought of Morpeth. I didn't want to meet anyone I knew. It was most unlikely that this would happen on a Thursday night in Morpeth.

This brought me to my second problem. What on earth was I going to say at home? What possible reason could I give for dashing home and going out dressed on a Thursday night? I turned over several reasons in my head at intervals throughout the day, but I didn't think I could use any. In the end I decided to stick as near to the truth as I could and simply give Jeremy a sex change.

I hadn't given myself much time when I said 7 o'clock. We didn't finish till 5.30. I ran all the way home.

'I'm terribly sorry,' I panted when I got in. 'I forgot till this afternoon. With all the upset on Sunday I forgot. Winnie Douglas's brother rang me on Monday. I used to know Winnie at school. Remember? I went to her party one Christmas. Well. She's having a bit of a reunion and she's asked me. They live in Morpeth now. I promised I'd be there by seven. I don't want anything to eat. There'll be something there.'

I flew around. My mother accepted my explanation but I didn't think I'd get away with the pale lavender grey suit, pale pink silk blouse, silk stockings and high-heeled grey shoes that looked smart but were agony to wear, so that it was with some apprehension that I went downstairs.

'You look smart,' said my mother. 'You should wear that more often; it suits you.'

I was more than ever glad of my mother's remarks when I got off the bus. How was it I hadn't noticed how good-looking he was in a fairish, intelligent sort of way? He came forward to meet me, handing me a loosely wrapped parcel as he did so. It was a box of chocolates.

'Would you like a drink first?' he asked.

'Yes,' I said, and we went into the Queen's.

I sat down and when he came back with the drinks he said, 'I'm surprised you wanted to come in for a drink. I'm even more surprised you asked for a sherry. I thought you were never going to finish the one you had on Sunday. The way you drank it, I thought it was laced with arsenic.'

'I didn't know you'd watched me that long.'

'Only because I was puzzled as to what you were doing there. I definitely got the impression that an ale house was not your Alma Mater.'

'I have nothing against them,' I smiled. 'I mean, I haven't any tracts hidden about my person or anything like that. It's just that the smoke hurts my eyes and drink doesn't seem to do for me what it does for others. It doesn't matter what people drink, they seem to be laughing and having a good time in seconds. I tried getting drunk last New Year. I went to a party and as I was staying the night I thought I'd use the opportunity to get myself blotto to see what it was like. It was awful. The more I drank, the more I felt I had the sins and cares of the world on my shoulders. I've no great desire to repeat the experiment.'

'Why are we sitting here then?'

'As I said, I'm not against drinking. And I thought you would like to come.'

In the end we went to the pictures where we ate some of the chocolates. When we came out he had a taxi waiting and in this I travelled home in solitary state. The first time I'd even been in a taxi. I would have loved to have taken the chocolates home particularly as I got there at 9.55 and everything was all right again, but I thought it wasn't politic. I got out of the taxi at Booth's Corner and gave the rest of the chocolates to the driver.

On Saturdays, round about lunch-time, a sort of inertia descended on the shop. I was standing near the Boss's office with no one in the vicinity when the telephone rang. Even before I picked it up I knew.

'Linda?'

'Yes.'

'I have a free day tomorrow. It would be nice if we could spend all of it or part of it together. Is it possible?'

'Yes.' I was as laconic as I had been on the first occasion, this time because I was fearful of the Boss's return.

'Good. Where and when?'

'Do you know Warkworth?'

'Yes.'

'I should be in the square at eleven.'

'Good show. Smashing. See you then. 'Bye,' and he rang off.

'Smashing.' It was the first time I'd heard the word used in that context. I scuttled away from the office. No one said anything.

The following morning, feeling a bit queasy, I decided to get off the bus at the top of the hill and walk down into the square. As I was early I had plenty of time. However, he was already there and, seeing me get off the bus he waved and walked up the hill towards me.

'You look as if you need a little something,' he said. 'Coffee or gin?'

'Gin,' I said.

'Shall we say coffee-flavoured gin,' he smiled. 'You have at least two choices. Yonder tavern. Ye Sun. Or this homely, bijou café on our left.' I had never, to this point, been in a hotel for any type of meal. The only meals I'd ever had out were teas in a café. I chose the café to be on the safe side. We were the only ones there and the proprietress clucked around us as though we were the first customers she'd ever had. I found it agreeable.

Sunday was still a day for visiting and I had made a loose promise to go to a friend's for tea. I'd toyed with the idea of saying I couldn't go after Jeremy's phone call, but then decided against it. He was beginning to fill my thoughts. I wanted to know more about him, but I didn't want him to know any more about me, and I didn't think it fair to question him if I didn't want to be questioned in return. So far we had met on a fairly equal footing. Our conversation had been general and though I hadn't his assurance I felt I'd done a reasonable cover-up job; but it couldn't last. What he wanted from me I couldn't imagine. Talking to him was easy – far too easy. And it was pleasant. I was afraid I'd give too much away too soon.

'We have the day before us,' he said. 'What would you like to do first?'

'Not quite,' I replied. 'I'm afraid I'll have to be back fourish. I've promised to go out to tea.'

'Oh. Ah. Well. We have the rest of the morning and part of the afternoon before us. What do you suggest? I have never been here before so I'm prepared to see all the sights.'

'I thought you said you knew Warkworth?'

'There I'm afraid I was guilty of a small lie. You always seem so breathless and anxious to put the phone down I feel as if we're spies making contact. I guessed that Warkworth would be relatively easy to discover. Your description was so apt I had no difficulty.' He smiled his kind, teasing smile and I had to grip the chair to stop myself melting.

'What about lunch?' I asked.

'What indeed?' he replied. 'We could ask the good lady here if she can oblige, or go across the road to the Sun, or go somewhere else.'

'Would you like to stay here?' I asked.

'I'm asking you,' he said.

'Here then,' I replied.

We made arrangements with the proprietress and, leaving the café, walked down the street to the river. We walked along the water's edge and paused to look up at the castle.

'Beautiful,' he said. 'Do you know anything about it?'

'Very little,' I replied. 'It's been there a long time.'

'Really?'

'Please. Do not poke fun at the guide. She's doing her best.'

'Sorry.'

'Next time you'll be asked to leave the footpath. Observe the position of the castle. See how well favoured it is for noting the approach of the enemy. It belongs to the Percys. The Dukes of Northumberland. It is mentioned, I believe, somewhere in Shakespeare and you can't go higher than that. In fact, Harry Hotspur was born there.'

'I am impressed and humbled. Pray do go on.'

'Well. The Percys lived here, I think, and kept Alnwick Castle as a fortress. I have a feeling the direct family died out. Then about two hundred years or so ago they surfaced. Smithson, I think their name is, or was. Anyway, they were also the Percys. Apparently both castles had gone to the dogs a bit in the interim and they could only restore one, so they decided on Alnwick.'

'Fascinating. One question, please. Do they pay you by the word?'

'You are the original stoney ground, aren't you? All right. I'll take the hint. Henceforth my lips are sealed.'

He laughed. 'No. Please. Truce. I beg of you. I expect you were good at history when you were at school.'

'No. Not really. I'm not interested in battles and things. No.

What I'm interested in is looking at the castle and seeing the people who lived there. Did you like history?'

'Till this minute, no.'

'Which school did you go to?'

He told me.

'That's a public school, isn't it?' I asked in awe. He nodded. Stories about boarding-schools, whether for boys or girls, held me spellbound. 'How marvellous,' I said.

He looked away. 'I hated it,' he said quietly. 'But, having said that, I'm glad I went. I'm glad I got through it all. I'm really quite proud to be able to say I went there.'

'What was it you hated?'

'The prefects' beatings mostly. When I was young – when I first went I was beaten by the prefects for the most trivial of reasons. Sometimes I didn't know why and it turned out I'd done something I shouldn't or not done something I should connected with the school. One of their unwritten rules that I didn't then know. I made up my mind that when I was a prefect I wouldn't beat little kids like that. I didn't even think I'd beat them at all. But when I tried that approach I was vilified for it. Well. Perhaps not as bad as that. They thought I was soft. Even the little kids I was trying to protect. There was a sort of cachet about having a good beating by some of the prefects. I was too feeble for words.'

'But you're still glad you went there?'

'Oh, yes.'

'And when you marry you will send your sons there?'

He paused. There was a sudden chill wind, though no leaf stirred.

'I never think of the future,' he said in a flat voice, and as he spoke I was suddenly turned to ice. My scalp tingled, my hair stood on end and I trembled with a dark fear. When the moment passed I felt as though perspiration covered my body yet my mouth was dry. I couldn't speak.

After a few seconds he turned and said, 'And where to next?'

'The . . . the bridge,' I replied, struggling to bring the saliva back into my mouth. The day had taken on a different significance. I had to hold on to it. Make it last.

'Is it far? We mustn't forget lunch and the fact that you have a bus to catch afterwards.'

'No bus. At least not till tonight.'

'But you're going out to tea.'

'I was. It was a loose arrangement. You know. Will you be along to tea on Sunday? Yes, unless anything crops up. That sort of thing.'

'And something has cropped up? Let me say at once I'm pleased. I'm not going to urge you to keep this appointment.'

'You could say something has cropped up.'

'What? Or is that an impertinent question?'

'I'm having a wonderful day. One for the memory book. There's no need to cut it short unnecessarily.'

'The memory book?'

'Yes. It's a bit silly really. I have a sort of mental memory book and sometimes, when I'm in bed I think, what shall I remember tonight? And I sort of bring out a memory and live it over again.'

'Is it secret?'

'No. Just . . . just . . . silly, personal, I suppose.'

'May I hear one?'

'Well. When I was at school I had this pash on the maths teacher. For some reason I was very good at geometry. I hardly had to think. You know. I could see the solution to a problem fairly quickly. One day he put a problem on the board. We had to solve it as a class. "Put up your hand," he said, "when you've got it." I sort of half put mine up and he gave a nod and a smile. That in itself was enough to keep me in bliss for aeons, but after a while he came up to my desk and held out a piece of chalk. He put his hand on my shoulder. The most marvellous feeling. He said, "Go out and show 'em how it's done, Linda." I think that was my first glimpse of heaven. I loved school but that's the thing I remember most about it.'

We didn't talk any more till we reached the bridge.

'Well?' he said.

'It's a fortified bridge,' I said. 'Fourteenth-century or older. Can you just imagine the packhorses coming over?'

'Or the soldiers. I suppose the idea was to clobber them with claymores or battleaxes as they came through the arch.'

'I expect so. Like it?'

He nodded.

The proprietress of the café welcomed us back like old friends.

'Don't rush over your meal,' she said. 'You can stay as long as you like.'

While we were drinking coffee, I fished in my handbag for a clean handkerchief, taking out a small book and laying it temporarily on the table as I did so.

'M.L.S.,' said Jeremy. 'What does the 'M' stand for?'

'Margaret.'

'Margaret. That's a beautiful name.'

'It is the way you say it. Like music.'

'That's probably because it is music of a kind. If your first name is Margaret, why are you called Linda?'

'I don't know. I've always been called Linda. Everyone calls me Linda. No. Correction. Everyone but one. One man I know calls me Leenor.'

As I spoke, I unconsciously raised my voice and said, 'Leenor!' in the way the Boss did.

'You startled me,' laughed Jeremy. 'Who calls you that? The man who answered the telephone when I first rang you?'

'Got it in one.'

'Why does he call you that?'

'When I first met him, he'd never heard the name "Linda" before and he refused to call me that. He said I must mean Lena.'

'Do you know what Margaret means? It means a pearl. I think it's a very suitable name for you. I think I'd like to call you Margaret. Would you mind?'

I shook my head. I was being drawn nearer and nearer the whirlpool that was him. I felt that shortly I must drown unless I fought against the current with all my being.

'And where would you like to go next?' I asked.

'What choice is there?'

'A walk by the river or the Hermitage.'

'The Hermitage?'

'It's a well-known place of interest, though not to me personally. However, I could find out.'

'I do not doubt that for one instant but I don't much want to associate myself with hermits at the moment. Perhaps the next time we come. Shall we settle for the river?'

The next time! The next time WE come. So there was to be a next time. WE. These were heady words that repeated themselves over and over again that glorious afternoon as we walked and laughed and laughed and struggled with a cumbersome boat with an affinity for the bank.

We went back to the café for tea. The proprietress wouldn't charge. She closed the café saying she was on the point of doing that anyway and after we'd finished eating her excellent scones and cakes she brought a fresh pot of tea and 'had a cup with us'.

As we waited for the bus I was to catch, Jeremy said, 'I won't telephone unless something untoward turns up. I expect to be free a fortnight today. Shall we come back and look for the Hermitage?'

I nodded. 'Yes, please,' I said.

The bus was there, its door open ready to admit me.

'Your eyes are shining like stars,' he said as he drew me to him and kissed me. 'I've wanted to do that since the first moment I set eyes on you,' he said as he let me go and guided me into the bus. Like a zombie, I took my seat. I had been sucked into the whirlpool finally and irrevocably and I wanted the moment back. I wanted to run the reel backwards. I had been taken by surprise. The moment had gone almost before I knew it was there. I wanted a still.

I could feel the lean body under the smooth cloth of his uniform, feel his warm breath on my face and the softness of his lips at first – softness which gave way to something far more complex. Something that lay deep, deep down beyond the point where the whirlpool was becalmed.

There were no boundaries, no restraints now in the feeling I had for him. No thought of consequences. And no hope that there could ever be anything permanent, no commitment for the future about our relationship. All I had was our next meeting. It would start at the point where the kiss ended.

I needed time and I needed an outlet for my energy and emotions before I could bring myself to the even domestic level of my everyday existence. I got off the bus some three miles from home, running and walking till arriving at our door provided nothing but relief.

Days later, how many I do not know, the Phoney War ended with a bang that shook us all. Hitler began his seemingly unstoppable march through Europe, and helpless to do anything about it, we were interested only in the news bulletins which followed each other with depressing regularity.

To a certain extent I was anesthetized against these events in Europe. My personal thoughts, dreams and feelings filled my mind to such an extent there was only a tiny space left for current happenings, however joyless and frightening these might be.

I thought of him all the time. What was he doing? To whom was he talking? Who were his friends? Where did he come from? Did he have any brothers and sisters? The information I had been so anxious we should not exchange I now wanted to know desperately. There was nothing about him now that I did not want to know. And I was jealous. I was jealous of everyone who saw him or spoke to him when I could not; jealous of everyone who knew him, above all, jealous of everyone who knew him in an intimate way, who knew of what pleased him and what vexed him, what he was like as a boy and why he had chosen to become a pilot. And I was afraid for him.

There was also an overpowering feeling that the future was being denied us all. Each day might be the last. For what reason were we now suppressing these emotional conflicts? These overwhelming sensations?

On the Sunday I dressed myself with the utmost care, bathing first in perfumed water, caressing my body in creams and powders that gave off a faint fragrance, putting on my carefully-looked-after, very best set of underwear, crêpe de Chine delicately trimmed with fine lace, gently smoothing on silk stockings, finally donning the dark blue silk dress adorned with deep red roses and slashed here and there with white. Over it I wore a light cream coat and on my feet the high-heeled shoes, which, though they complemented the outfit to perfection, were still painful to walk in for any length of time. But I knew that, when the time came, I would never notice the discomfort.

This time I went all the way down to the square in the bus. Aquiver with the anticipated excitement of seeing him again I peered out of the window this way and that so I might get the first glimpse of him as soon as possible. By the time the bus stopped in the square I still had not seen him.

Disappointment weighed me down like lead when he didn't come forward to hand me off the bus. I looked around the square. There were people there, but none of them was him. How dull and stupid and getting-in-the-way they all were. I stood at the fountain looking about me. Which way would he come? How would he come? I walked round the square in the futile hope that he would suddenly appear full of concern for not having been there the moment that I arrived.

We hadn't said any time. It wasn't 11 o'clock yet. That was it. I was early. I went back to the fountain to wait. I waited and waited and kept on waiting. All day I waited by the fountain. I could not bear to leave it lest he came. I was neither hungry nor thirsty, being filled only with the longing to see him. Heavy with disappointment I got on the last bus.

To the numbness of what was happening in Europe was added this other numbness. Sometimes my heart would lurch when the telephone rang, but it was never for me.

I wrote to him. Every night I wrote a letter out in rough and copied it on to thick, good quality paper I'd bought specially for him. And every night after I'd sealed up the letter I posted it into the heart of the living room fire. He had said he would not telephone. He had said that before he kissed me. Possibly that kiss had told him many things. Possibly he had found me childish and dull and the kiss had confirmed how unsophisticated I was. When he had guided me on to the bus, had he been dismissing me?

I had to force myself to listen to the news.

Then came Dunkirk and the plea for ships, any ships, and here again we were helpless. We could only hope – and pray.

Some of the survivors of Dunkirk were sent to a camp not far away from Ashington and word sent out that invitations for the men to visit our homes would be welcome. A friend and I teamed up and said we would be willing to entertain two young men for the afternoon.

We met them at the appointed place. They were young soldiers, totally withdrawn and passive. Where would they like to go, we asked them. They shrugged. They were willing to go wherever we suggested. Our choice really was limited, Morpeth or Newbiggin. We decided on Morpeth.

Once we'd got there there wasn't an awful lot to do after we'd walked around the town and I suggested we went on the river. The

43

boats for hire were full of years, rheumaticky and slow-moving. It wasn't a very sensible suggestion, having regard to the ordeal the young men had suffered, but what else was there? The two young men sat patiently, silent and withdrawn at either end of the boat while my friend and I did our inept best with the oars.

We returned a silent group and made our way to the bus station.

Suddenly my heart turned over – I saw him. Jeremy. He was walking a way ahead with his back to us, walking towards the main road. Without a word I set off at top speed running and dodging the people in the bus station. I caught up to him when he was about six yards from the corner and grabbed his arm. He turned.

It wasn't him! I couldn't believe it. It *was* him. It *had* been him. Some cruel deity had dissolved his face into another. I wanted to shake him and scream at him, 'Take that mask off. Take it off. You ARE Jeremy.'

My mouth stayed open while he stared at me and still I held on to his arm. I was aware that a tall slim girl with a mane of blonde hair had come up to him and taken his other arm in a proprietary way. He ignored her and continued looking at me. I dropped his arm, feeling foolish.

'I . . . I . . . thought from the back that you were someone else. I thought you were Jeremy Browne.' The young man's face cleared slightly.

'Jeremy Browne?'

'You know him?'

His face softened. 'Yes,' he said. 'I did.'

4. War-time Civilians

The war news got worse. Invasion threatened. Gloom everywhere, but under it all there was anger. Anger against what had happened. Anger that prevented us from thinking anything other than whatever still had to come we would win.

'In the event of invasion,' the form sent out by the voluntary food organizer said, 'EMERGENCY RATIONS will be available. The complete ration should suffice for seven days, but in your own interests it should be treated as a RESERVE only to be consumed in case of real necessity.'

The price of the ration was fixed at six shillings (30p) and, as far as we were concerned, it was to be obtained from Pearson's – 15 High Market. Each householder had to provide his or her own wrappings for tea, sugar, biscuits and margarine and his/her own basket or container to carry the goods away, which were:

1 tin corned beef
1 tin baked beans
1 tin condensed milk
2 oz tea
1 lb sugar
3¾ lb biscuits
4 oz margarine.

Weight all told was approximately 8 lb. Ration books to be produced to obtain delivery. All personal documents had to be put in a single container in a safe place ready to be picked up in an emergency.

My mother provided our own emergency kits. She had been saving 'solid silver' coins for some time and she now had a £5 bag for each of the four of us. Added to that she had four bags of rations containing tinned meat, sugar, condensed milk, tinned meat puddings, baked beans and biscuits. These were all stacked in a cupboard in the living room. We also had warm clothes at the ready.

The country was also prepared for invasion. All names of places had been obliterated and signposts removed or painted over. I don't know how much this set Hitler back but it certainly flummoxed me. I got lost even on roads I thought I knew well. This made me feel very disorientated.

Pillboxes were put up in unexpected places in the country, giving the feeling of the war being brought to our doorsteps. Old cars were put in strategic positions to form road blocks to stop or hinder any advancing army. My brother joined the newly formed Local Defence Volunteers (LDV). Churchill talked of fighting in the streets. It seemed a distinct possibility.

Then they bombed London and Coventry. We went to the

pictures more to see Movietone News than to see the film. 'Look what they've done to our city,' the reporter said, tears in his voice, and we watched with lumps in our throats, the tears smarting our own eyes.

Life in the shop went on. Some of the men went away and were replaced by girls. Being responsible for ration books and coupons was an added extra to my other jobs and at first the whole system was haphazard, so much so that there were customers who came in and said they were rationed with us and got the appropriate goods when, in fact, they weren't. It did not matter so much at the beginning when food was still fairly plentiful, but soon it was becoming increasingly scarce. This was particularly true of sweets and tinned goods not then on points.*

As the new registration period approached I felt it would be best if I reorganized the ration-book system as far as it affected our shop. It was difficult to do this in between the other necessary jobs, and one evening when the shop closed at 5.30 after everyone had gone but the foreman who was checking the back shop doors, I kept on working in my little office under the stairs, intending to keep on till the last minute.

'Come on,' said the foreman when he returned to the front shop and saw that I was still there. 'I've got a home to go to.'

'Look,' I said, 'would you mind just letting me stay behind for a few minutes to finish this job? I'll not have a chance tomorrow. There's only the front door left and I'll see that it's locked when I go.'

The foreman hesitated. 'All right,' he said at last.

When he closed the door, the noise echoed through the shop. From where I sat it looked long and lifeless. There was a feeling that it was waiting for the dust to settle before the noises and scuttlings of the night took over. I nearly ran away from them there and then, leaving the ration books to muddle through as before.

However, gripping the edge of the high Victorian desk, I thought better of it. I gave myself time to become accustomed to this large

*'Points' were coupons entitling the possessor to buy from a range of goods each worth so many 'points'. It was a flexible form of rationing, unlike the weekly allowance of staples

hollow building and concentrated on the tiny office under the stairs into which little daylight ever filtered. It, at least, hadn't changed.

I brought down the light on the pulley till it was about two feet above the bench, to which I moved. Actually I didn't have to move. I simply made a quarter turn. The office wasn't big enough for me to move. With the shaded light down, the rest of the office was in near darkness.

I gazed at the scarred bench without really seeing it. What was really wanted was a complete organization of the ration books with an overall ledger where every customer was listed alphabetically alongside information which gave the address, the number of books and the kind, any extras allowed, any changes, whether they were on a load (and if so which one) or came to the counter.

It was a long, boring job. Working it out had been pleasant. Carrying it out was another matter, but I went on doggedly and painstakingly, unaware that outside the light was waning and darkness setting in.

Suddenly I was startled and alarmed. There was a commotion at the foot door. It was being opened and heavy footfalls, several heavy footfalls, were making their way into the shop. I froze. A gang! Burglary!

Suddenly – the voice of the Boss. 'What the hell are you doing here? Do you know what time it is?'

He approached the little office. With him came a warden and a policeman.

'I . . . I . . . er . . . was just organizing the ration books,' I stammered, shaken.

'Organizing the bloody ration books at this time of night! We'd had our suppers, look ye, when the pollis come to the door. The pollis. It gave the wife the fright of her life.'

'I went for him,' put in the warden.

'Aye, and the warden an' all.'

The warden was feeling a bit aggrieved. Lights were his responsibility.

'I came along here,' he put in firmly, and in command, 'all unsuspecting. I had been given no official word that the shop would still be working at this time of night. I couldn't believe me eyes when I saw this light and the *blackout not up*. I thought something was seriously wrong so I got in touch with the pollis.'

At that moment while my sins were being spelt out, working in the shop without authority, contravening the blackout regulations, I had a sudden desire to laugh as something else flashed into my mind. Uncle Lance told me a story about this same warden. He had brought a man out of his warm house in winter because, he said, there was a light showing under the door.

'Ye don't bloody mean to tell me,' said the man, incensed, 'Hitler's bloody well comin' over here on his hands and knees.'

'What are you doing here anyway?' asked the Boss. 'Who let you in?'

'No one,' I said. 'I told the foreman I would follow him out in a minute. It took longer than I thought.'

The Boss sighed. The sigh said more about the trouble he had to endure because of recalcitrant menials than words could express. 'Get your things together,' he said.

The policeman had remained silently in the background hitherto. As we shuffled ourselves round a bit I saw that it was a young man whom I knew and whose company I'd been in several times.

'Am I being arrested?' I asked.

He bit his lip and put his hand to his mouth momentarily. 'Not this time,' he said in a low voice. 'I left my handcuffs at the station.'

'You've been lucky,' said the warden. 'We've all been lucky. If there'd been a raid tonight there's no knowing what would have happened.'

I felt decidedly foolish as I walked through the shop under their gaze.

'Where on earth have you been?' my mother asked when I got home.

I did my best to give a rational explanation.

I finished my self-appointed task by going in early to work and taking some of it home on one or two nights. When I'd finished there was nothing I didn't know about the books. I tried to explain my system to one of the men.

'Do you know what I think?' he said. 'I think it's a pity you hadn't a bit more work to keep you occupied. If you had my job you wouldn't be able to play around like that. You know your trouble,' he went on. 'You take far too much upon yourself. You get above yourself. You forget just what your job is.'

In spite of restrictions, the dreadful war news and the shortages of food, there was still a fair amount of food and gifts in the shops for the second Christmas of the war. In September we had been told there was to be no more cream and after Christmas no more bananas. Petrol, now called Pool Petrol and dyed, was rationed. (Undyed petrol, detected by random inspection, meant that the driver had bought it illegally on the black market or was using petrol reserved for war purposes). We ourselves were allowed five gallons a month.

We had a large 25lb turkey for Christmas. We kept hens and had the produce from the allotment and the garden which, even pre-war, had kept us in vegetables throughout the winter. Cheese was still plentiful, especially as this was a mining community (miners were given an extra ration of cheese). Oatmeal was also plentiful. We were all fond of oatmeal (fortunately) and my mother made large quantities of oatmeal scones and oat cakes. We also frequently had herrings done in oatmeal.

Clothes-wise, siren suits and pixie hoods had now become part of the scene.

So in the second year of the war, we still had a fair standard of living. Indeed, in August 1942 it was said officially that the health of the nation was better than it had been before the war and there was no malnutrition. By this time sweets and tinned goods were on points, clothes were rationed, there was talk of rationing fuel and cigarettes and tobacco had disappeared from the shelves in shops. Most shops now displayed little but empty shelves and old adverts.

We were saddened and distressed by the war news and by our own personal griefs. Billy's fiancée's brother, Bobby Little, had died from bomb-blast when he was little more than a recruit. He was expected home on his first leave when the news came that he was dead. My friend, Joyce, had married her boyfriend, Billy Tippins, he of the Rothbury incident which I described in *The Pit Village and the Store*.

At the outbreak of war he joined the Merchant Navy, the service which, I believe, had a higher casualty rate than any of the armed forces. Theirs was a job of hardship, physical discomfort and danger.

Admiral Doenitz took over from Admiral Raeder in January 1943.

Doenitz believed the only chance of Germany's defeating Britain was to cut the Atlantic lifeline to America. Therefore he decided to put as many U-boats as possible (every one if he'd had his way) in the North Atlantic. The Germans called this the 'wolf tactic' and the British called the group of U-boats that carried out the attacks wolf packs. To begin with, these tactics were very successful. A lookout U-boat or German reconnaissance aircraft would report a convoy and U-boat HQ would order all nearby boats to close in. When enough were assembled (maybe thirteen or more), the attacks would begin and the escort vessels could do little to prevent the slaughter that followed.

It was to one of these wolf packs that Billy fell victim. His ship *Toward* was torpedoed. In fact it was a rescue ship which, in the event of an attack when the convoy scattered, stayed put to pick up survivors. A boat-load of twenty-six survivors from *Toward* were landed in Canada before they were returned to England. One of the survivors, an engineer, wrote to Joyce and said that the last time he saw Billy he was in the water, 'but he must have died instantaneously,' he said. 'No one could have survived in the Atlantic in that temperature.' Devastated, Joyce waited several weeks before writing to ask if she could have official notification of her husband's death, and she received this reply written on an official buff form:

2 May 1943

Madam,

With reference to your letter of 8 May respecting Mr W.G. Tippins ex *Toward*. I have to state that the list of crew from which certified extracts relating to deaths are issued, has been returned for amendment of certain particulars.

Immediately the amended document is received in this office the required extract will be forwarded to you.

I am, madam, your obedient servant,
(signature)

for Registrar General

Some time later she was sent this, the only letter she has concerning the death in freezing winter waters of this kind, loving, courageous young husband and father. It is an official buff form measuring 4 inches by 6½ inches. It reads:

B&D 32
General Register and Record Office of Shipping and Seamen, Cardiff.

16 March 1943

This is to certify that according to the records of this office
Mr William Tippins
Age 26
Born South Shields
of the *Toward*
Official number 147862 is supposed to have died on 7 February 1943

(undecipherable signature)
Assistant Registrar General

401 W279 5m 6/42 R.D.C.O. 254 (Gp 39)

One day Margaret Cotterill came into the shop white and drawn. The previous night they'd had a telegram to say that her brother was among those lost when the *Hood* blew up. A colleague was killed in the thousand-bomber raid over Cologne.

These were only a few among the many.

In the winter of 1941 a shocking thing happened. A woman was murdered and her body was hidden under a seat in Green Lane and banked with snow. The murderer, a soldier, was not caught for some time.

In the midst of this there were happy days, however. The dance halls were full, as were the picture houses. In common with many of my friends we made up small parcels to take to the wounded in military hospitals, visiting those whose families were too far a way to come and see them.

At my own home, we kept open house on Sunday afternoons and evenings for members of the forces and my friends to visit. My cousin, Jack Summers, would come and play the piano for us in the sitting-room, when we would sing and do the hokey-cokey and other dances suited to a large number in a smallish room. On many winter evenings we played monopoly around the dining room table.

It had never occurred to us to have anything in to drink on these occasions, and they seemed none the less happy for that. The great stand-by as far as food was concerned was paste sandwiches. Sometimes we were helped out in this respect with the occasional emergency ration book.

In September 1942 my brother was married. Margie was at that time a staff nurse in a hospital in Glasgow. Her home was in the picture postcard village of St John's town of Dalry in Kircudbright-shire, and thither we, the wedding party, travelled by train the day before.

The ceremony itself was memorable. Margie was a beautiful bride and the countryside was at its best. The newly married couple walked from the church, followed by the wedding party, between ranks of villagers come out to wish them well, to Margie's home, Smithy House. It was a warm, family wedding wrapped around with much laughter and love.

The following month my call-up came. I said my farewells to the entirely impassive office-under-the-stairs and spent the afternoon of my remaining day of civilian freedom at a Blyth cinema, where they were showing *Gone with the Wind*. In the evening I went through my wardrobe. My hats were carefully stored in boxes, the crowns stuffed with paper. My suits, dresses and coats were shrouded in bits of old sheeting, my blouses and underwear carefully laid away between sheets of tissue paper, my two pairs of silk stockings firmly screwed into their airtight jar and my shoes stuffed with paper and neatly stacked away in boxes. My bank book was given into my mother's safe-keeping. My preparations were thus completed.

5. Recruit

'Now, whatever you do, don't go on the guns.'

'There's no fear of that. I expect to be a pen-pusher. Not much danger there except from writer's cramp.'

I was about to walk out of civvy street. I had said my goodbyes and had given my promise to write to the rest of the family who, very properly, were now doing their bit towards the war effort. Now I was saying goodbye to my mother. We kissed and she stood at the gate to wave me off.

This was 23 October 1942, and a glorious autumn day it was too. Dearly loved autumn, full of colour and changing pictures, trees beginning to show their dark, lacy structure against the pale sky, gardens browner than they were, the dew still throwing up diamond patches on the dark grass. Carrying my suitcase I scuffed and crunched my way among the leaves that had fallen from the park trees. At the bus station I met up with Evelyn Todd. She too was going into the Auxiliary Territorial Service (ATS).

In Fenham Barracks we waited with other arrivals till all had assembled. We were each given a mug of hot cocoa, and while we drank it an officer gave a little speech of welcome before handing us over to the care of a sergeant and a corporal. Speaking slowly and carefully the sergeant said the first thing she was going to do was take a roll call, and in so doing she was going to put everyone in order preparatory to their going for a medical examination. Here for the first time I learned that my name was followed by that of a girl named Swallow. The sergeant paused when she reached this point and said, 'Now. One Swallow doesn't make a Summers.'

We laughed, partly to receive the tension. Throughout our three weeks together, whenever a roll call was taken (and this was often – very often) the person taking it could not resist this reference to Summers and Swallows, and after the first two or three times, the obligatory laughter strained our facial muscles somewhat. Only one sharp-eyed roll caller made capital out of the fact that I was smaller and lighter in build than my colleague.

'In this case,' he said, 'we might say that one Summers doesn't make a Swallow.'

As the sergeant called out names the corporal saw to it that we girls stood in line in our proper places, one behind the other. To my distress I found myself immediately behind two girls, obviously friends, who looked decidedly shop-soiled and who smelled. I wasn't too happy about their peroxided hair either. I kept as far away from them as I could, but the corporal wasn't having any.

'Move up,' she said. She meant to sound kindly but I heard the steel in her voice and moved forward a fraction while, at the same time, trying to attract the corporal's eyes in order to bring her attention to the state of the two girls. The corporal, however, was concerned with the group as a whole and with the finished job. She had no time for individual dilemmas. Thus I could only stand, a tensed figure, withdrawing physically and emotionally as far away from the two ahead of me as possible.

We were led, the roll call having finished, to a corridor where there were several forms placed end to end. The corridor was hardly long enough for us and the sergeant made us shuffle forward till we almost touched each other.

'Now,' she said, 'take off your clothes except for your bra and panties and put them, in order, on the forms provided.'

My distaste turned to horror when the two in front, without hesitation and not in the least self-consciously, began to peel off their garments and throw them as they came off on to the form. The skin of the girl immediately in front gave me cause for concern, and her underwear was dirty.

'Fold your clothes. Remember, they *all* have to go on the form,' said the sergeant as she walked up and down. The girl in front made a token effort and rolled the things she had thrown down into a loose ball.

I looked helplessly at these garments as the sergeant approached on her perambulations and tried with my eyes to draw her attention to the state of the girl ahead. But I was no more successful with her than I had been with the corporal.

'Come along, slow-coach,' she said to me. 'The others have nearly all finished.' She looked me over. 'You've got neither more nor less than anyone else,' she said. There was no smile on her face, nor in her voice.

I loosened the buttons of my carefully laundered white blouse, rolled down my stockings, then took off my jacket, blouse, skirt and underwear, carefully keeping each garment over my arm. Finally I was ready, my clothes neatly folded over my arm. It was then that I became aware that not only had the sergeant and corporal been watching my antics, but so had most of the assembled company, their gaze possibly directed to me because of the interest being shown by the two in charge. I felt myself crimson all over.

The sergeant came over and said, 'I told you to put your clothes on the form.'

'But, Sergeant . . . – '

Ignoring me, she took my clothes, put them on the form so that they overlapped the loose bundle of the girl ahead and, head erect, marched rather than walked away. I choked back my anger and I looked fixedly ahead.

I passed my medical, but five girls didn't, among them the two girls who had been ahead of me in the queue. They were taken to the sick bay. I returned to the corridor, singled out my clothes and began to dress. Usually dressing was a joy. I love the fragrant smell of clean laundry, the delicate feeling of fine material against my skin. Now I felt they were contaminated. I would rather have been putting on the coarsest hair shirt, could I be sure the latter was clean.

The meal we were given in the cook house was good and well served. Afterwards we collected the suitcases we had been directed to leave behind and, carrying these, we walked to our barrack rooms where we were each allocated a bed, a cupboard, a soldier's box and three biscuits, hard square pads which, when placed end to end, formed a mattress. The rest of the afternoon we spent collecting kit. We were to get only one uniform. The other we would get when it was decided which branch of the army we would be sent to.

In a short while the deflated kit bag I'd been given filled out like a large sturdy sausage balloon. The expert eye of the corporal in charge of uniforms decided my size and, as the skirt she gave me fitted to her satisfaction, I got the jacket that went with it. At the end of the counter I was requested to walk past a sergeant armed with a measuring stick and a piece of chalk. As I passed my skirt brushed the chalk indicating that it (the skirt) needed shortening. Accordingly it was taken from me. The greatcoat which reached almost to my ankles somehow missed the chalk so I was allowed to keep it.

The remainder of the afternoon was spent in a demonstration of how to fold blankets and sheets into a neat square, to be placed on top of the stacked biscuits so that a straight line resulted when the room was inspected. We were also taught how to lay out kit. After tea we were free except that what uniform we had was to be made presentable for wearing the following morning, at which time there would also be a first kit inspection.

The morning was given over to jabs in the medical room, and I was among those who subsequently fainted.

On Monday we were subjected to a number of written tests which I enjoyed very much, in spite of the new clothes, which caused me to itch, and the new shoes, which were also giving trouble. My heels had blistered and burst but I felt I couldn't complain.

Also on the Monday we were given a short talk on jobs available within the ATS and afterwards, with the printed sheet before us, we had to make our first, second and third choices. The words *kinetheodolite operator* had a lovely flowing rhythm about them, I thought. I had no idea what a kinetheodolite operator was but, with such a music in its name, it couldn't be other than interesting and I put it down as my first choice with driver and clerk second and third.

Later in the day we were introduced to marching drill. This was something of a necessity because wherever we went, we were marched there. In marching drill I met my Waterloo. I have always had the greatest difficult in telling my left from right and have had to devise my own code to cope with what I now realize is possibly a mild form of dyslexia. On the square I was hopeless. I would put my right arm out with my right foot and got out of step and hitched to get back in again which I never did. My blistered heels didn't help.

Monday and Tuesday nights were miserable affairs. I couldn't sleep for scratching and my heels were beginning to fester. Evelyn, when she saw them, felt they were serious enough to be reported to the corporal-in-charge, who sent me to the MO. The MO was sympathetic, but it was not my feet which held her attention; it was the reddened state of the backs of my legs.

'Been scratching?' she asked.

'Yes,' I said. 'It's the new clothes they've given us. I would rather have washed them before I wore them.'

'Let me see your hands.'

I held out my hands for inspection. They too were red between the fingers.

'I'm afraid,' said the MO, 'you've got scabies.'

'SCABIES! Oh, no!'

'Yes,' answered the MO then, seeing my distress, she went on: 'It's not an uncommon disease. We'll soon clear it up.'

Tears rolled down my cheeks. The only thing I knew about scabies was that only very dirty people got them. No one I knew had ever had them. The tears fell faster.

'You'll have to go into the sick bay,' the MO went on, 'and the rest will help those heels of yours. They could have become quite nasty. I don't know how you walked around. They must have been painful.'

The MO's sympathy was obvious, but it had no effect on me. I was now crying openly. The MO saw to it that an orderly helped me pack. Together we walked to the sick bay, the orderly trying all the while to bring me to a more cheerful frame of mind by recounting the sufferings, and often eventual deaths, of others who had been much worse off than I.

The medical orderly, into whose hands I was transferred, seemed to be made up of a number of different-sized balloons, none of which had been fully inflated. She was an amiable young lady determined to look at life through indelible rose-coloured spectacles. She was able to maintain her placid outlook because, most of the time, she did not hear what was being said. She appeared to go effortlessly through her day, emerging unruffled at the other end, as though she had been programmed.

She led me to the ward with heavy determined steps saying, as we went along, 'You'll like it here. Everybody likes it here.' She stopped at a door already opened and added. 'This is it. The scabies ward. This is where we clean you up, isn't it lasses?' This last question was addressed to three girls who, issue-pyjama-clad, were sitting on a bed in the corner. Except for this three, the remainder of the beds were empty.

'That's right, Florrie,' they called back in unison and on cue. I looked at them briefly. Through my now–swollen eyes I recognized the two girls who had stood ahead of me in the corridor queue.

'You can have that bed,' said Florrie, nodding straight ahead. 'We'll make it up while you're being scrubbed down. Just put your things down, take your closes off, get into your jim–jams and come into the bathroom. It's just across the corridor. The lasses will show you, if you can't find it.'

I found the bathroom on my own initiative. Florrie was waiting for me, sitting on a stool and sunk into her own flesh so that she looked like one of those dolls that rock when they are touched. The bath was filled to the regulation 5 inches.

'Right,' she said. 'Into the bath and I'll give you the once-over.'

'Can't I bath myself? Shouldn't I have my bath things?'

'No to both, flower. You don't need 'em. I bath you. Don't worry, I'm used to it. Hop in.'

I got in because there was nothing else I could do. Florrie took a piece of strong-smelling yellow soap and a worn brush, not unlike a small scrubbing brush. Indeed, that had been its original design.

'Right,' she said. 'Brace yourself. Here we go.'

'You're not going to use that on me?' I said, looking at the brush.

'Sure am.'

'But you can't. It's been used on other people.'

'Of course it has. How d'you think it got like this? Back first.'

'Please, oh, please, no. Can't I get my own nail brush?'

'No time. We're behind already. Besides, this is the one I always use.'

Florrie was just about to attack me (no other wording seems appropriate) when she dropped her arm and laughed.

'We're behind already. Get it?' and she laughed so much the balloons shook. Finally she recovered sufficiently to begin her work. For such a soft-looking person she had enormous strength. She scrubbed me firmly, ignoring my contours, with all the vigour she might have used on a kitchen floor. She did this with me standing because, she said, it was quicker and more thorough in the long run. It was with the greatest difficulty I kept my balance.

'There,' she said with satisfaction when she'd finished, 'that's better.'

I couldn't have blushed noticeably if I'd wanted to; I was scarlet all over. Florrie flung a rough towel over me and rubbed vigorously with the same abandon she'd shown with the scrubbing brush. This part of the operation over, she threw down the towel and took a generous handful of sulphur ointment and spread it over certain areas of my body. At the sight of my red buttocks, however, she had to pause to allow herself to shake again.

'Behind already,' she laughed again.

By the time Florrie had dressed my heels and I had sorted my things, it was lunch-time. Because of the lump in my throat I could do little else than swallow the custard and a small portion of the sponge pudding. Florrie, who helped clear away the dirty plates, looked at my still-full plates and said, 'That's right. You'll feel much better now you've enjoyed a good dinner.'

Still engulfed in my private affliction, I kept to my bed and closed my eyes that I might not have to involve myself in conversation with the other three. For a little while, silence reigned. Then Florrie's heavy tread could be heard at the other end of the corridor. Suddenly, in ringing tones, she yelled, 'Scabie parade!'

The others quickly got to their feet and made for the door. Startled I stayed where I was. Florrie appeared at the door.

'Come on, pet,' she said to me. 'Jump to it. We haven't got all day. At the double.'

'What for?' I asked.

'You heard. Scabie parade. Bath.'

'But I've just had one.' It was no use. Florrie had gone. This time I took my sponge bag, determined that Florrie should use my nail brush. Florrie, however, was well into her stride by the time my turn came. She dealt with me with the restraint of an avalanche. Although she said 'Yes, yes,' in soothing tones when I tried to be purposeful about the brush, she went on using the same brush she'd used on the others. 'Yours is too small,' she said, 'and not strong enough, sugar.'

We had scarcely settled down again when Florrie reappeared. 'Into bed, lasses,' she called in what she imagined was a whisper. 'Senior commander.'

'What?' asked the girls, as they moved quickly to their own bed.

'Senior commander. Boss woman. Weekly visit.'

Florrie disappeared like the Cheshire cat, and footsteps were heard in the corridor. A senior officer and a woman whom I guessed (correctly) was in charge of the sick bay appeared at the door and stood on the threshold. The officer, somewhat rigidly, kept her distance though she did move her head forward slightly in the direction of the ward inmates. She turned and said something to her companion who replied. 'Yes. Two went out yesterday and one came in this morning,' then added in a whisper that must have reverberated round the sick bay, 'It was a *very dirty* intake.'

I slid further down into the sheets, bit my lip and squeezed my eyes tightly together.

When the afternoon cup of tea came round I was more able to eat the biscuit that came with it. 'Thank God you've stopped crying,' said one of the girls. 'We thought you were never going to dry up. I'm Bet, this is Lou and that's Nance. What's your name?'

'Linda.'

'Nice name. What were you crying for? It couldn't be 'cos you've come in here. It's smashin' here. We're having a smashin' time, aren't we, lasses?'

I didn't have to reply. Evelyn stood at the door.

'I'm going home on a pass,' she said. 'I'll call at your house if you like. Is there anything you want?'

'Yes, please. Another pair of pyjamas and a small scrubbing brush. A new one if my mother can get it. We have to have one for the baths here. Don't tell her about the scabies. Just say it's my heels.'

Hardly had we finished tea when the corridor was filled with Florrie's clarion call, and for the third time that day I stood to be scrubbed down and anointed with sulphur ointment.

About 10.30 Evelyn appeared. 'I've got the things you wanted,' she said.

'What did my mother say?' I asked.

'She said if Linda was rationed to a saucer of water a day she'd contrive to have a bath in it,' she replied.

On the second day of the scabie parades, in the morning, without a word, Florrie took the new scrubbing brush I offered. We were just about to start the afternoon session when word came there was an officer waiting to see me.

'I'll do her first,' said Florrie, 'but the ossifer will have to wait. After all, there is a war on and this is a sick bay.'

Soon, brick red and in clean pyjamas, I was back in bed and the waiting officer was conducted in. Not unnaturally, perhaps, she hesitated at the door before gingerly she entered the 'dirty' ward.

She was a tall well-made girl whose movements, rather at

variance with her somewhat masculine figure, were dainty and fairy-like. Her uniform was new and she had only one pip. She didn't look very sure of herself and almost before I knew what I was doing I blurted out: 'This should never had happened. The whole idea of the medical, surely, is to separate those who are all right from those who are not. One glance at the two girls should have been enough. I didn't want to embarrass them. It mightn't have been their fault. But I tried to tell both the corporal and the sergeant with my eyes. The sergeant should have known. I wasn't being awkward when I wouldn't put my clothes on the form. She should have wondered why, instead of taking them from me as she did. And she put them on the forms without even glancing at where she laid them.'

The officer stood uneasily at the bottom of the bed.

'Yes,' she nodded. 'We realize that. It was an oversight. Rest assured it's been rectified now. Your bed and your bedding have been taken away and fumigated and your soldier's box properly cleaned out.'

It didn't seem to me to be the answer. She had glided off the point I was trying to make. We fell silent.

'Has anyone told you you have a high IQ?' she asked.

I shook my head. I'd never heard the letters IQ before, but having regard to where we were I presumed she was talking about my blood pressure. I knew a bit about high blood pressure. My father's Aunt Martha had high blood pressure. It cropped up almost every time she was the subject of the conversation. 'Martha should remember she has blood pressure and not go gallivanting up there to help them to clean that chapel out.' 'Martha wants to think on she has blood pressure. A hundred and forty aprons she made for the sale of work this year . . .' Aunt Martha was chapel, the speaker C of E.

'Are you surprised?' asked the officer. I nodded. As a matter of fact I was surprised. Aunt Martha was what was termed a noble-looking woman about five inches taller than I and about twice as heavy and she always had bright rosy cheeks whilst I, according to my new pay-book, my AB64, was 5 feet 2 inches tall, weighed 108 pounds, had a maximum chest measurement of thirty-three inches, grey eyes, light brown hair and a fresh to sallow complexion.

Besides, I always thought I had low blood pressure. I was always under the impression that this was the reason for my sluggishness in the morning, my reluctance to greet the new day with a song on my lips and joy in my heart. Of a truth each rising bell I die.

It was the officer who again broke the silence.

'I'm afraid you can't train as a kinetheodolite operator. You see, you didn't know what a sine or a cosine was. That means your maths are not sufficiently advanced.'

One thing for sure, I thought, she didn't get her pip for hospital visiting. I couldn't think of anything to say aloud.

'But you did well in mechanical aptitude,' she went on. 'Very well. You finished the paper and got it all right. In fact you did well on them all, but I'm not supposed to tell you that. There aren't so many vacancies on the mechanical side as there were. There are only three RDF' (later known as radar). 'You didn't put down for one but they think you would be very good there. So you can have one of the three vacancies if you want it.'

'What's RDF?'

'I don't know much about it. It's a bit hush-hush. I know you have to work on a gun site and it's the nearest you can get to active service. That's why you've got to sign a form to say you volunteered.'

'Hush-hush? Active service?'

'No. I didn't actually say active service. I said the nearest you can get to it. Of course, you can still be a driver if you want, or a clerk. Someone else, another officer, will come to see you and she will bring the form with her should you wish to sign.'

Weighed against a hush-hush job, 'the nearest I could get to active service', driving and clerking didn't stand a chance. I signed.

I had my stipulated number of 'sulphur' baths. These were followed by three Vaseline dittos after which an MO was called in to inspect my person. He pronounced me cured and Evelyn was given permission to help me carry my kitbag to the hut. In fact, she did all the carrying. I still felt very sorry for myself.

I was released on a Monday, the second of our initial training. For the others the interim had been spent in dental checks and the like. Before I could do any more I had to catch up with these checks and was detailed to report to the dental centre the following morning.

Inwardly trembling I walked rather slowly to the dental centre, regardless of the cold stinging rain, and I was finally directed to a room into which very little light penetrated. It was warm and a little steamy, for a coke stove burned in the centre. This surprised me: I thought no fires at all were allowed in the camp before 5 p.m. I sat down, trying to estimate how long it would be before I had to face my ordeal.

In the dimmest corner a slightly build man occasionally got up to tend the stove. He also kept tally of whose turn it was. I tried to place him. He wasn't an orderly, I thought. He was dressed in complete outdoor uniform. I watched him at the stove and saw, or thought I saw, that he was suffering to talk to someone. I went up to the stove as though to warm my hands and then went over and sat where he was.

'It's nearly your turn,' he said affably. 'You'll not have much longer to wait.'

'What about your turn?' I asked him.

'Not me, pet,' he said. 'I'm a mark-three coward. I would faint at the door. The thought of that chair makes me weak. If they came to get me I'm not above kicking and screaming and even biting, to stop them from taking me in.'

I smiled. 'You're kidding.'

'I'm not. However if I can keep my head above water I won't have to go in. I'm trying to get out. Out of the army I mean. I never thought I'd pass the medical, but I did. With flying colours, they said. I tried to tell them they were making a mistake; they were reading somebody else's medical sheet. They were, too. I'm sure they were. But you try to get the army to admit to its mistakes.'

'What are you doing here then?'

He tapped his head. 'Using me loaf. When you get into places like this, there's a process you've got to go through whether you like it or not. They put you in one end and somehow you can't get out the other till you've been through the lot, if you see what I mean. I nearly died the death when they told me I had to come here. But look at them. They come in in a trance. They need somebody to give them a shove. The orderly's never here. She's after one of the dentists. So I make meself useful. Keep the fire going and that, and keep the customers moving. Not too obvious, you know, to draw attention but enough so that they'd miss me if I wasn't here. There's an art you know. It's one of these things that looks easy but takes thinking about. You've got to know a bit about human nature.'

'You're a student of human nature then?'

I wanted to smile, but he was so deadly serious I thought it might give offence and so I kept my face straight. He had a very soft, gentle voice, just above a whisper. His round, open face was almost childlike. His hair was already showing signs of giving up the struggle for existence and his moustache was at variance with itself, part sulking and refusing to grow at all, part growing with the utmost reluctance and part flourishing, full of *joie de vivre*. Nor could the bits that did grow agree about the colour.

Before he answered he got up and spoke to a man in the corner. 'Your turn,' he said.

'Well, like I said,' he went on when he got back, 'I use me loaf. Notice things. Not like me sister. Honest. You never met anybody like me sister. No kidding. She's absolutely tasteless. When I say that I mean she has no taste whatever. I mean, we've never tried to eat her or anything like that. I mean the other thing.' He stopped, took a watch out of his pocket, shook it, got up, pulled me up with him and said, 'NAAFI break.'

But it was to the cookhouse that we went. His expression grew even more serious as he neared the door. We went into the business part of the cookhouse.

He stuck his head round a recess and spoke to someone within. 'How's your leg?' he asked. There was a reply and he tut-tutted in sympathy with the speaker.

'If it had been anybody else,' he said when the voice stopped, 'meself included, they would have been in bed. How you manage is a mystery. Mind, it's a good job you do. This place would be lost without you.' The outcome of all this interest was two mugs of cocoa and a generous plate of new bread dipped in hot dripping and seasoned.

Replete we returned to the waiting room.

At intervals during a mournful recital about an accident his sister had suffered, the business of the waiting-room continued until it was time for us all to pack up and go for the day.

'You see,' he said, 'there's worse places. Just tell them you've got to come back tomorrow. Nobody minds. You're here to get fitted out, be put in an A-1 condition (or what they think is A-1) and be sorted out into the kind of job you're going to do. They're bound to make a mistake, of course. I don't know what theory they work on, but you'll find yourself in the job for which you are least suited. It has something to do with the British climate, a stiff upper lip and the British character. It made people like Churchill and they think it will make you.'

For three further days I visited the waiting-room to listen to this new-found friend's philosophy of life. Actually, I had intended to take my turn on the Thursday feeling that I'd done very well to make the visit last so long.

'You'd be better waiting till Monday,' he said.

I agreed. Something else was bothering me. The itch had started up again at the back of my knees. I was due for a 12-hour pass on Saturday and I decided to ignore the itch till then. I didn't want to lose out on my posting.

On the Saturday I bought some Dettol to put on raw on the backs of my legs. It smarted something awful but it was better than the itch. In the end it got rid of the scabies. It also took the skin off my legs.

On Monday the young man didn't turn up. I never saw him again.

'Open up,' said the dental officer as he put the metal tube with its asthmatic sucking noise inside my mouth. 'Wider,' he added as he went on peering into the cavity and poking round with his probe and mirror. 'I see you've already had some dentistry done.'

'Agk,' I said.

'Mm,' he went on. 'You've got an unusual jaw. Peculiar really. Teeth don't seem to meet anywhere.'

As he continued his inspection and remarked on the strangeness of what he saw I had a sudden vision of God in the celestial workshop removing his protective apron and saying to the Angel Gabriel, 'That's me lot for today: 3,041 Africans (assorted tribes), 10,000 Chinese (various), 8,322 Europeans (multi–styled), 700 Asians (that'll larn 'em. I've had a complaint from that quarter), 22,003 Indians (diverse castes), 19,656 Americans and the odd sprinkling of Australians. Not bad for one day. I've done better of course. However, put on your halo and we'll call it a day.'

'And what shall I do with these odds and ends? Put them in the wastepaper basket?'

'Let me see. D'you know, I think you've enough for another one. Put them together and we'll make Linda Summers.'

I couldn't control the snort.

'That didn't hurt, I hardly touched you! For goodness' sake relax,' said the somewhat tetchy dental officer.

I spent the 48-hours' pass we were all given prior to our postings on a visit home. I changed into civvies, took my uniform to the store tailor and asked him if he could do anything with it. He measured me as for a suit and said I was to leave it to him. I took a pair of very comfortable dark red walking shoes with thick crêpe soles to a cousin of my father's, George Barnfather, shoemaker and cobbler, and asked him if he could dye them and make them look as much like my army issue as possible. I managed to buy a very nice forage cap and a dark khaki silk shirt and some extra Van Heusen collars.

The uniform fitted to perfection when I got it back and the tailor had replaced my buttons with a very fine set indeed. The shoes were also perfection. I wore them throughout my service career.

Actually, as far as uniform was concerned, as soon as we left initial training camp we soaked our stockings, shirts and collars in bleach to lighten them to a café au lait colour. Most of us had our collars stiffened at a Chinese laundry. To this end we 'won' enough collars one way or another to be able to change into a clean one every day.

The following Monday I journeyed to Oswestry. There was some slight difficulty in transit and I did not arrive at the camp till just after midnight. A sleepy duty officer accompanied by a sergeant saw to my needs. I signed for my bedding, went to the cookhouse for something to eat and made back to the hut.

In the glow of the dim pilot light I made up my bed, a bottom bunk. An icy blast from an open window blew straight on to the spot where I hoped soon to be sleeping. I closed the window. In the deserted ablutions I imprisoned my hair in some sixty pipe cleaners to ensure an all-over frizz next day. The water was hot. I could not resist taking a bath. Cleansed and warm I returned to the sleeping barrack-room. The window had been re-opened and once again I closed it and got thankfully into bed. A few minutes later the ceiling above me heaved, the occupant on the top bunk jumped heavily out of bed, re-opened the window firmly and climbed weightily back into bed. I waited, intending to get up again, but the next thing I knew I was being shaken into consciousness and an imperious voice was demanding that I get up. Still stupid from sleep I mumbled, 'Time is it?'

The voice said, 'Six-fifteen.'

'Jus' go ere,' I said and slid down again into the sheets to avoid the gale coming in at the window. A firm hand reached out, seized the bed clothes and pulled them back exposing me, my pipe cleaners and my issue pyjamas to the icy wind, the curious gaze of several pairs of eyes and a dark-haired, very irate corporal. Why, the corporal wanted to know, was I not up and dressed like the rest?

'Get up,' she commanded. 'Get up at once. We're leaving for breakfast in three minutes and you're going with us.'

'Have a heart, Corp,' said a thin, red-headed girl. 'She's just got here. She can't have been in bed much more than three hours.'

'She's got to learn. You've all got to learn. There's a war on. Or hasn't anybody told you yet? Mummy is a long, long way away. Now,' she turned again to me. 'Up. Breakfast. And when you get back I want all this (indicating my kit) put away, your floor polished, bed made, shoes and buttons polished. And,' she said eyeing the others, 'she polishes her own bit of floor and makes her own bed.' She was no taller than I, this corporal. She wore a flash on her arm advertising the fact that she came from South Africa.

Watched by twenty-nine pairs of sympathetic eyes I got up and made my bed, wrestling with blankets and sheets that would not fold into the regulation square. In an agony of embarrassment and mounting inadequacy, with two left hands and forty thumbs, I finally dressed, pulling out pipe cleaners with lumps of hair still adhering and cramming my cap on my head. In silence we were marched through the darkness to the cookhouse. Before she dismissed us the corporal informed us we were to appear for fatigues at 07.00 hours before mustering at 07.40 hours to be taken to the lecture room. With the others I joined the queue for porridge. The noise, the cooking smells, the little puddles of tea and crumbs already on some tables and my recent feeling of humiliation didn't help the porridge to look appetising. I settled for tea and bread and walked back to the hut in the friendly darkness, allowing the cold air to cool my burning cheeks. I polished my buttons, polished my floor space, went to the ablutions, washed and, thankful no one was near, tended the backs of my legs which were still sore. I did my hair and in the midst of those rushing about around me, redressed with care. When I returned to the room it was deserted and beautifully clean. I transferred the things from my kit bag into the soldier's box and struggled to fit my suitcase under the bunk. It was 7.35 by this time. I went to find the corporal to explain about my late arrival and not knowing about reveille and to say I would see that I wasn't late again. In the ablutions the corporal was waiting for me. So was my fatigue and the implements with which to accomplish it – a pail, a grey cloth, a scrubbing brush and a square of hard yellow soap.

'I'm sorry . . .' I began.

'You're late,' said the corporal severely. 'Very late. But that does not mean you can skimp your fatigue. I want it done thoroughly and WELL. You will get hot water from the tap. Use the soap *very* carefully. It has to last all week. Use the scrubbing brush with VIGOUR. That is how you'll get the seats clean. Wash out the cloth METICULOUSLY when you've finished.'

'The seats?'

'Yes. Your job is to clean these toilets.'

I gazed aghast at the row of ten toilets. 'But . . .' I gasped.

'You haven't time to stand with your mouth open. Report to me when you've finished. I shall inspect your work then.'

'But, Corporal . . .'

'My name is De Silver. Corporal De Silver. And stand to attention when you speak to me. Do you hear?'

'I was . . .'

'Stand to attention I said. Now get on with your fatigue. JUMP TO IT.'

I jumped, but it was a nervous reaction. I bent down to pick up the pail.

'The answer is "Yes, Corporal De Silver".'

I put the pail down again and stood to attention.

'Yes. Corporal De Silver,' I said.

The corporal strutted out and I had the silent ablutions to myself. I walked over to one of the toilets and pushed the door open. The sight was not reassuring. X number of ATS had used that toilet throughout the previous twenty-four hours, and I was a bit squeamish about toilets.

For a moment I contemplated the task before me. With care I took off my jacket, rolled up my immaculate sleeves and gazed at the first lavatory. Gingerly I dipped the floor cloth into the water, squeezed it delicately with the tips of my fingers and moistened the seat with the water remaining. Taking the soap by my finger and thumb I guided it carefully round the seat. As we neared the first bend it fell foul of a crack in the wood, slithered from my fingers and into the bowl where it lay half in and half out of the pipe that led to the waste.

I determined to act quickly. I would not stop to think. I would plunge my hand into the water and retrieve the soap. I removed my gold watch and identity bracelet ready for action. I closed my eyes and plunged, but try as I might I could not force my hand below the surface of the water. Then I remembered my coat hanger. I brought it from the hut and, with its help, tried to manoeuvre the soap up the side. I tried the stab direct, plunging the end of the hanger firmly on the soap and forcing it up the side, but with each inch I forced it through the water the coat hanger slipped a little nearer the end of the soap, till, before it reached the surface the soap had slithered free and was back in its retreat. I tried the stab oblique, pushing it up the side, with even less success. I tried edging it out with the curve of the hanger. Slowly and patiently I brought it nearer and nearer the surface, but time and time again it evaded capture and lay leering at me with the utmost contempt from the bottom of the bowl. I tried two coat-hangers and brought it clear of the water, but in the second that I put down one coat-hanger in order to pick the soap up, it escaped. By this time the water was milk white and I had to resort to blind stabbings not daring to pull the chain in case the soap disappeared altogether.

Then I remembered my toilet soap. I had with me several cakes with which to eke out my rations. I recognized defeat when I saw it.

In my fight with the soap I'd been vanquished. I got a tablet of my own and rubbed it up and down the scrubbing brush to obliterate any marks of identification in the hope that it would pass as a substitute for the yellow soap entrusted to my care. Thereafter I contented myself with squeezing a certain amount of water on each seat, shaking that article up and down, removing the surplus moisture with a cloth and pulling the chain.

I was putting on my jacket when a sergeant appeared.

'What are you doing here?' she asked. 'Shouldn't you be somewhere else?'

'Yes, Sergeant,' I answered. 'I didn't get here till the early hours of the morning when everyone was asleep. I didn't know about reveille. I had to unpack my kit. I was late for fatigues, so I had to do mine after the others had gone.'

'You don't have to burst into tears about it.'

'I wasn't going to.'

'Where should you be now?'

'I have to report to Corporal De Silver.'

'Ah. Yes. Corporal De Silver. Well. Right. I'll see Corporal De Silver and report that you've finished. Then where are you supposed to be?'

'I don't know.'

'You're one of the new people then. RDF? I thought so. I think we can restore you to the fold without too much trouble. Hurry up and put those things away then come with me. I think you should be in hut 307.'

When we arrived at a door with 307 painted on it in white, the sergeant turned to me and muttered something.

'What?' I asked.

'Your name.'

'Oh. Summers.'

'Ah,' she said, 'the last rose of.'

She opened the door and went into a room awash with khaki. She came to attention and saluted smartly.

'Private Summers, sir,' she said. 'Delayed.'

'Thank you, Sergeant,' said an officer at the other end of the room. The sergeant saluted again and left.

I stood still. Jeremy. He was fair with a golden fairness and taller

70

and broader and he wore a different uniform, but he had the same considerate charm.

'You haven't missed anything,' he said. He looked at the list lying on the table before him. 'Come in, Private Summers, and find a seat.'

Most of those assembled were sitting on forms at tables. The rather angular fair-headed girl who had tried to plead for me earlier edged a little way along and, thankfully, I sat down beside her.

'My name is Douglas,' he said. 'Roger Douglas. But I'm afraid you can't call me Roger and I can't call you . . .' looking around the group, 'Mary or Davinia or Dorothy. I'm Captain Douglas and you,' looking at me, 'are Private Summers. Now I expect,' he went on, 'that you feel hard-dealt with this morning. I'm afraid the harsh truth is that if you are to be successful on this course, you are going to have to do a lot of hard work and have many disturbed nights.

'We've looked down the list and it makes impressive reading. On paper at least, this emerges as one of the best intakes we've ever had, and looking at you, I am not disposed to think the lists are lying. Nevertheless, the weeks ahead of you are going to be difficult ones. You are going to work harder than you've ever worked before. Sometimes we shall have to start as early 07.30 and sometimes we shall finish as late as 21.30 hours. There is a great deal of technical material to be assimilated, operation duties to master, maintenance to know about, ditches to be dug, cables laid, and lectures to attend on aircraft recognition among other things. In addition I'm afraid you'll have to do fatigues. I tried to get you off – your course is so strenuous – but it wasn't possible. Also you will have to work every Saturday morning and sometimes Saturday afternoons and even Sundays. Church parade on Sunday, by the way, is obligatory, except on certain religious grounds.

'A liberty truck leaves the camp every evening 18.30 hours but I doubt whether you'll be able to avail yourselves of it most evenings for various reasons. This is a very large camp, but you will be concerned with only part of it. There is a NAAFI and usually, once a week, a film show in the cookhouse and on Sunday evenings there is often a dance, also in the cookhouse.

'Every Saturday morning there will be a test. The pass mark is 60 per cent. I expect you all to pass each week. For those who might be

71

having an off-day and fail one test you will be allowed a resit on Monday evening following. If you fail again, you will be transferred to another, new course, unless it is felt that perhaps RDF isn't for you, when you will be sent for other training elsewhere. When you have finished this course most of you will be sent to a gun-site already in existence or you will go to make up the personnel of a new unit. In either case you will be part of the Royal Artillery, whose motto is "Ubique" which, as I'm sure you all know, is Latin for "Everywhere". You will also be known as GL or OFC. The GL stands for Gun Laying and the OFC Operator Fire Control, both names given to RDF in its infancy.

'Perhaps there's one thing more I should say. Rumour has it that those who work with RDF are sterile. I cannot vouch for this and I do not advise you to accept this supposition as gospel, nor to test its validity.

'As far as Ack-ack is concerned, contrary to anything you have believed hitherto, its primary function is not the destruction of enemy aircraft. We leave that to the fighters who find it easier. The principal aims of Ack-ack are to prevent accurate bombing, to prevent enemy aircraft reaching their objectives, to keep enemy aircraft at a high altitude and deter them from flying in a straight even course for bombing. If a bomber can't fly low or straight, its chances of doing serious damage are lessened. Of course, we in Ack-ack do shoot down planes, but not in anything like the numbers achieved by the RAF. A shell must burst on or very near the target to be effective, and a plane can suffer a fair amount of damage and still function. When it comes to giving data for the guns, a plane has only to deviate slightly after the data has been given to escape unharmed. On the other hand, a plane has to fly straight and at a constant speed to bomb accurately. When it does this, it has a real chance of being hit by Ack-ack. Gunfire also tells fighters where enemy planes are. Sometimes one or two rounds are fired to alert fighters. Ack-ack breaks up formations of enemy bombers so that the fighters can attack them more easily. Sometimes we can't fire at targets because of the fighters overhead. Thus, you will see we work in harmony with RAF Fighter Command. And we do help keep up the morale of people in an air raid by just firing.

'Lastly, I want you all to hold your heads up. To be considered

72

for this work at all you must have passed through a process of selection, and further, in deciding to volunteer you are making a valuable contribution to the war effort. You will know something about active service before the war is over and the great thing about RDF is that in the heaviest air raid you'll never know you're in it and you'll never know the bomb that hits you. Any questions? Right. I know you are all going to do well, but just the same, the very best of luck to you all.'

In the afternoon we were kitted out in battle dress and taken to see the dem. sheds, huge places with mock-up sets where we would learn to operate the various pieces of equipment with which we would have to deal. As we walked out into the closing stages of the winter afternoon I looked out over the camp and saw in the reddening sky a distant blue hill. Something in its shape struck me and I found myself overcome with a feeling of homesickness, the very last thing I'd expected to happen. The painful yearning to be where there were mountains, my mountains, the Cheviots, was all-consuming, filling me to the brim with the desire to be near the sound of water plashing and swashing and bubbling over stones, to be in the midst of majestic, yet gentle, uplands and trees. It is good to be where there are trees, mountains and water. The air is pure. Nothing and no one hems you in. Life is free: restraint forgotten. And to be among one's own people! Here, everything was alien, a purposeful, workaday wartime world – no flowers, no bird-song, no books. It was a bad attack of homesickness and, do what I could, I couldn't get rid of it nor minimize it.

This longing didn't stop me from writing notes, or doing the written test at the end of the week, or digging and laying cables or actually working the equipment, but it did affect me when I was asked to speak, to get up and explain what I had just done. The lump would come into my throat, try as I might to stop it, and the words that came out were strangled or mangled to such an extent I was almost inaudible and my embarrassment was acute.

"In training. Digging a trench"

6. Training

Gradually, we were grouped in workable teams and after the first fortnight I found myself more or less settled with Ellen Bousefield, the slim fair-to-ginger-haired girl, Joy Evans, a very composed young lady with the most beautiful speaking voice I'd ever heard, Madeleine Habberley, a very attractive girl and Betty Hammond her friend, also attractive.

We operated an RX and TX (receiver and transmitter) together with a power unit under the eye of a number one. Ellen measured the angle of sight on a goniometer, Joy the range and I the bearing. Madeleine and Betty worked the transmitter. It was also their job to start up the power unit.

We began our training on the operationally obsolete Mark I Receiver. The main difference between it, the Mark I Star and Mark II as far as the actual operation went was the bearing. As the bearing operator I sat with one leg either side of the bearing column and took a mean, i.e. with the bearing column handles I turned the set from one side to the other and watched the little cone on my

74

cathode ray tube. It sank, peaked and sank. I stopped the set at highest point of the cone and gave this as the reading. In later models the column with its handles was superseded by a little handle situated below the tube.

Christmas Day that year fell on a Friday. Normally we would have worked late on the Thursday, but as it was Christmas Eve we were going to finish at 5 o'clock so that we would be able to have tea and catch the 6 o'clock (18.00 hours) Christmas liberty truck. We were to have a full day off on Christmas Day with a full day's work to follow on Boxing Day. We were also to have a late pass on Christmas Eve: like Cinderella, we had to be back by midnight.

On the Wednesday before Christmas, up to my ears and eyes in mud, I leant on my spade and surveyed the trench I and two colleagues had just dug. Water was already seeping into it.

'Just think,' one girl said (I'll call her Mary), 'tomorrow night at 5 o'clock we'll be free to grab what's on offer and squash into the liberty truck. Squash seems to be the operative word. The entire camp seems bent on painting Oswestry a delicate pink at least.'

'I'm not,' I said. 'I've worked out every detail of tomorrow night. There won't be time for anyone to have a bath. All that hot water going free. If I stay behind I can get in a mugful of that curious concoction the cookhouse calls cocoa. I daresay I could get a pailful if I wanted it. No one else will. I'll keep it hot by the stove and have a bath, and remember, I'll have a choice. Usually I always seem to get the leaky one – you know, the one they keep for arithmetic books. I have it on authority that the prototypes, the models for all those problem baths, are here at Oswestry. Bath A fills at a steady rate, bath B has a faulty tap and fills at different rate, bath C fills at rate X but has a leak . . .'

'And if the hot tap fills twice as fast as the cold tap and the temperature of the hot tap is 50 per cent less than that of the cold tap . . .' put in Mary.

'Well, anyway,' I went on, 'I'm going to enjoy it, then I'm coming back to sit on my soldier's box in front of a roaring stove, to drink the cocoa, even if I have to spoon it out of the mug, have a bit of cake, NAAFI doughnuts and anything else I can scrounge, and read *Mansfield Park*.'

'Sounds bliss,' said Mary. 'I must admit I wasn't relishing

risking ankle and shin to get into that truck and further risking the body beautiful to get a drink of doubtful vintage before they run out. It's just that I thought we had to. Part of the training. You know. Stiffens the sinews.'

'Me too,' said her friend. 'I must admit I thought there might be a better way to pass the evening, but apart from staying behind to polish my buttons yet again, I couldn't think of one.'

'Mind if we join you?' asked Mary.

'Love it. We can anticipate Christmas and share my cake,' I said.

'Sorry I can't bring anything other than NAAFI doughnuts and rock buns. I'm not getting a parcel. My prudent, practical, prospective mother-in-law has managed to get a towel for Christmas and she's putting it away into the bottom drawer she's preparing for me,' said Mary.

'I'm not getting a parcel either,' said her friend. 'Mummy and Daddy each sent half a guinea. I'd love to stay behind too.'

Christmas Eve dawned dark and wet. It was still dark when we left the hut, every soldier's box in place, every uniform correctly hung, buttons agleam, the floor polished to mirror-perfection. By midday the rain was pouring down. We marched through it to the barrack room to get our eating irons and stood aghast at what we saw. Our floor, our beautiful floor, was muddied over with the marks of numerous pairs of dirty boots; our bedding, those neat symmetrical squares of a few hours ago, had been thrown into heaps against the wall. A small army of men were dismantling our bunk beds and carrying them out to be loaded on to a three-tonner. Replacement bunks were already standing out in the pouring rain.

Corporal De Silver appeared.

'Don't stand there with your mouths open,' she shouted. 'Out. To the cookhouse. At the double.'

'But . . . what's happening?' asked Sally Bates, who was standing nearest her.

'At the double. Didn't you hear me!'

We went, wondering. No one we met in the cookhouse seemed to have any idea of what was happening either. However, during the afternoon, although no official announcement was made, it was generally accepted that the beds had been wanted urgently for a hospital and that our beds had been chosen because, although they were bunks, they were high bunks.

When we returned after lectures we found the room had been refitted with low wooden bunks. Those who slept on the bottom bunk would have to slide into bed. The activity in the barrack room was tremendous. Those going out had barely time to make up their beds, change and dash to the cookhouse for a quick mug of tea and anything that could be gulped down at speed.

'Leave your hot water bottles out. We'll fill 'em,' I said.

As we had the whole evening before us we three lit the stove then walked to the cookhouse and took our time over tea. We returned with three pieces of cake liberally spread with margarine and jam. In the hut we swept the worst of the mess up from the floor, filled the hot water bottles and put them into their respective beds, placed our soldier's boxes round the now hot and radiant stove, looked over the various comestibles for the feast then went out to see what else we could forage in the NAAFI and the cookhouse. As we had borrowed extra mugs we had both coffee and cocoa to keep hot on or near the stove. We had amassed quite a feast, and filled with pleasure at the thought of the evening before us we went to have our baths, drawing lots to decide who should have which bath. We returned warm and glowing, walking leisurely along the corridor that connected our hut with the ablutions, swinging our sponge bags. Our hair, newly washed and regimented into curlers, was completely covered in khaki scarves turned turbans. We wore greatcoats over our freshly laundered pyjamas, and our feet were encased in woollen socks and boots.

Corporal De Silver stood at the entrance to the barrack room.

'Oh! There you are,' she accused. 'I've been looking for you. I want this room cleaned up, the floor scrubbed and polished ready for inspection before anyone in this hut goes to bed tonight. Each one of you has to scrub her own bed space and polish it tonight. I will inspect the room personally before I go to bed. When you have finished yours I will inspect them if you decide to do your bits before the others.'

Mary was the first to recover.

'But, Corporal,' she said. 'It's Christmas Eve. Tomorrow is Christmas Day. Couldn't we leave it till Saturday?'

'My name, Private Ramsay, is De Silver. Corporal De Silver. No,

Private Ramsay, we cannot leave the barrack-room till Saturday. There's a war on. Don't you understand that yet? War does not distinguish between Christmas Day and any other day. That room is to be cleaned up tonight. That's an order. Is that clear?'

'Yes. Corporal De Silver.'

'And in the unlikely event of my not being around when the others return, you, Private Milvaine,' she said to Joan, 'will inform them of what has to be done.'

'Yes, Corporal De Silver.'

We walked into the room, the long room, and looked about us. It housed, in all, 30 girls.

'I can't believe it,' I said. 'I just can't.'

'I can,' said Mary. 'Bitch.'

'I can't tell them they've got to scrub and polish a floor before they go to bed. Imagine them coming back full of Christmas cheer and being met with that,' said Joan.

'And some of them,' I said, 'might be the worse for wear, to say the least. We might even have an alcoholic mutiny on our hands.'

We looked at the stove, already beginning to redden at the bottom and, round it, the feast.

'Well,' said Mary. 'It's no use hanging around. Better get started.'

'I don't feel I can just do my own bit,' I said. 'It would make the rest look even worse.'

'Nor me,' said Joan.

'Is it to be the lot then?' asked Mary.

'Might as well.'

Mary sighed. 'Dear God!' she said.

We changed our greatcoats for denims and set to work. To speed things up I tried using my hairbrush as a substitute scrubbing brush. I dipped it in the water but as soon as I applied it to the floor the bristles collapsed so that the wood of the brush and the lino met. I flung the miserably inadequate brush down.

'Damn!' I said. 'Blast! Bloody hell!' – actually, the first time I ever remember swearing.

'Is that the best you can do?' asked Mary.

I stood up, put my hands on my hips and looked at the bucket of water, already dirty. 'Do you know what I think?' I said. 'It would be better if we evolved a system. We'll divide the room into three and use three buckets. One bucket lasts no time. For the first third, you slosh water on and scrub, Mary, and Joan, you wipe up after her using the clean water. And I'll bring fresh water. We'll move the pails one up. I'll take the dirty water away and bring clean back. Next third we'll move around one and the next we'll change again.'

By the time we got to the bottom of the room, the top of the floor was dry and we began polishing. We could not manage the rich, dark glow that had hitherto prevailed, but we did make the floor shine. At last it was finished.

'Well, who's going to summon our revered Corporal De Silver?' I asked.

'She put you in charge,' said Mary to Joan. 'It's up to you but I'll tell you this – if she utters one word of criticism, or we have an inch to do over again, I'll push what's left of this tin of polish into her stupid face, even if it means spending the rest of the war in the Glasshouse.'

'Or facing the firing squad,' I said.

'At the moment,' said Mary, 'even that.'

Corporal De Silver scanned the room. She walked slowly down one side and up the other, inspecting the floor.

'It needs at least two more coats of polish,' she said, paused and added, 'before Saturday.' She paused again. 'But for tonight it will do.' She looked at us.

In spite of ourselves we stood to attention and said, 'Yes, Corporal De Silver.'

Without speaking, we put away our materials, laid newspaper stepping-stones on the floor, took off our denims and went to the ablutions to clean up. Standing on newspaper in front of the stove, we drank the cocoa. Of the two drinks it was the better equipped to withstand the delays of the evening and was not markedly different from what it would have been four hours earlier.

'Have some cake,' said Mary.

'I couldn't,' I said. 'Has anyone a large sheet of paper?'

Joan provided a sheet of plain foolscap.

In large letters I wrote,

DO NOT DARE STAND ON THE FLOOR
DO NOT DARE TO SAY THANK YOU
DO NOT DARE TO UTTER THE WORDS
'A MERRY CHRISTMAS'

I read it over and then added,

AT LEAST NOT TILL TOMORROW

We put it on a prominent place on the floor near the door.

'Listen,' said Mary. 'They're coming back,' said Joan. We got into bed quickly. I pulled the bedclothes over my head.

In spite of Christmas Eve, Christmas Day was quite a happy one on the whole. We were allowed a fire all day, had an egg and bacon breakfast, roast meat, veg. and Christmas pudding lunch and ham and Christmas cake for tea. There was a dance in the cookhouse in the evening and if we didn't enjoy ourselves, we gave a very good imitation – having eaten, drunk deeply, laughed noisily and talked shrilly.

On the Wednesday evening following I was washing my smalls in the deserted washing/drying room when suddenly I started to cry and I couldn't stop. This must have lasted about half an hour. When it was over I felt strangely cleansed and light. The awful yearning ache had gone. I finished off my washing and went back to the room a new person.

The course was drawing to its end. Although I had been robbed of speech in the oral parts of the course, I had done consistently well in the weekly exams, never getting less than 90 per cent. On the Thursday Captain Douglas told us that they'd make their selection of those who were to stay behind to train as number ones, i.e. NCOs. He said it had been very difficult as at least half the course qualified, and there were only four vacancies. I was not one of the four.

New Year's Day was to be a working day like any other, but again, on New Year's Eve special liberty trucks were laid on to take would-be merrymakers out of camp. This time I elected to go with the others.

One of the casualties of our free day on Christmas Day had been the lecturette that, normally, each member would have given. As this was not part of the course proper but was more concerned with potential NCOs it had been omitted. On New Year's Eve in the morning we were told that next day was to be a working day when we would each be called upon to give this belated talk.

That night we crammed into the liberty truck, were spewed out at Oswestry where we went round from crowded pub to crowded pub wishing everyone a happy new year, crammed ourselves back into the truck, were spewed out again, sang 'Should Auld Acquaintance be Forgot' in an alcoholic nostalgia and got into bed.

The next day we assembled for the lecturettes, each to be of three to five minutes' duration. Ten minutes before we were due to speak we 'drew' our subject from a box and went into a side room to do what preparation we could.

When my turn came I drew 'Cathode Ray Tube Supplies', which I took to mean how the signal, having left the power unit as electricity, finally arrived at the cathode ray tube in the RX. Just as I was due to be called in there was a hiaitus. It was almost breaktime and we were sent off for coffee and told to return in half an hour. I spent that time studying my notes for all I was worth.

When my name was called on our return, I walked forward to my place. Mary Bruce, a large plump friendly girl sitting in the front row, smiled at me and nodded. It was heart-warming and I suddenly felt calm. I began my lecture. As I talked I became aware of when my listeners understood what I was saying and when they did not. When I sensed the latter was happening I went back and explained, pausing, to see that the meaning had sunk in. I drew diagrams, explaining, explaining, explaining, filled with nothing but the desire that they should understand. When I had finished the applause was warm, prolonged and genuine. One or two asked questions and I was able to answer them. For some reason, Captain Douglas had been replaced by another officer, a woman. 'That five minutes lasted thirty-seven,' she said.

By the time the morning session was over, Captain Douglas had returned. He called me to one side and asked me to report to his office as soon as I'd eaten. I was ushered into his office within twenty minutes. The woman officer was there too.

'I hear that was a splendid lecture you gave this morning,' he said. 'I'm sorry I missed it. I am told that the instructors could not have done better. More. I think it's true to say that you got some points across that we did not. We've just looked through your records and nowhere can we find that you've done any teaching.'

'I haven't, sir.'

'None at all?' It was the woman officer who spoke.

'No, ma'am.'

'Remarkable. Well. I don't know what you plan to do with the rest of your life, but if you don't teach it'll be wasted. You have a gift,' she said.

'Thank you, ma'am.'

'The strange thing is,' said Captain Douglas, 'that you should have changed into a swan so late in the course. There's never been anything wrong with your written work, but your oral work has left something to be desired. We weren't prepared for this morning's *tour de force*. Can you offer up any explanation?'

I couldn't put into words what had happened. In any case, I thought it neither the time nor the place.

'I had an attack of laryngitis and a slight sore throat, sir,' I said. 'I spent some time in the sick bay during my initial training and I think I left before I felt completely fit. I was afraid that, if I complained, I would be taken off the course and I didn't want that to happen.'

'You feel well now?'

'Perfectly, sir.'

'Well, I'm afraid this morning's performance has come too late to affect the issue as of now. But I felt I had to speak to you about it. I really shouldn't tell you but we'll give a strong recommendation that you are promoted to number one as soon as the opportunity offers and also that you shall have an opportunity to become an instructor, although you may well decide you'd rather remain on site. I hope you were not dismayed that your name was not on the list. But your turn will come, I'm sure of that. Any questions?'

'No, sir, thank you, sir.'

He nodded, then went on, 'Oh, by the way. I heard about the floor. I tried to persuade them to leave you all undisturbed over the holiday, but officers are not the all-powerful creatures you think. But there are compensations. In the years to come one Christmas will dissolve into another – but you will always remember Christmas Eve 1942.'

When I got outside, Ellen was waiting for me. 'I wanted to tell you that was a smashin' talk you gave. I've also come to invite you to the NAAFI. Captain Douglas hasn't proposed or anything like that, has he? What else could bring those roses to your maiden cheek? Or is it a secret?' she asked.

'No secret, I suppose. He was just complimentary about the talk.'

We had reached the NAAFI by this time, queued for coffee and joined a group at a table. I felt at peace with the world.

Later that day we heard our postings. Ellen, Joy, Madeleine, Betty and I were to go as a team to help make up a new battery, 625 Heavy Ack–Ack. We were told to present ourselves at 09.00 hours the following day at hut number 40, which was at the other end of the camp, there to receive further instructions. Reveille on Saturday was one hour later. Even so we should have had ample time to get to the hut, but Corporal De Silver was even more difficult to satisfy than usual over the fatigues. I had been given the last job of all. I had to wait till all the other jobs had been inspected, then I had to sweep the entire floor, report to Corporal De Silver, who would then inspect that it was properly swept, after which time I had to burn the rubbish in the incinerator. I waited in a rising fever of anxiety lest we were late. In the end it was decided the others would go ahead. While I swept the floor Corporal De Silver disappeared and when I had finished my task, she had to be looked for.

As I approached the door of hut 40 I was aware of the ominous silence which told me that someone of importance was speaking and was being listened to with complete attention. I attempted to enter unobserved and to that end slowly and gingerly turned the knob. The door, however, was in no mood to co-operate and it let out a piercing squeak of betrayal. All eyes in the overcrowded hut, including those of the speaker, turned on me. The speaker was also, obviously, the person-in-charge. He looked me up and down slowly from the toe of my boots to the crown of my cap. I shrank so much beneath the scrutiny that I thought I might crawl out of sight under the door.

Finally he spoke. 'Your name,' he demanded.

I was undecided. My hand fluttered up a few inches and fell back. Should I salute or shouldn't I?

'You have a name?' the man went on.

'Yes, sir. Private Summers, sir.'

A junior commander sitting at a desk checked the list before her and nodded. The officer looked down at the list.

'Ah,' he said. 'GL. I'll have more to say about that in a minute. In the meantime you're late. This is 09.15 hours, not 09.00 hours. Take a seat.'

There wasn't one. No one moved to make way for me. A girl was sitting to my immediate right and, in obedience to the officer's command, I lowered myself till the extreme edge of the upper part of my right leg was on the edge of the girl's chair. I remained in this very uncomfortable position for the rest of the meeting.

'As I was saying,' went on the major, for such he was, 'you are a unit and you're going to be the best unit in the British or any other army. To do that you have to train. Train, train, train. And that is what we are going to do. As a unit. And when I say unit, I mean unit. There is no one part of this unit any better than any other. I don't care what your instructors have told you. None of this mystery and superiority as far as trades are concerned. GL is no different from any other part of the unit. I will have no inflated ideas of superiority in this unit. Is that understood? Right. You will muster on Monday at 04.30 hours on the parade ground near the GL dem shed ready to march off at 05.00 hours. You will have your kit at hut 34 by 12.00 hours tomorrow. All bedding, etc., to be returned to stores by 04.00 hours on Monday. Anything you have left after that you carry yourself. We are going from here to a practice camp for one month. During that month it will be my job to turn you into an eager, fit, efficient, alive, force. And, by God, I'm going to do it. Understood? Now Sergeant Smith has something to say to you.' He sat down next to the JC at the table.

Sergeant Smith was obviously already known to a fair number of those present because, when he appeared on the platform, the tension in the atmosphere lessened noticeably. He was not exactly misshapen; rather, he was badly cast, as though he had been fashioned in a hurry by a kindly but slapdash architect. His head was somewhat too big, his eyes tended to protrude. But when he smiled his warm smile, which he did often, he showed beautiful white teeth and he became attractive. In fact, it was only when you first looked at him you thought him odd; after that you never noticed. He had a slight hump, his shoulders were too broad, his hips too narrow and his legs too short. He was obviously well liked by those who knew him and those who did not liked him on sight anyway.

'Well, lads and lasses,' he said. 'Welcome. I think the best way we can get together is to have a concert here in this very room tonight at eight o'clock. Now we can't have a concert if we haven't any acts so I want some volunteers. In fact. I've got some already. Gunner Morton is going to play the spoons and — '

'Me?' interposed someone, presumably Gunner Morton. 'I never said — '

'You've just volunteered,' went on Sergeant Smith, and everyone laughed and clapped, including the major, 'and, as I was saying, Bombardier Jones is going to sing for us — '

'No,' came a voice from the body of the hall.

'Oh, yes he is,' went on Sergeant Smith, 'we all heard you volunteer' (laughter) and 'Lieutenant Brady is also going to give us the benefit of his rich baritone voice' (more laughter). 'He has also volunteered' (prolonged laughter and clapping). 'But I'll need some more. Don't be afraid. If you can't take part you probably know someone who could and is too shy to come forward. But don't you be too shy. You tell me who they are. I'll do the rest.'

One or two names were shouted at him above the general noise and Sergeant Smith wrote something down on an envelope he fished out of his pocket. Presently he left the stage and the major took command once more. I was by this time so uncomfortable I could think of nothing but perservering till the meeting was over. When we were dismissed I stood up and managed to stifle a yelp of pain just in time – pins and needles.

'I think I'm crippled for life,' I said to one of our number as we walked towards the NAAFI. 'What did I miss anyway?'

'Nothing that you won't know off by heart in time,' she answered. 'He gave us a sort of family tree to show where the battery stood in the hierarchy. Also the names of the officers. The JC is Miss Gaitskill.'

'And what was that about us not being superior? I've never felt superior. Have you?'

'Well. You know these things get about. If you're a GL you're supposed to be brainy and all that mularky. I'd heard that before I came here.'

'Well, I've never felt superior since the day I first tried on that initial bit of khaki. I had the impression that all the training, especially that bit concerned with Corporal De Silver, was to make you feel inferior.'

After lunch we had the offer of a lift. I cannot remember now where we were dropped off, to be picked up two hours later, but I seem to remember it was a smallish town. There was really nothing there to distinguish it from any other town of similar size. We looked at the shops and, in so doing, tended to become absorbed as individuals in whatever interested us. Thus I was alone in looking at the contents of one shop window located in a narrow side street off the main thoroughfare. The proprietor had, apparently, long ago decided to ignore the fact that he had a shop window and the dust of ages had settled on the contents where it had lain undisturbed for some time. In one corner I espied a monocle. I went into the shop.

When I opened the door an ageing bell shook as with the palsy and protested feebly at my entrance. Undeterred, I went into the darkened interior. It was almost as dusty as the contents in the window. I walked towards the counter looking around me. It seemed that no customer had disturbed the musty air since the beginning of time. Presently a curtain moved and a small sparse man, dressed in a dowdy black suit and high wing collar, merged into the area in front of the counter.

'Good afternoon,' I said.

The man pulled a dark grey handkerchief (which had no doubt once been white) out of his pocket and wiped his mouth.

'Good afternoon,' he answered, then went on. 'The one sure way to get a customer is make a cup of tea.'

'Oh, I'm sorry,' I said. 'I didn't mean to disturb you.'

'No need to be sorry,' said the man. 'I'm not complaining, just stating a fact. What can I do for you?'

'The monocle in the window,' I answered. 'How much is it?'

'Monocle?'

'Yes. The one in the corner.'

The man thought a bit. 'The window?' he said, at last.

'Yes, over there. In that corner,' and I pointed in the general direction. 'To be sure,' said the man. He went forward and opened a little door at the back of the window and then paused, as though in preparation. Finally, he dived into the window space and returned with the prize in his hand.

'Did it give much trouble?' I asked sympathetically.

The man almost smiled. 'I soon get the better of it,' he said. He blew the dust off the monocle and then stood back a little to allow the cloud to disperse.

'How much?' I asked. The man continued looking at it.

'Sixpence?' he said at length.

'Is there a ribbon or something to go with it?'

'There might be.'

'Would that be sixpence for the lot?'

'It might.'

'I'll take it,' I said. 'And while you're looking for the ribbon, d'you think you might have anything else of interest?'

'That depends,' he said.

By the time he'd found the ribbon, he had spread before me a lorgnette minus lenses, a long black cigarette-holder with a silver band and a silver purse on a silver chain. I bought the lorgnette and the cigarette-holder. I was to regret for a long time to come that I didn't also buy the purse but, at the time, I couldn't afford it.

'Where on earth have you been?' the others wanted to know when I caught up with them.

'Sorry. I wandered down a side street and got lost,' I answered.

We decided to go to the concert early to be sure of a good seat and to that end were at hut 40 by 19.40, only to find that the room was already packed to the door with soldiers of both sexes. The only vacant spaces were on the platform and immediately in front of it, where there were a number of fairly comfortable seats still empty. These, we guessed, correctly, were for the officers. Most of those present were sitting on forms which meant that, in theory at least, there would always be room for one more. The second-back form was the one least crowded and after much squeezing up and rearranging we were finally accommodated in conditions that promised maximum discomfort.

It was certainly a receptive, convivial, if somewhat noisy audience who awaited the arrival of their martial pastors and masters. By 20.05 the front row was filled and the evening's entertainment began. Sergeant Smith was compère and he was given a tumultuous welcome when he appeared on the stage to announce the first number. Messrs Morton, Smith and Brady had been augmented by Gunners Jones (two 'Albert' monologues) and Holdsworth (card tricks with Sergeant Smith as stooge). Of them all perhaps Gunner Morton on the spoons was the best, but, regardless of performance the applause they got would have done credit to a first-class music-hall artiste. We had, like everyone else in the back rows, abandoned the forms and stood where we could get a better view. Sergeant Smith came on to do his piece. He carried with him a toilet roll. We clapped loudly, stamped our feet and started to laugh before he'd ever opened his mouth. After a while he held up his free hand for silence, bowed and said, 'Ladies and gentlemen – Little Nell.'

He pulled the free end of the toilet paper till some of it cascaded on to the floor and then, as if reading the bit hanging down, he said in sombre tones:

> 'Nell was a grocer's daughter.
> She knew how to handle the hams.'

It was the only bit of the recital I actually heard; most of the monologue was said amid the laughter of the audience. It went on interminably. Nell's mother, fickle and obsessive about insurance policies, was given to marrying a succession of men from various trades, each of whom met his death in one verse. At the end of each verse Sergeant Smith wiped the mock tears from his eyes and shook his head at the catastrophe which had befallen the victim of the moment, then looked up and said brightly, 'So the girl's mother married again,' and sent another tug of paper rolling to the floor. He frequently forgot his lines and had to be prompted by the good-natured audience, most of whom, it appeared, knew the poem better than he did. For his second piece he elected to do a dramatic rendering of 'The Death of Nelson', performing all the parts himself. To assist him in his endeavours he had a gummed paper moustache and an admiral's hat in black crêpe paper. With the hat sitting straight on his head he suddenly clutched himself in the region of his diaphragm and staggered about the stage.

''Ardy,' he roared, then clutched his throat and groaned as though he was working the throttle on a motor bike. 'Hi am 'it. Hi am wown-dead.' He turned his hat to the side and stuck the moustache on his upper lip, keeping it approximately in place with one finger as he didn't trust the gum, and stood to attention.

'Not seeriyowsly, Hi 'ope.' He turned the hat back to first position, took off the moustache, gripped his middle, tottered a bit more and said, 'Mort-alley, Hi fear.' Once again he resumed the guise of Hardy. 'Then all ower 'opes is coll-opsed.' When it came to 'Kiss me, 'Ardy,' he had us whistling and stamping encouragement.

The concert ended with the 'Corpse de Bally Oswestry' doing 'Voices of Spring' – i.e. the whole company with their trousers rolled up above their knees, little tatty paper skirts round their waists and paper flowers in their hair, prancing round the stage. It was hilarious at first but I thought they spoiled it by playing to the gallery too much. The church choir back at home did it better. I felt hot, sweaty and exhausted. I had clapped and cheered with the others. My jaws and my feet ached and I longed for fresh air, but mindful of the major's words of the a.m. I decided to do what everyone else was doing.

'I always thought,' said Ellen, 'that Nelson was shot in the back.'

'I think you're right,' I said. 'They used what I think is called "dramatic licence".'

'I don't know about the dramatic bit, but I would certainly agree about the licence,' Ellen replied.

Next morning we were fully occupied getting our kit to hut 34. I felt it necessary to keep back my pyjamas, toilet things and a change of underwear. It wasn't till I met up with the rest in the dark watches of Monday morning that I realized everyone else had been content to leave out only those things that they could stuff into their pockets. I had to tie up my left-over belongings in my gas cape – the only one carrying a parcel. In the cold and dark we drew up in ranks, roll calls were taken and all being presumed present we marched out of camp en route for Oswestry and its station.

"Sheepskin mitts could be folded back to become mittens"

"Leather jerkin over battledress"

"Leather gaiters"

L. '86.

Battledress

7. Practice Camp

In Oswestry station, almost three miles from the camp, a troop train awaited us. We were herded in and bidden sit where we were told, but there proved to be more room than was at first thought and after a reshuffling of places we, Ellen, Joy, Betty, Madeleine and I, had the carriage to ourselves. Hardly had we started when it began to rain so that what we could see of the landscape became increasingly cheerless. Before long the windows steamed up and there was nothing to be seen without effort.

What with dashing from lecture room to dem sheds, digging, fatigues, polishing floors and buttons, tending to one's laundry and learning notes, these seemed to be about the first quiet moments we'd had since we'd teamed up, and I began to see my colleagues as personalities. Ellen had made an impression on me from the first. She had early learned the necessity of standing on her own two feet and it showed. She had a mordant sense of humour and a penchant for saying what she thought. She did not suffer fools gladly and the fools were left in no doubt as to her sentiments. I liked her. She was a loyal friend and an entertaining companion. She had the clear skin and light blue eyes that usually go with light golden/ginger hair. When she smiled she showed a perfect set of gleaming, even white teeth.

As I have already said, Joy had the most attractive voice I'd ever heard. Even when she was angry she did not speak loudly or unattractively and because of this, I suppose, in repose her features retained their serenity. She had been educated at a convent, a boarding school, where, at night and in the morning, the girls shrouded themselves in white tent-like arrangements under which they dressed and undressed. As far as I know she had no job between leaving school and coming into the forces. Her father was a high-ranking officer in the army and her brother was a captain therein. I admired her tremendously for her integrity and her calm self-assurance, although we often ruffled each other's feathers. Or, I should say, my feathers were ruffled. Hers did not alter noticeably. One of the inconsequential things we disagreed over was the pronunciation of medieval. I cannot remember how the difference came about, but Joy pronounced it 'med-ee-val' while I pronounced 'medi-ee-val', and she told me I was wrong. Secretly I thought her pronunciation was right, but I had learned mine at Bedlington, where I went to school, and I felt that to accept her pronunciation would be disloyal to my own particular little-known but much loved alma mater; so I stuck to my guns.

Madeleine's father was either a major or a colonel. She had come into the ATS straight from school at 17½ and had taken a clerical post until she was old enough to transfer to Ack-ack. I thought at first that with her military background she had been avid to join the colours at the first opportunity, but later, on further acquaintance, I feel she joined up so that she was free to do much as she wished. She was very attractive, even glamorous. She had large blue eyes and thick lashes. These eyes and lashes alone could play havoc with the hearts and desires of almost all the men we met up with, which was pleasant for me because there was always an agreeable number of left-overs. However, her eyes were not her only good feature. The rest of her face matched up, the whole crowned with an abundance of blonde hair that waved and curled. Regulations demanded that her long tresses be imprisoned in something that kept it in control and above her collar. Like most of her fellow female military personnel, she rolled it round an old bootlace or something similar. In her case, it deceived nobody. It wasn't difficult to imagine it cascading, rippling and curling down her back and over her shoulders.

Madeleine was very intelligent but she used her intelligence in a way that was new to me. Two things had stood out in my life hitherto; education, which was important for its own sake, and work. The great thing was that, whatever you did, you should work hard at it. The more capable you were the harder you should work. Madeleine used her intelligence to give herself the lifestyle most agreeable to her in the circumstances. The most enduring picture I have of her is her lying full-length on her bed while we rushed round preparing for the next event, whatever it was, and talking the while. She would appear removed from us all and then, suddenly, she would interpose with a remark that shed a radiance on what we'd been saying, showing up its weak points or its humour, hitherto hidden.

Betty and Madeleine had met up earlier, and when Maddy decided to transfer to Ack-ack Betty elected to go with her. She, too, was attractive, with dark eyes and hair and a clear olive skin, but she was overshadowed by her friend. Madeleine was at home with anyone of us, but Betty only liked to be with her. Madeleine chose to work on the transmitter where she became the number three in charge. Betty worked on the TX as number six, to be with Maddy.

Our number one, Kay, we'd met briefly. She had come straight from school into Ack-ack and had been selected for training as a number one, at the end of which she had been appointed to a team – us. As we were strong individuals in our own right, I had a feeling we were sometimes a bit overpowering. However, Kay came from Wakefield, Yorkshire; she wasn't easily overpowered.

At first, our talk was mostly confined to guesses at where we were going. At no time during my service, until I got my last two promotions, was I ever to learn beforehand where I was going and why. I was simply detailed to get myself ready for a kit inspection (all moves were preceded by a kit inspection, when you were put to the trouble of separating the things you should have from those you shouldn't) and then muster outside battery office at 07.00 hours – or earlier. I never knew where I was going till I got there. Most often I never knew why I'd been sent. The disconcerting thing was that the people to whom I'd been sent sometimes didn't know either.

Inevitably the talk turned to boyfriends. Both Ellen and Madeleine were engaged. The latter, when asked, passed round the photograph of a very handsome young airman indeed.

'Gosh,' I sighed, looking at it. 'He's smashin'. I'll bet you're head over heels in love.'

'What about your boyfriend?' Ellen asked me.

'Haven't got one,' I replied. 'I have not yet found anyone willing to prostrate himself before me, overcome by my beauty. I have walked over no greatcoats, army or otherwise, nor has anyone thrown himself in front of a train for love of me.'

'Ah,' they said in unison and Ellen pulled out her handkerchief and delicately mopped up a non-existent tear.

Gradually the talk died down and we became quiet. Packed lunches were brought round and we chewed our way through them before stopping briefly at a station to be given tea from a canteen at the far end of one platform. After the meal the atmosphere became stuffy and we were sleepy. At intervals we rubbed circles in the steaming windows and looked out on to the dripping landscape. At one point we seemed to pass near a great deal of water. Finally, the order came to detrain. We got ready and sat expectantly on the extreme edge of our seats. Nothing happened. After a time, the train slowed down and jerked to a stop. We made peep-holes again in the steamed-up window and peered out. A sparse cottage or two, a few mournful sheep, a country road. Nothing more. The train moved forward slowly and jerked to a stop again. Betty looked over to the corridor side.

'Some people seem to be getting out,' she said.

'In this rain?' said Maddy. 'They're fond of a treat.'

We jerked forward again. The door at the end of the compartment was opened and a voice shouted, 'Everybody out!'

We got up and stumbled on to an insecure wooden platform which was about the length of a carriage. A most undisciplined and unprincipled wind blew in gusts and never from the same direction twice. It slapped into our faces, whipped round our legs and up our skirts. And the rain wasn't much better. It was a time for chin-straps and gas capes, only I couldn't put mine one. The foghorn voice of the sergeant major roared above the rain and wind. We mustered on the road, ready to march off. Before we did so, however, there was a commotion. Someone had fainted. I got a glimpse of a blonde girl being helped into one of the baggage wagons. Then we set off.

The rain permeated everything. It found the chink between my greatcoat collar and my neck and trickled down, saturating my shirt collar and travelling on in little icy rivulets, down both my back and my front. The hem of my coat, the front of my skirt and my stockings above the knee were sodden. The rain easily found its way inside my shoes. We squelched on, overtaken by the baggage wagons that liberally bespattered us with mud. Occasionally we were urged on by a sergeant or an officer.

'C'mon. Pick 'em up there. You're out of step. Left. Left. Left, right, left,' till the dreary afternoon gave way to dismal dusk and a grey mass lay flattened before us on the horizon. Then came the order 'Right wheel!' and we marched into camp where we came to a halt, around us a drab huddle of buildings, ahead of us a rocky drop to a turbulent, grey sea.

We were stood at ease while hut numbers were given out and orders issued about the collection of bedding and kit, the daily ration of coke and the hot meal that would soon be available in the cookhouse. I sprinted to my hut; I'd had enough of sleeping on a bottom bunk with the lumpy outline of the heavy occupant overhead a mere few inches from my own slender anatomy. I had more bumps on my head than I had when I left civvy street – and not bumps of knowledge, either. I got my top bunk. I was agreeably pleased to find the stove already lit and roaring and the chill off the room. In spite of the stipulated ration of one hod of coke per hut per night, both stove and hod were full. It was then I noticed that the room already had an occupant; one of the top bunks had a tenant – the girl who had fainted, scarcely visible above the bed clothes.

I saw to my bedding and kit, went to the cookhouse and returned to the hut a little later than the others because I'd had to take my greatcoat to the drying room. The hut was full of warm bustle and friendly chatter. The girl who had fainted had by now recovered sufficiently to be sitting up in bed. From the empty plates on her soldier's box it seemed that she had eaten.

Standing behind my bunk, my arms resting on the bed I had just made up, I gazed at the girl, fascinated. She was the first of four 'blondies' I was to meet on Ack-ack. She looked, I thought, like a delicate bloom in a bed of thistles. All the poetry I had ever heard, or read, likening girls to flowers on summer days, suddenly made sense. Many of my friends were attractive, even beautiful, but none of them could be described as flower-like. Everything about this girl was pale and slender, a flawless porcelain skin, pale yellow hair, light blue eyes. She wore flimsy, sleeveless art-silk pyjamas in pale blue that brought out the colour of her eyes, and which added to the general air of frailty. She looks, I thought again, like a cornflower in a field of ripened grain. That anyone so fragile should be subjected to the rigours of a gunsite! Of course, she would have to volunteer, but even so, someone had blundered.

The girl was gazing critically into a looking-glass intent on plucking stray hairs from her eyebrows. Around her, kit was being unpacked and already a number of photographs had been put up. The talk was generally of boyfriends and engagement rings. Suddenly the girl put the looking-glass down, and extending one long, slender arm, exposed the nicotine-stained fingers of her left hand.

'Ma bugger,' she said in a voice reminiscent of a corncrake, 'cost twenty pun.'

The chatter ceased abruptly. All eyes were turned on the speaker and then on the ring. The latter stared back at us, glassily and brassily defiant. Joy recovered first.

'It's . . . er . . . very nice,' she said.

'What's his name? What is he?' somebody else asked.

The girl threw back the bedclothes and jumped lightly down to the floor and pulled off her pyjamas.

'Reginald,' she said. 'Reginald Courtenay. Posh name. He's a pilot.'

I watched wide-eyed, oblivious of everything in the room. The girl stood there, long slender white body, small breasts, long slender white legs. She reached through the space between the bunks, got her clothes from her soldier's box and dressed, talking all the while in her croaking voice. I didn't hear a word. I watched rooted to the spot. The girl put on a gossamer suspender belt, stockings, pink art-silk camiknickers and on top of that, her uniform. I couldn't remember having seen anyone in the nude before. Since I'd joined up, like the others, I changed my clothes modestly, when I couldn't do it in privacy. Many had become adept at removing pyjamas and putting on underwear underneath the sheets before they got up. And here was this girl exposing her naked body, dressing and undressing in front of us all as if it were the most natural thing in the world. The girl's voice cut across my thoughts.

'Well,' she said, 'that's me ready. If anybody comes round just cover up for me, loves. D'ye mind, pet, putting the light off while I take a shutter down to get out?'

'Get out?'

'Yes. I'm going through the window.'

'What's the matter with the door?'

'Nothing. But you never know who you might run into. Besides I like to keep me hand in. If I was to keep on going through the door I'd lose the knack. See?' We didn't, but we were too nonplussed to do other than what she'd asked. Hardly had we got the shutter back up and the light back on when an officer arrived accompanied by a sergeant. We assured her, too hastily, that everything was all right. The officer wasn't looking for trouble and this hut was the farthest away on the camp. She said, 'Good,' and left.

We were all in bed, the lights out and the blackout down when Blondie returned the way she'd left.

'What cheer, lasses,' she said as she walked over to her bunk, making no attempt whatever to walk quietly lest she disturb anyone already asleep, 'Put out your mugs ready for tomorrow morning. I've arranged for us to have tea.'

The following morning as reveille sounded a man who looked as if he had spent the night in a coal-hole came self-consciously into the room, and with an awkward grin and a somewhat shaky hand filled our mugs from the pail he carried.

It was good tea, he told us. By that I suppose he meant it was thick, strong and stewed. It also smelled faintly of engine oil. All of this was a little too much for me, and as soon as I could I opened the window a little and allowed the tea to fall on the place beneath.

'I'm sorry for whatever is expected to come up there,' I said to Ellen. 'I couldn't honestly say that tea reminded me of the dew from heaven above, but I did it in self-defence. It was the grass or me.'

'You needn't bother about the stove,' Blondie told us from her bed as we prepared for breakfast. 'I'll do it if you bring my breakfast back. It's all right. I've spoken to the one in charge today – the ginger-haired one with the squint.'

While we did the necessary fatigues and got ourselves ready, Blondie ate her breakfast and got into her battledress and cleaned out the stove. When she'd finished, she climbed up on to her bunk, sat there for a few minutes and then jumped down, letting out a yell of pain.

'Oh, my ankle,' she moaned.

She refused all assistance and bravely decided to hobble to see the MO on her own. After we'd attended the morning's lectures setting out the programme for our stay (fatigues, manning practice, guard duty and marching drill) we went to the NAAFI for break and there was Blondie already sitting down, her foot swathed in bandages up on a chair, a mug of coffee and two NAAFI doughnuts already before her on the table.

This ankle troubled her for the rest of our stay. It was extremely painful during the day but the pain eased off when we began to prepare for tea and she turned her thoughts to the trip out through the window (where, over her rainbow, there was an endless supply of smashing lads). This brought an immediate, though by no means permanent, cure. Incidentally, we never heard of Reginald Courtenay, pilot, again. Nor, I think, did we ever see the ring again.

Because of my stay in the sick bay, my days spent in the dental waiting-room and the requirements of the course on radar, I had not really had any experience of marching drill. This deficiency was remedied at practice camp. The barrack square had been levelled off on the most appropriate piece of land, which was on top of the cliffs. On one side, at one corner, it was easily accessible from the main camp throughfare, but the corner horizontally opposite was supported on what had become a quagmire, mostly as the result of incessant rain.

On the days we assembled on the square for drill, chin straps were a must and coats had to be buttoned up as far as possible, for the wind blew in strong gusts and carried with it flurries of stinging rain. My uncontrollable urge to push my right arm forward with my right foot persisted. I moved off on my right foot when it should have been my left. I turned the wrong way and I marched out of step. On my first day the sergeant (male) concentrated on me almost exclusively. His comments, his witticisms, his criticisms were easily heard above the wind and I was completely routed. Hundreds and hundreds of ATS had come under his tutelage without his ever learning one name, but, within ten minutes, he knew mine.

'Right. Next we are going to change step. All except Private Summers who will, no doubt, delight us with a solo performance and about turn. Ready. Atten . . . SHUN! By the left QUICK MARCH. Left. Left. Left, right, left. Private Summers! Are you deaf or merely dim-witted? LEFT! LEFT!'

And so it went on.

One day he made a discovery which he felt he had to impart to the squad that stood before him. In spite of my determined effort to get everything right, I had again defaulted and again been held up as a horrible example of inadequate education at my mother's knee.

'I have heard,' yelled the sergeant, 'that one of our number aspires to wear the very badge of authority you see on my arm. I am told she has been recommended. I can hardly believe we have sunk so low but it is my duty to see she is given all the training she can get. Private Summers, OUT!'

I stood still, uncertain whether I had to obey a command or laugh at a joke I could not see.

'Private Summers. I have long wondered about those ears of yours. OUT, I said!'

Tentatively I moved forward.

'Private Summers,' roared my self-appointed mentor, 'you must come smartly to attention, thus,' and he came noisily to attention, 'and march forward thus.' (Again he illustrated what was required of his backward pupil.)

I did my best and finally the sergeant stood back and said, 'Now, you're in charge.'

I gazed aghast at the khaki sea before me. My tongue stuck to the roof of my mouth because all my saliva had dried up.

'Private Summers. It's cold out here. Are you going to let 'em freeze to death? Turn 'em. Turn 'em!'

They were fairly near the grotty end of the square which fell away to squelch and mire. I decided to set them off so that they marched to the other end of the square, which would give me time to collect my thoughts.

'Squad,' I squeaked. 'Squad. Atten . . . shun.' They obeyed.

'Right turn.' They turned – and faced the nearby mud and sludge.

There was nothing else for it.

'Quick march.' And to my horror the monster before me came alive – an inexorable khaki being which I had brought to life with only two words. Total paralysis set in, and I was stricken dumb as they moved relentlessly towards the end of the square.

'Wheel 'em. Wheel 'em,' said the sergeant. In the nick of time I found my voice.

'Right wheel,' I commanded and, without hesitation, they turned and marched down into the squelchy morass.

Nor did I fare much better on the sets. Although they were now obsolete as far as active service was concerned, I had my first practice at getting on to a real, live target on what must have been a prototype GL Receiver. It had a sighting telescope which almost made it a museum piece.

'Put Private Summers on as acting number one,' the GPO (gun position officer – the man in charge) said to the sergeant overseeing our practice training. Above the camp a tame RAF pilot was doing a stint – flying round and round the camp pulling a sleeve. The sleeve was our target. As far as I know the pilot only had one line of dialogue when it came to communication with us here on the ground: 'I'm pulling the bloody thing – not pushing it!'

In the RX I relayed the information I'd been given to the rest of the team: 'Search bearing – to bearing — '

We searched and we searched. Back and forward went the cabin. Up and up went the elevation. Suddenly, we got it, and there, with a bit of juggling was the nice clear image on my tube.

'On target,' I said smartly into the mouthpiece clamped in front of me. 'Bearing . . . Angle of sight . . . Elevation . . .'

'Take another reading,' commanded the GPO. We went through the drill and I reported back.

'Bearing . . . Angle of sight . . . Elevation . . .'

In my euphoria at getting on to the target I didn't realize that according to my information the plane hadn't moved an inch. (The No. 1 had to be able to see the target before the others could find the height and angle of sight of a plane. We gave the present position – the predictor worked out the future position.)

'Number one,' said the GPO, 'have the cabin held steady and get out on to the sighting telescope and have a look at your target.'

I opened the door. A sudden gust of wind flung it against the side of the RX and me with it. Battling against the elements, I clawed my way up the little ladder leading to the telescope and clinging on for all I was worth, looked through the lens. At first all I could see was a grey heaving mass – the sea. Then I made out a darker object – a boat of some sort – my target.

In fact the goniometer had gone beserk. Long ago it had reached the end of its allotted life, and when it registered 'Elevation' it was really 'Depressing' – going down.

Whether it was to look for signs that the report they'd been given on me was correct, or whether a kindly officer wished to give me the opportunity of showing I was made of better stuff than was apparent on the barrack square was not made clear, but, early one afternoon, the subaltern sent for me.

'Ah. Summers,' she said. 'One of our batteries in the same brigade is at practice camp not far from here. They have challenged us to a friendly game of netball and we have agreed to accept the challenge. I would like you, therefore, to get a team of volunteers together to muster, with your PE kit, at the guard room at 14.00 hours on Thursday. You and the team will be excused afternoon duties. Sergeant Payne and I will accompany you. Now, I don't want your list to be drawn exclusively from the OsFC. You must involve the plotters, telephonists, girls on the predictor, cooks and orderlies. Today is Tuesday. You should have the team made up by tomorrow. Bring it to me then. Any questions?'

There were several things I would have liked to ask, among them, Why me? Slim and agile I might look but organized games was not my forte. However, I had learned by this time that 'Any questions' was a form of dismissal. I said 'No, thank you, ma'am,' saluted and left.

There was just time to tell the others the gist of the sub's order, before afternoon parade.

'Rather you than me,' they said.

I got a sheet of foolscap from battery office and wrote out a note calling for netball volunteers, the volunteering having to be done by 19.00 hours. I myself had no intention of playing whatsoever. I pinned the note up in the cookhouse and refrained from looking at it till I went to take it down in the evening. The list was crammed with names: Zazu Pitts, Funf, Mona Lott, Churchill, Minnie Mouse, Big Lil, Stinker, Toeless Mike the slowest draw in the west, Claude, Ali Oop, Alf Hart, Norah Titsoff, author of the 'Baby's Revenge', and so on down to the bottom of the page and up the sides.

'So much for volunteers,' I said when I returned to the hut where the others were putting the finishing touches to their evening toilette. 'I'm going to detail you whether you like it or not. And whether *she* likes it or not, it's going to be one hundred per cent GL wallahs.'

Blondie finished applying her lipstick. 'I'll volunteer,' she croaked.

'You?'

'You heard.'

'But . . .' Good manners stopped me from saying more.

'You'll have to take her,' said Ellen. 'She's the only volunteer you've got, or are likely to get.'

'Well, that's me ready,' said Blondie, ignoring Ellen's remarks. 'Night-night. Don't forget to leave the window,' and she was gone.

'Hurry up with that list,' said Ellen. 'I want to get to the NAAFI before it closes.'

'I wonder why she wants to go,' I mused. 'Not to play, that's for sure. At least not to play netball. To say I'm suspicious is to put it mildly.'

'I'll tell you what,' said Ellen. 'Put down the team. We'll back you up. With Blondie and Jo that makes seven. It'll be easier for everybody if there's just one team. And Blondie never does anything anyway. Nor Jo for that matter, but don't say I said so. It shouldn't take much ingenuity on your part to cook up a few noble and patriotic reasons for the sub. In the last resort you can show her the list, but I guess all her enthusiasm for equality for all lived and died in that speech. I don't for one moment think she'll even comment.'

At 14.00 hours the following day we piled into the tilly, carrying our PE kit. Blondie had been to see the MO that morning and as a result, her face was adorned, here and there, with dots of gentian violet.

'Why they're called "shorts",' I grumbled to Blondie some time later, 'I shall never know. They're only about an inch shorter than my skirt. Who designed them anyway? You can hardly call them attractive.'

'Oh, I don't know,' replied Blondie who had tied a belt round her middle almost to suffocation, to emphasize what she insisted was a seventeen-inch waist.

We walked out in pairs, I and the opposing captain leading. It was a Sabbath day's journey to the pitch. A fine rain was falling.

'What's all this in aid of, may I ask?' I said.

'To keep up morale,' my opposite number answered.

'Whose morale?'

'There you have me. I wouldn't know.'

'Are you the athletic type? I'll tell you straight off, I'm not. My greatest wishes are that you won't give us too much of a trouncing and that I don't forget which goal I'm playing towards, as I once did, in olden time,' I told her.

'That makes two of us then. I had to look the word netball up in the dictionary. By the way, what's the matter with the tall girl?'

'Blondie? Gas-rattle Blondie?'

'Yes. I expect that *is* her name. Why is she dotted with gentian violet?'

'Dotted or dotty is the operative word, and in a nutshell I don't know and I haven't got round to asking. This Olympian contest has been somewhat on my mind. It may be that she has contracted some sort of pestilential disease, or that she found the bottle lying around in the medical room and thought she'd use it, or scrounged it off the medical orderly because she liked the colour. I wouldn't worry about her. She's here because she volunteered. I still haven't found out why. Certain it is, she won't do anything. And, as I said, please don't worry about the score. We expect to be beaten. Well beaten.'

The pitch was on a wind-swept stretch of ground. *The only sort there is around here*, I thought. A sergeant had rounded up a fair number of spectators but, somehow, only three had arrived at the ground, and one of those had craftily escaped from spud-bashing, knowing that in the circumstances she would not be dragged back.

From the beginning the game belonged to Blondie. She was here, there and everywhere. Nobody else stood a chance. As attack, she scored all the goals and saw to it that the ball never reached the other girls at all. By half-time we were leading 10 goals to nil.

'You're a wonder, Blondie,' I breathed in admiration, 'but this is a friendly game. Play it down a bit.'

In the end, we won 17 to 4 and we walked off to change and have tea and buns in the cookhouse. Blondie came up to me.

'Fancy giving the tilly a miss and coming with me to a place I know?' she asked.

'We can't do that,' I said, 'they'd miss us.'

'Who would?'

'The sub for one.'

'Come off it, sunshine. You don't think for one moment the sub or the sergeant are coming back with us. Why do you think they arranged this little get-together?'

'To keep up morale, I was told.'

'Bloody hell! You're supposed to have brains. Where d'you keep 'em? This'll have been cooked up so the sub and her little echo can have a night on the tiles. Like everybody else they're bored to sobs in that dump. Of course they're not coming back with us. You'll see. Look. Let your back hair down for a change. You've spent your life in a morgue. Get a little adventure into your days.'

I hesitated. Actually, I was flattered that Blondie had picked me out to be her confederate on what promised to be one of her nocturnal wanderings. Like the others I was puzzled as to what she did in this wasteland where signs of any sort of night life were non-existent. At the same time, I was also flattered, although I'd never have admitted to it, that it was I who had been selected to raise the team, and I did not want to scupper any chance there might be of promotion.

The sub collected us together and, after a few words of praise for our afternoon's performance, she said that unfortunately neither she nor Sergeant Payne could go back with us. We had proved, however, that we could be trusted to go back by ourselves.

'Told you,' said Blondie, and after asking Ellen to cover up for us she took me to the ablutions. 'Now,' she said, 'keep the door open and stand behind it, but up on the ledge so that your feet can't be seen.'

'Why do you have to do everything the hard way? Why can't I just go in and close the door?'

'Finesse, love. It pays in the end. If anything goes wrong, Ellen will come and fish us out. On the other hand, they're not above sending someone round to see that no one has thought of going to the ablutions, the obvious place, till the tilly has gone.'

We stayed there till there were noises which indicated increased general activity. The male guards were now on duty and, with practised ease, Blondie smiled at the man those tour of duty it was, and we were soon out on the open road. Walking was pleasant and we continued in silence for some time till I said, 'I've just realized something. I wondered what it was. It's stopped raining.'

'There now,' responded Blondie. 'Enjoy it while you can.'

'You surprise me,' I said. 'This afternoon you were wonderful. And here you are now, striding out. If anyone had asked me yesterday, I would have said you were incapable of walking five yards, let alone even recognizing a netball ball.'

'You live and learn,' said Blondie, 'and I've learned that you take what you can get at the moment you can get it, and make the most of it. The time will never come again.'

We talked for some time in this vein and then the conversation flagged. The daylight had gone and, as yet, we had seen neither moon nor habitation and the going was rough. My spirits had flagged with the conversation. I had been a fool to agree, I knew that now, as I had known it at the time. However, nothing could be done about it. I just had to go on. It began to rain again, the insistent, all-pervading rain that we had come to know so well. Misery was beginning to set in when Blondie said, 'Here it is.'

All I could distinguish was a low, dark building which might have been a barn.

'Where?' I asked.

'There in front of you. The canteen.'

'That?'

'What else did you expect? This isn't the metrolopse.'

As we drew near it was possible to see that it was a cottage. I took out my torch, the better to examine it, and saw that propped up against the rain barrel there was a piece of slate on which a message had been written in large letters in chalk; but the rain had obliterated most of them and what was left made no sense.

Blondie opened the door as one sure of her welcome. After we were both on the other side, she fought her way through a heavy curtain into a room lit only by the leaping flames of a friendly fire. Near the fire was a plump woman standing over a dish placed on a chair. From her waist up, part of her bosom was clamped into a whalebone prison, while the remainder burgeoned under, and over, a white woollen vest. At the moment we entered the room she had one red, fleshy arm raised and was in the act of applying a flannel to it.

'Oh, it's you,' she said to Blondie. 'I was just having a wash before I opened.'

'That's all right, flower,' said Blondie. 'I brought a friend. We don't mind.'

The woman looked at me but said nothing and continued with her ablutions. She and Blondie exchanged friendly comments till the operation was complete, and the woman had donned a blouse which she had been warming in front of the fire.

'I expect you're hungry,' she said as she waddled out with the dish. 'Sit up to the fire till I'm ready.'

The fire was warm and agreeable. The darting flames hypnotized me and I became oblivious of everything else. Blondie jerked me back to the present with the news that the meal was ready. On the table behind us was a huge brown pot of tea, two steaming cups already poured out, a plate with a slab of farm butter on it and a jar of home-made strawberry jam. The woman was clutching a large loaf to her ample middle.

'I just made it this morning,' she said. 'Who wants the crust?'

'You have the first,' Blondie said generously. 'I'll have the next.'

The bread, the butter, the jam, the tea and the fire were absolute heaven. The woman, apparently, had never heard the word 'rationing'. She cut bread till we could eat no more.

'It's been a wonderful meal,' I said. 'I really couldn't eat another bite.' We sat back for a while and I was just about to say we ought to leave when the door opened, and a man came in followed by a boy dressed to look like a man. I never learned their names, nor what relation they were to each other.

Blondie gave the elder an immediate welcome. I knew this did not mean much and it gave me no clue as to whether the man was a stranger or an acquaintance. Their hostess appeared from the next room and, with an eye to business, said, 'What'll you have?'

The two newcomers went to the door where I saw, for the first time, two crates of soft drinks. They took the bottles out and looked at the labels before they made their choice. Finally, the elder said,

'Dandelion and burdock.'

'Me, too,' said the younger.

'You'll have cherryade,' said the elder, the voice of authority. The elder paid, and before they came to the table they removed the bottle tops and took a swig at the contents. Blondie moved a little way along the form she was sitting on and the elder man accepted the implied invitation and sat beside her. After another swig from his bottle he moved nearer Blondie and nudged her and grinned. The two of them giggled and the boy joined in. The elder took another swig keeping his eyes on Blondie all the while.

'You didn't get wet then?' Blondie said.

This caused them both to slap down their bottles and laugh loudly.

'No,' the elder said, when he was able. 'Us didn't.' He nudged Blondie again and the three of them fell to laughing.

'I thought you might because it was raining.'

'Hear that?' the elder asked the younger and again they exploded into mirth.

I felt I was missing out on something, but couldn't see what it was. When they had recovered they sat in silence for some time, conversation having been exhausted. Then the elder man took a determined swig at his dandelion and burdock, put the bottle down and put his arm around Blondie who didn't object. He squeezed her, took another drink with his disengaged hand and laughed again. It was unreal. I wondered if perhaps I had fallen asleep and was dreaming.

'Ouch!' I sat up with a start. Something had pinched my side. Moreover, an arm was being held somewhere in the middle of my back. The boy was grinning up at me. It was his arm.

Cheek, I thought and moved away as much as I could. The arm followed. *He must be all of 14*, I reasoned silently. *I wonder if he's been brought here to be taught how to sow his wild oats. Well, not on me he isn't. I refuse to be a wild oat.*

I attempted to draw Blondie's attention to the passage of time without effect. The room was warm and Blondie had removed her jacket as well as her greatcoat. As I was growing apprehensive about the possibility of her removing more, I made a determined effort to go. I paid for my share of the tea and asked how I could get back to camp. The elder man said,

'Dun't matter. 'E knows.'

I realized I was to have an escort. *Over my dead body*, I thought. 'I can manage,' I said firmly, but they ignored me and when I went out into the night, the boy went with me. As soon as we set off, he took up his proprietary position with regard to his arm and flung it around my middle. Unfortunately, with the extra girth provided by my greatcoat he could not get it all the way round and his hand was left hanging limply somewhere in my lumbar region. Also we tended to knock against each other, and the hand held against my back, having no anchorage, moved with each step.

A fitful moon periodically let us in on a desolate road and bleak landscape. Neither of us spoke. The rain fell harder. The wind was mean and attacked from all sides. Holes suddenly appeared under our feet. We plodded on silently although the rubbing against my back nearly drove me to screaming pitch. The road stretched on to eternity. Hours seemed to have passed. Suddenly the boy said, 'There she is,' and, in the fidgety moonlight I discerned a black mass ahead. I broke free from my associate and ran towards it. I thought I heard him running after me and, floundering and staggering, I redoubled my efforts. I had no pass, so I couldn't go through the guard-room. Instead I had to skirt the perimeter and enter the camp by the cliff where there was no barrier because it was thought none was necessary. Stumbling into ruts filled with water, hanging on to shoes that the boggy ground would fain have sucked from me, I covered the stretch along the camp's boundary till it stopped at the cliff edge. On hands and knees, I felt my way over the rocks, while below, the sea lashed itself in fury against the cliff, spitefully covering me with spray. I reached the level of the camp and heard a voice call.

'Halt. Who goes there?'

I could just discern ahead a shrouded figure. 'Foe!' I called. 'And don't hesitate to shoot. It'll be a relief.'

The man came up.

'What on earth are you doing here at this time of night?' he asked. 'Never mind. Get behind me. Which hut is it? I hope to God nobody sees us.'

We made the hut. Lit with a small manning bulb, the room looked and felt warm. The stove still retained some heat. Everyone was asleep. I walked gingerly over the polished floor on newspapers laid out like stepping stones. On top of the stove were two mugs of still-warm cocoa, not yet solidified. I took off my sodden coat and hung it up, undressed and rubbed myself down with a towel, got into my pyjamas and drank the cocoa. I had almost finished when Blondie slid in through the open window. I looked at her in amazement.

'You're not even wet,' I said.

'No, flower,' she replied. 'I got a lift here on the back of a lorry – covered.'

'You did what!'

'Sh.'

Ellen stirred and opened her eyes. 'You're back,' she said.

'We are,' I said as I put down my mug and slid between the sheets.

'Did you enjoy yourselves?'

'Yes,' I answered. 'We met two smashing fellas,' and I pulled the bedclothes over my head.

The days passed with agonizing slowness. Most of us had numbered squares, one of which we crossed off just before getting into bed, each night. After an age three weeks had passed. Three weeks of rain and wind. I had had no idea till then how many varieties of rain and wind there were and how many differing types of uncomfortable weather they could make between them.

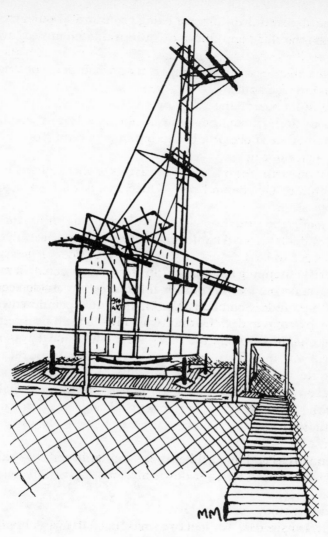

Receiver (RX)

Finally we had only five days to go. Our spirits rose and the weather cleared. On one glorious spring-like afternoon Captain Wright took those members of the camp who wished on a walk along the cliff top and the shore. It was delightful.

We had also heard of a nearby village with a café where tea and home-made cakes were still to be had. It sounded like a miracle. I went with the others and found we'd been told no more than the truth.

Also in a shop, I saw a small brass tray. I had been looking for something to take home with me for my parents, but, like Mother Hubbard's cupboard, the shops were bare. So that this was a tremendous find. I bought it. It cost 5 shillings (25p).

And in no time at all, after that, we were separating for our first leave.

8. First Leave

This was it. I was on my way home. Supressed excitement quivered through me as I got into the branch-line train that was to take me to a main-line station. Soon I changed trains for the penultimate part of this exciting journey. Usually when I'm travelling I get the feeling I should be going the other way. This time I was more concerned with my watch than what was going on outside the train. The minutes snailed their way till finally I noted a change in the tone of the rhythm of the train and, looking down, I saw the dark water of the Tyne. It thrilled me more than I can say. This thrill was to remain with me throughout the years I lived away from the north-east.

A man sitting opposite smiled at me and said,

'The Tyne, the Tyne, the coally Tyne,
The best uv aal the rivers . . .'

I sighed with pleasure as I looked around me in Newcastle Central station. I still had another leg of my journey to go and for this I made my way to the Haymarket. On the way there I had a call to make. The cigarette holder I had bought puzzled me somewhat. The hole for the cigarette was not round but elliptical. I decided to call in at a tobacconist and ask why this was.

'It's for Turkish cigarettes,' he said. 'They're a different shape.'

'Do you have any?'

'Why, yes. I do have a packet. Abdullah. They are more expensive than the others.'

I bought a packet of twenty and laid them carefully inside my gas mask case. They were safe there.

With trembling, mounting excitement I looked out of the bus window as we snaked our way through Sheepwash, up the bank, and at last into Ashington, past the Long Row, Bothal Schools and High Market till finally I was deposited at the bus stop outside the first block of Seventh Row.

I got off the bus, grinning my welcome. Ashington carried on as if nothing had happened. As if I'd never been away for an endless thirteen weeks. No band played. No flags fluttered. Little children had not been lined up to bid me welcome. The shops round about had not even put my photograph in the windows surrounded by even the most wilting of laurel leaves. However, when I staggered home, my welcome was all I could have desired.

Having been fed and talked myself to a standstill, I decided to walk abroad, to travel the length of Station Road and beyond to find out how the villageship had struggled on in my absence. There was a distinct lack of recognition as I walked up the Main Street, once so thronged with acquaintants. Even the Store seemed to be working efficiently, exactly as though it had not lost its most valued employee.

All my friends were, by this time, in the forces or on munitions. Together with my mother, I visited most of my relatives, spending two days at Wooler. In the privacy of my room I tried the monocle on, making faces detrimental to my features in an effort to get it to stay in place. One morning, after giving an elaborate and detailed account of my projected plans, I furtively walked round by the Dene and on to Sheepwash, casting looks this way and that in case I'd been followed. Finally, after a detailed search of the immediate vicinity, I stationed myself behind a tangled mass of bare branches and twigs that afforded cover but was also a peephole on the world beyond and there took from my bag the Abdullah cigarettes, the holder and some matches.

I found the aroma very agreeable. After one or two experimental puffs, I extinguished the cigarette and carefully returned it to the packet. My mission accomplished, I walked boldly home.

The days had gone by with remarkable rapidity, especially considering their previous slow progress. Before I knew where I was, my last evening had arrived. I was due to report to Liverpool's Lime Street station at 09.00 hours the following day. Because there was no train that went direct from Ashington to deposit me conveniently at Liverpool at 08.55 hours, I had, perforce, to leave Ashington the evening before on the last train to Manors – the 9 p.m.

We'd had our evening meal. My kit was standing packed ready to be picked up. Propped against it was my gas-mask case which now had yet another content – a packet of egg sandwiches.

I had never loved my home more than I did at that moment. Never been more loath to leave its cosy warmth and the people sitting round the fire, my mother and father, Billie and Margie. The clear orange-red flames flickered and danced in the bright fireplace while outside the wind howled and moaned in an ecstasy of fiendish glee that I would soon be out there to be battered and tormented.

The clock on the sideboard cleared its throat preparatory to striking the quarter-hour and in so doing, reminded us that it was time to go. My father shut off the wireless. My mother finished the end of her line of knitting, stuck the ball of wool on the end of the needles and wrapped the whole lot up in a tea-towel. Billy and Margie put down their books. The condemned woman stood up and went to get her greatcoat and took a last look round the room.

The wind was worse than we thought. In a huddled bunch we braced ourselves against it and made our way in the blackout to the station. Conversation was impossible. When we got there, the Main Street was deserted except for two policemen trying shop doors and a solitary warden who warned my father to be careful with his torch.

When we reached it, the darkened station was deserted and the station clock invisible in the blackness. We compared watches in the torchlight and decided the train wasn't due for another fifteen minutes.

'It doesn't look,' I said, 'as if any trains were expected here ever again.'

This was regarded as defeatist talk and I was subjected to a little cheering up.

'You'll be back before you know where you are,' said my brother. 'Three months soon passes.'

'I'd be better see if I can find a porter or something,' my father said and disappeared into the darkness.

'What a night,' Margie said after a time. 'There'll be a few people minus chimney pots and slates by tomorrow.'

Father came back with the news that the 9 o'clock was still running and would be here shortly. We all stamped our feet, taking what shelter we could and said, 'What a night,' and talked about likely damage again and looked as far along the line as we could. Presently we heard a clanking noise above the sound of the wind.

'Here she is,' said my father. 'Now keep back,' he commanded as if we had all surged forward when all we'd done was tell each other that this was the train.

My father opened the nearest carriage door as the ticket collector made his tardy appearance. Billy temporarily abandoned Margie to lift my kitbag into the dimly lit compartment which at first sight seemed empty but had, in fact, one passenger in the extreme corner. The ticket collector, anxious to get back to his fire, called, 'Hurry along there,' and my mother said,

'Goodbye. Now don't forget to write.'

I said, leaning out of the window, 'No, I won't. I'll write with my new address as soon as I get back.'

At the guard's command I put up the window and pulled down the blind to comply with blackout regulations, and slumped heavily into the nearest corner seat, hands in pockets, chin sunk into collar, eyes fixed ahead. The train chugged away, gathered a little cautious speed, uncertain of the effect the rocking wind would have on its aged structure, then slowed down for the next station. It made several stops while I sat with fixed gaze, rigid except for the motion of the train.

After a while I moved the side of the blind a little to peer out into the night. The figure in the corner, a sailor, encouraged perhaps by this show of activity said, 'I too feel miserable, but I hope I don't show it as much as you do.'

Without looking at him I answered, 'If I look miserable it's because I *am* miserable.'

'How far are you travelling?'

113

'To Liverpool.'

'I thought girls weren't allowed to travel overnight.'

'Going on leave they're not supposed to, but it's up to you when you return. In this case it's my first posting. I've just finished training, had a leave and now, at the end of it, I have to report at the RTO at Liverpool at 9 a.m. tomorrow. This was the last train out of Ashington station tonight. The Liverpool train leaves at 03.00 hours. Imagine!'

'At the rate this train's going it'll take you all your time to catch the train at 03.00 hours. It doesn't go to the Central anyway. They don't trust it that far. You'll have to get out and change at Manors.'

After a time the train stopped and there was a staccato of banging doors.

'I do believe this is Manors,' said the sailor, and in confirmation came the guard's voice:

'All change. All change.'

He took my kitbag. 'I have a better remedy for curing the blues,' he said. 'It's recommended by doctors,' he went on as we walked along the platform. 'No one can feel miserable while eating chips from a newspaper. We still have aeons of time. I know a chip shop not far from here. Let's dump your kit with the porter and see if it's open. Better still, you stay with the porter and I'll go and see. It's a rotten night.'

'No. I'll go with you.'

We found the porter in a warm little shoebox of an office. He gladly agreed to look after the kit and even suggested we come back there to eat our chips, if we got any, as things were quiet and we weren't likely to be disturbed and it was *such* a night. He further volunteered the information that we would need some paper because if they were frying tonight you had to take your own. He found some stuffed in a corner behind the coal pail and said that it was clean enough inside.

As we went out I found myself smiling. 'What a friendly soul he is,' I said.

My companion put his strong arm round my shoulders, and we bent our heads to the wind and went on to find that the chip shop was open.

'I felt a bit like Scott of the Antarctic,' I said, once we were inside the shop.

'You'll probably feel more like Montgolfier on the way back,' he countered.

Back in the porter's little office we wedged ourselves into its rather stuffy warmth, unloosed our greatcoats and shared our chips with our host.

'I wonder why chips always taste so much better out of a newspaper?' the sailor mused.

'Perhaps printer's ink brings out the subtle flavour,' I suggested.

The porter launched into a discourse on Chip Shops I Have Known and then offered us dark lukewarm tea, which we declined, saying that buying tea would give us an excuse to go to the forces' canteen. When we'd finished eating and wiped our greasy hands the porter told us a train was almost due but if we cared to wait there would be another later. We thanked him and decided we would take this one.

At the Central station we made for the Forces' canteen and managed to find a table. Like the porter's office the canteen was warm and stuffy. It was full of people in uniform. They came and went so that the swing doors seemed forever in motion. The kitbags and gas-mask cases on the floor made crossing it with a hot cup of coffee something of an obstacle course. Here and there were small groups carrying on a low conversation. One or two sat head in arms on the table, trying to sleep. A few gazed vacantly into space and at one table a blonde in WRAF uniform sat holding hands with a soldier. They neither spoke nor looked at each other but sat motionless as though sculptured in stone.

'I wonder what it is about stations,' I mused, as I sipped my coffee, 'that inhibits people so much. Is it the atmosphere of parting, do you think? We're a chatty family but at the station we were reduced to saying the same inane things over and over again, such as "Don't forget to write".'

'I don't suppose it matters so much what you say as how you say it,' he replied. 'Talking about writing is safe and helps to preserve the great British tradition of the Stiff Upper Lip.'

We passed the time in friendly talk until I suddenly found I had only ten minutes before my train left. We reached the platform and the train with little time to spare, and the sailor went ahead along the corridor opening doors to find a relatively empty compartment. He found one in which the only occupant was a young soldier stretched out on one side fast asleep.

'This should do,' he said, then added: 'I hope he hasn't passed his station.' He shook the soldier urgently and the sleeper returned briefly to dim consciousness.

'Sorry, mate,' he said, 'but where are you travelling to?'

'L'p'l,' said the speaker and returned to oblivion. A whistle blew. He turned to me and, taking one of my hands in both of his and holding it tightly for a few seconds, said softly, 'Goodbye, dear Linda. I hope you'll be happy. Bless you.' After kissing the hand he turned quickly away. I felt a sense of panic at his going and went to the door leading to the corridor. I wanted to call him back.

At the door he turned briefly, waved and jumped down on to the platform. I ran along the corridor. As I reached the door it was snapped shut by a porter and I was cut off from him by the blackout.

Surprisingly, I had a very comfortable journey. Usually, day and night, the main-line trains were crowded. On these occasions often the best you could do was sit on a suitcase or a kitbag in the corridor and be stepped over, knocked into or brushed past an average of thirty times per hour. At night you did your best to sleep in spite of it all.

Some people managed this sleeping so well that they hardly waked or moved when they were knocked into or stepped over. There was a curious smell on the train at night, a sort of 'tired' smell, not bad or good or musty. Just distinctive.

During air raids the speed of trains had to be reduced to fifteen miles an hour and, of course, during the hours of darkness, in raids, the train had to be totally blacked out. This blackout isolated us from the rest of the world.

I arrived in Liverpool well before 9 o'clock. After I'd tidied myself up I reported as per instructions to the RTO then waited with the others to be transported to my first posting as a bona fide fully operational GL wallah.

9. First Posting

Our first posting was to a camp in the Wirral peninsular.

Happily for me marching drill had become a thing of the past. Now, the first thing we had to learn was to 'take post'. This meant that we had to be at our posts and ready for action within two minutes. We began this training by running from the parade ground towards the sets for all we were worth, Captain Wright behind us urging our stiff limbs on to greater effort.

When we had more than halved the time it originally took us we then extended our running to actually being on the sets. This also had to be honed down to two minutes. Finally every parade ended with the words 'Take post', when we galloped hell-for-leather to our posts. The long catwalk increased the pace at which we GL could run once we'd actually got on to it.

Other than that the alarm would go at various times of the day, when we had to drop whatever we were doing and gallop as aforesaid. This also was practised till we could move from any part of the camp and be ready for action in two minutes.

The last training we had in this direction was at night. In the quiet still hours the alarm bell would clang and we had to jump out of bed and be on duty before the bell had stopped its racket, which it did after two minutes. Most girls wore some arrangement of curlers in their hair and tin hats had to fit over these. This was uncomfortable to say the least. In GL we weren't allowed to wear our tin hats on the set. At first we put them underneath, but before long we didn't bother to wear them at all. We simply flung a scarf over our heads to be put on again, turban-style, at the first opportunity. We got into slacks and boots and put the rest of our uniform on as we ran.

So thoroughly was this urgency drummed into us that, even today, I still leap out of bed when I'm wakened by the postman's ring, putting my dressing-gown on as I slither downstairs. Similarly, I drop whatever I'm doing and rush headlong to answer the urgent shrill ring of the telephone.

There were changes. A day was known as a 24 hours. A 24 hours ran from 14.00 hours one day to 14.00 the next. Weeks were replaced by 8-day cycles. For us on GL it meant:

1. MANNING
2. Fatigues/fire picquet/guard duty
3. STANDBY, MAINTENANCE of GL equipment
4. Fatigues/fire picquet/guard duty
5. MANNING
6. Fatigues/fire picquet/guard duty
7. STANDBY AND MAINTENANCE
8. 24-HOUR PASS

We took over our new duties at 14.00 hours when we mustered for parade. Those on MANNING (i.e. on duty on the sets to take post in the event of a raid) spent the afternoon in practice tracking with the predictors and guns. It was a very boring exercise, lacking any sort of aerial activity. Those on manning duty were not allowed to go anywhere which was further than two minutes from the sets.

Fatigues consisted mainly of spud-bashing. Mountains of spuds. The NCO in charge of the fatigue wallahs had to ensure that the potato peelings weren't too thick and all eyes had been removed. Fire picquet and guard duty came round less frequently. Apart from some cooks and orderlies and all battery-office clerks, all personnel did duty in the guard room and in the sentry box. Girls were on duty during the hours of daylight or from 08.00 hours to 20.00 hours in summer. The men took over in winter, during the hours of darkness or from 18.00 hours to 07.00 hours. The guard room was always tidy and swept, but never really clean. It had a somewhat grey appearance and the suggestion that it was never properly aired. A women's team was made up of four ATS, the guard commander (an NCO), and three guards who worked one hour in the sentry box, one hour as runner and one hour off. It was a deadly boring job. You began with the idea that you were going to catch up on reading and letter writing, but sooner or later, the inertia of the guard room took over and you began to count the slow seconds till it was all over. The hour in the sentry box was worse. In the middle of winter not even long johns and sea-boot stockings kept out the cold.

The guard commander's job was to write up the log book and to march the guard next on duty to the sentry box and say, 'Guard. Guard, halt,' when the GL spoken to came to a smart and noisy halt. Then, 'Old Guard, one pace forward march,' and, when it was me, 'Left – er – right – er' ('left' out of the sides of the mouths of both guards). 'Left turn. Two paces forward, march! Halt. New guard. New guard left – er ('Right' from the guards) right turn. Two paces forward, MARCH. Halt right – er (yes. Right) right turn. One pace forward – MARCH. A-BOUT TURN. Old guard. Old guard forward MARCH. Halt. Old guard fall out.'

I am happy to say no one ever watched this hourly pantomime. When it was my turn I felt a right nit.

On maintenance days we maintained the machinery, as the name suggests. Strangely enough, I became quite an authority on the power unit which supplied power to the RX and TX. I could strip it down, clean out the sump and do all necessary maintenance only having to ask REME to lift out the batteries when necessary. We kept the power unit in sparkling condition. I can well understand the care and affection some steam-organ and road-roller drivers lavish on their machines and what pride they take in keeping them clean when they themselves are hardly distinguishable beneath their oily covering. One job I did on maintenance, which required all my courage and nerve but which was taken for granted, was cleaning the aerials on the Mark II Receiver. A very slender and insecure ladder ran from the aerials down to the receiver and, thereafter, down the side of the set. I have no head whatever for heights and felt very giddy indeed and as if my body were made of a mass of swirling water as I clung to the slightly swaying ladder, forcing myself to climb it rung by rung. My relief was great indeed when, at last, my feet touched terra firma. Of course, doing maintenance had to be juggled so that it fitted in with manning.

The morning pararde was at 08.30 hours when all our floor-polishing, bed-making, boot-cleaning and button-polishing was over. At that parade any details for the day, and any news, were read out. I have stood on that parade ground in all weathers from tropical sunshine to arctic gale and not once were conditions considered bad enough to have the parade in the NAAFI or the cookhouse. We were a hardy breed.

The time sacred to the checking of the dials was 09.00 hours, when RX, TX guns and predictors were 'lined-up'.

In the dead of winter when the blood almost froze in our veins, the NCO (number one) together with number three had an extra duty to perform: each hour in the night they were summoned by a tap on the window from the runner on duty in the guard house. They had to get up and, with the aid of lethal looking torches, make their way to the power unit, set it in motion, then separate for the RX and TX respectively there to turn the equipment round so that it didn't freeze up.

Sometimes, instead of practice on the sets, we had lectures in the cookhouse. These were on aircraft recognition. This was a must, but it wasn't a great deal of help to us on GL. The aircraft that we saw were spots on a tube. For us, the official way to distinguish friend from foe was the IFF signal (Indication Friend or Foe) which, when the plane was ours, followed the cone that was the target. This IFF code was secret and changed from time to time.

We also had to muster for gas drill wearing our gas masks. Mine always steamed up. I felt suffocated by the hot rubbery smell.

Occasionally we had visiting lecturers. One was a Russian on a goodwill tour. He was a smallish man in a grey suit with a thick mass of black curls, and he was heavily bearded and moustached in the same curly black growth. He wore round pebble glasses which partly concealed two fiery blackcurrant eyes. A slit of pale forehead and the end of a fleshy nose was all that was visible of his face. His speech was rather thick and difficult to distinguish, which was hardly surprising when you think of the jungle it had to negotiate before it burst forth. We had been primed beforehand to ask questions afterwards as a compliment to him. Accordingly, therefore, when he had finished speaking, one of the gunners stood up and said, 'Sir. Is it true what we hear about Russian women, that they wear dark, coarse clothes and do manual work and they are big and look more like men?'

I thought the lecturer was about to explode (and who would have blamed him).

'Rooshian veemen,' he spluttered, 'are the most voomanly voomanly veemen in se verld,' and stalked out, furious.

The sergeant got up on to the platform after the lecturer had disappeared. He looked at the silent battery before him. 'It was a bloody stupid question,' he said, 'but I always thought they were.'

A woman lecturer once came to talk to us girls. I forget the subject she was supposed to talk on, but it didn't matter. She was hung up on a song then popular, 'Would it be wrong to kiss when we both feel like this?'

'Yes,' she said vehemently, 'it *is* wrong. It is totally and absolutely wrong. He was married. He had a very good wife at home who looked after him. There was nothing right about it. Or about her. She was a no-good adventuress splitting up a happy home and causing untold misery.'

And so she went on. We all sat looking at her in stunned silence. I wondered if her husband had gone off the rails and she was taking it out on us.

The men got a film or talk on VD. This was very hush-hush and not spoken about but we knew they got 'something' which we didn't. One day we girls were summoned to the cookhouse. With a great deal of innuendo and embarrassment the sub introduced a woman, a nurse, and said she was here to answer our – er – er – intimate questions. The things we wanted to know about – er – er – intimate things. We knew. We didn't, but her red face and hurried exit gave us a clue. 'Right,' said the nurse, 'just fire away. Nothing embarrasses me. I have seen it all.'

We looked at her. She was fairly tall, and of commanding bearing. I thought she looked more like a matron than a common or garden nurse.

'Come along. Come along,' she chivvied. 'I have come here specially. It was a special request and I have put off a great deal of other work and commitments to oblige.'

Still we sat there mute. Tongue-tied. The colour mounted in her face. We could no longer look at her. Nor could we look at each other. We shifted uneasily.

'Are you going to ask questions or aren't you?' Her eyes flashed. 'I was given to understand there were things you wanted to know. Well for goodness sake have the gumption to speak up. I can't answer till I know what the question is.'

Thick tangible silence.

'For the last time, are there any questions?'

There were none. Our tongues clove to the roofs of our mouths.

'Really,' she said drawing herself up even more, 'this is too bad. An utter waste of time. I have been totally and completely misled. Who is in charge here? Conduct me back to the officers' mess,' and she stalked out. Like sheep waiting for a shepherd, we stood there till any angry sub came to tear a strip off us collectively. She had gone to a great deal of trouble to get this highly qualified and experienced nurse and we had let her down. Still confused, we were dismissed.

From time to time we had medical inspections and once a month we girls were subjected to a rather undignified, and as things turned out, perfectly useless test called an FFP – Free From Pregnancy. We lined up in close formation in our bras, pants and gym shoes. When our turn came we went into a room and in the presence of a woman officer, we were given an examination by an MO.

There were, on most sites, three ATS huts, one for GL, one for cooks and orderlies, and the third for predictor operators, telephonists and clerks. Among the compulsory fittings of each hut was a bath list. Ours was a rather ragged and not every illuminating document, the product of the hut NCO. Harassed at intervals by those in authority, she was constrained to borrow a sheet of paper and a ruler from battery officer, a pen from one of our number rich enough to own one, and, even more difficult to come by, ink. Thus equipped, with painstaking care she produced her literary effort.

Looking at its blank, rejected visage, the interested visitor could not be criticized for considering us unclean, walking abroad as did our prehistoric ancestors unwashed and unkempt. However, with an impending inspection from one of the great ones of the earth, the military moguls, the wearers of pips and crowns, ribbons and medals, it became a different matter. Ticks appeared like mushrooms overnight. Total ablutions had become a primary object of life around which the daily task, the common round of a gun-site, evolved.

Inspection or no inspection, I had a daily, yearning desire to submit my elfin figure to five inches of water in which to wallow. In training camp we had three baths more or less serviceable. On the majority of sites we had but one. Feverishly, therefore, I would dash thither after tea. The door was locked. A strident voice paused in its refrain to inform me that Poppy was next. The hunt was on and Poppy, tracked to her lair, revealed that Joan was next and so it went on till the final aspirant to total ablution was reached and I took my place next in the queue. At about 9.30 when I had done nothing but wait, a dark figure came to ask was I next with the bath because if so the water was cold and something had happened to the light.

Shivering in a modicum of cold water, performing my ablutions by the flame of a guttering candle, splashing that flame out, fishing for damp matches on the sodden floor and ending my bath in total darkness, had less than no appeal. The answer was to do without tea – or try the showers. The trouble with the showers was that they were in their infancy. Actually, there was a dichotomy here. The *design* of the showers was in its infancy. The showers themselves were in their dotage. Thus the plumbing was erratic, caught as it was between the primitive knowledge at the plumber's disposal and the irascibility and cantankerousness that is the prerogative of age. After the vain struggle with the hose-pipe arrangement, the frantic turning of levers, the decision to abandon the fight was arrested by a blinding jet of ice-cold water. Thereafter there was a choice. Hissing, scalding steam or icy jet, both capricious, both intent on scarring for life. The end was not in doubt. The strife over, the battle lost, the rout was inevitable. Towel and clothes had been soaked in one or other of the deluges.

They were there, of course, those frustrating ablutions, for a purpose. They helped mould the British Character. They helped make the GL wallah what she was – cross, defeated and going at the edges. The Romans would not have approved.

Apart from the men's quarters – about which I knew nothing – the battery office, the officers' and sergeants' messes, the command post, guns and the sets, there was the cookhouse and the NAAFI. In winter, until 17.00 hours, the only heating to be found in the camp was in the cookhouse. Those with sufficient acumen swarmed round it like flies; and like flies before a swatter they suddenly disappeared, one knew not where, when an officer or sergeant appeared. The cookhouse had a stage at one end. Every Sunday it (the cookhouse) catered for both body and soul. We ate there (as we did every day), we had a church service there and we had a dance there in the evening.

Then there was the NAAFI where, from 19.00 hours till 21.30 hours, chips, and sometimes bangers, could be obtained singly or in any combination. There were also doughnuts and rock buns, beer and coffee on sale. Cigarettes and a small range of confectionary, both of which were on ration, were also sold. The important question, never far from the inner man/woman, was, 'Has the NAAFI convoy got through?'

Also nightly, the NAAFI was given over to housey-housey, so that whatever was going on, whatever little secret conversations were being exchanged in the dark corners, it was done to a penetrating background of 'Legs eleven' and 'Kelly's eye'.

Saturdays and Sundays were not completely obliterated by our eight-day cycle. There was a parade at 14.00 hours on Saturdays but, except in an emergency, work was kept to an absolute minimum. Beds were allowed to be made up earlier than usual and those on pass were allowed to go early.

On Sundays blankets did not have to be folded. There was no hut inspection. Those on a 24-hour pass could stay in bed till 14.00 hours if they wished.

Also on Sundays we attended church, but with a difference. Sunday finery had been replaced by battledress and heavy boots. We did not converge on the place of worship individually. We were detailed to go and lined up on the parade ground in threes, right dressed, turned and marched off. Not till we got to the door were we allowed to break step. No minister, verger or sidesman stood there to greet us; only the sergeant, alert for skivers. In the building the Norman arches had been replaced by cookhouse rafters or NAFFI beams, and the odour of sanctity by the lingering smell of porridge and cooking fat or the unmistakable traces of the previous night's smoke and beer. The organ was replaced by the subdued clatter of pans behind the scenes.

But when the visiting padre opened up his attaché case and set up his small altar, it became church for those who wished it. Things spiritual should be able to rise above adverse temporal surroundings. Usually, I gave up at least part of this time to meditation pondering the meaning of God and Christianity.

There was a general feeling of catharsis in the camp after church parade, even among those who had managed to get themselves excused, and NAAFI break became almost a celebration. After break we did the essential drills and the afternoon was free.

Monday evenings were make-do-and-mend nights when we were supposed to do our personal mending and darning. The subaltern came round to inspect the work we were doing and to check that the underwear not then being worn was clean and in good repair. Except for those on 24, no one was allowed out of camp on Monday nights.

In every eight-day cycle we were allowed two passes, one till 23.00 hours and one, a late pass, till midnight.

This then might almost be said to be the end of our training. We had been taught how GL worked and how it was operated, we had been drilled that we might obey commands quickly and efficiently without demur, we had put into practice our recently acquired technical knowledge re. GL and lastly, we had been moulded into a unit with our own mores, our own team spirit and our own jargon. Captain Wright was largely responsible for this last phase of our training. He was, I now realize, a well-set-up, good-looking man with a moustache trained to make him look fiercer than he probably was. But I never thought of him as a man. He was the one in command. You jumped at his bidding.

Six days after our first coming to camp it was announced that we would now operate as a battery and leave would start. Names had been put in a hat and a rota resulted. We, the team of which I was a member, had been among the first out of the hat. One week after I'd torn myself away from the parental hearth I was back again and the tidy hall was once again cluttered with my kitbag and impedimenta.

'Sparks' for trade-tested OsFC, the wearing of which was discontinued c.1943

10. The Trail

I walked from the TX with Madeleine and Betty. The ground was sun-splashed, the sky a pale blue with here and there airy white balls of cotton wool. Although it was still only February, it seemed that spring had stopped playing fast and loose and was here to stay.

'Spring is in the air,' I said.

'What an awe-inspiring thought that is,' responded Madeleine.

'I wonder what the folks are doing at home this minute,' said Betty. 'Just beginning to think about tea, I expect. It was marvellous getting that leave. Don't you wish you were home, Maddy?'

'No, thank you,' said Madeleine. 'I'm perfectly happy to be where I am. As for home, I think it was a shock to the system to see me back so soon.'

'I know what you mean,' I said. 'Don't misunderstand me, I was as welcome as the flowers are supposed to be in May but underneath it all I was just a teensy bit suspicious that they'd only just settled down after my last leave. Going home on leave is not quite the same as living there all the time. It takes a bit of time to fit into the organization. Things you would have been told off for when you were at home all the time, you aren't told off for when you're on leave. They put up with it. They forbear. It sets you apart, if you know what I mean.'

'I don't feel like that at all,' said Betty.

'I suppose I would if I thought about it,' her friend replied. 'Are we all going to that dance tonight? It's free to the forces.'

'Magic word that, *free*. Methinks it hath a pleasant ring,' I said. 'However, it's not entirely free. It depends on how great is your regard for your person and how much you enjoy being strained to some rough khaki chest.'

'It's a live band,' put in Maddy.

'Literally I suppose you're right, but perhaps not always animated,' I said. 'But live or not I'm afraid I must pass this one up.

I've other fish to fry. Next time perhaps.'

Later, when we lined up to be inspected before we got our passes, I stood in the darkest part of the room. We wore greatcoats, but I was taking no chances. I was wearing my khaki silk shirt.

With a number of others I made for Liverpool where, at the station, we went our separate ways and I made for the Adelphi Hotel. As soon as I got through the outer doors I took off my greatcoat and looked about me. I was in unfamiliar, alien territory. I took a deep breath and went to the place where I thought I'd be likely to get information – the reception desk. In answer to my question I was told I could have coffee there and I was directed to the lounge. It was large. There were a number of easy chairs and small tables. I wandered in and sat down. There were four other people there, all elderly, two men sitting by themselves and a couple. All had drinks before them. The two men were reading. The couple could have been part of a tableau. No one took the slightest notice of me. Presently, a waiter appeared. He, too, was elderly.

'Yes, madam?' he said.

'Could I, that is, may I have some coffee?' I half mumbled, not sure of myself.

'Certainly, madam,' he said. 'Will that be all, madam?'

I nodded. 'Yes, thank you,' I said.

He brought a table to where I was sitting then went off and returned presently with a tray containing a coffee pot, a container with a small amount of sugar, milk, cup, saucer and a folded bit of paper. After putting down the tray he stood respectfully to one side obviously waiting for something. After a bit of cunning metal detective work, I connected his waiting with the piece of paper and picked it up. It was the bill for the coffee. Two and sixpence (12½p)! Half a crown for one cup of coffee! I could get fifteen cups of NAAFI coffee for that.

'Do I . . . er . . . do I pay now?' I asked.

'Yes, madam, if you would be so good,' he said.

I fished out the half-crown and gave it to him with the piece of paper. He still appeared to hesitate, but in the end he said, 'Thank you, madam,' and tottered off.

In fairness I must say there were two cups in the pot, but also in fairness I should add they were small cups. And the coffee wasn't like Mother NAAFI made, but that was no reflection on the Adelphi.

I sat over those two cups of coffee the best part of three hours. When I'd come to terms with the shock to my pocket, I read my pay book from cover to cover six times. I took out my purse and, without taking the money out, counted how much I had. I worked out (in my head) how many lots of coffee I would get for a week's work if I were paid in that currency. After check and counter-check I made it just less than six and a half. I went through the contents of my sling bag twice. The couple got up and left. Others came and sat down and ordered drinks and every time the waiter came in I put the coffee cup to my lips in case he came and took the tray away.

Apart from the waiter no one spoke to me or even noticed I was there. Finally I took the monocle, the ribbon of which I'd slung round my collar, from my breast pocket and put it in my right eye. I inserted a Turkish cigarette in the holder, lit up and took one or two puffs being careful to blow the smoke out straight away. The waiter came in while this was going on and he brought over an ashtray, laying it silently on the table. After I'd smoked about an inch, I carefully stubbed out the cigarette and returned it to the packet. I intended that these cigarettes should last the duration.

At last I got up and left. When I got to the station, where there was a little more light, I found I was just ahead of another GL wallah, Dorothy Alter.

'That wasn't you I saw coming out of the Adelphi, was it?' she asked. 'I thought it was but couldn't be absolutely sure.'

'Yes, it was,' I said, 'Like George Washington, I cannot tell a lie.'

'Why did you go there?'

'For coffee.'

'Good Lord! Forces canteen not good enough?

'It's not that,' I answered. 'I have nothing against the forces canteen or their food, which is smashing. They make the best bangers and chips I know. And I like the prices they charge. But I know all about these places. What I want to see and know more about is high living and I don't think I'll ever get a better opportunity than I have now. I don't care if I have nothing left for the rest of the week.

'Do you know I once had a date with someone and he suggested taking me out for a meal and I was on pins in case he suggested a hotel and I put my foot in it. We never ate in hotels or stayed in hotels. It was considered an unnecessary waste of money. I was quite keen on this chappie and I didn't want to let myself down in front of him. We went to the café, as it turned out. Then, when we all met up at Liverpool to come here, I got in ages before anyone else and I thought, *I wonder what it's like to have breakfast in a hotel*. When I got there, this man looked me up and down and said, "The cheapest breakfast here is three shillings and sixpence" (17½p) and I slunk out, although I could have paid this wretched three-and-six. So I've made up my mind, I'm going into hotels and I'm going to keep going in till I can walk in as if I owned the place. For the present, give me the hallowed air of the coffee lounge at the Adelphi. As a matter of fact it was penance there tonight, but this uniform is a sort of magic cloak. It gives the open sesame to things you might not otherwise have had and I mean to take advantage.'

'I'm with you, I'm with you,' she said. 'Would you like a partner, or do you prefer to walk alone?'

'I prefer a partner, a kindred spirit.'

'Good. You've got one. By the way, how much was the coffee?'

'Half a crown.'

'WHAT!!'

'Yes. It was a shock, but I think I bore up very well. After Corporal de Silver, that drill sergeant and Captain Wright you don't shake easily.'

'And how much tip did you give?'

'Tip? What do you mean, tip? I bought the place.'

'Tip. T.I.P. TO INSURE PROMPTITUDE. You're supposed to leave one.'

'There I defaulted. Not a brass farthing did I leave.'

'I don't know how you can hold your head up! You'll be known all over Liverpool tomorrow as the woman who didn't tip at the Adelphi. It's worse than not ordering Guinness.'

This was friendship at third sight. Ellen's had been friendship at first sight. That was one of the marvellous things about life on a gunsite – the number of friends one had, each different and each bringing out a different facet of one's personality. It was hardly surprising in a way. The army had sorted us out into similar types.

We had all come into radar (when the Americans came they called it radar – Radio Detection and Ranging – and we adopted the name) because we were deemed suitable. Thus we were similar in at least one respect. Also, we had to work together in teams. At the beginning of our training we worked with several groups of girls till we finally settled into congenial teams. As far as I know we each had a brief interview with a sergeant instructor asking us, in confidence, if we were happy with the team to which we had been assigned. Was there any one member we would prefer not to work with? Thus, a great deal of ground work had already been done to see that we were a homogeneous unit capable of working together with the best possible results. There was a standing joke that the army put you in the job for which you were least suited. It did not happen in my case, nor did I hear of anyone else complaining in that way on GL. Naturally, there were some people on GL and on the site whom I liked better than others, but there were none whom I disliked.

I was to make one other particular friend – Vida Jackson. Vida was like Dorothy and Ellen in some ways. She had a forthright personality and decided views about some things. With her, too, it was instant friendship.

We three, Dorothy, Vida and I, were drawn together for another reason. While we all wanted to get married we had no desire to make a full-time career of domesticity, and there seemed no choice at that time. It was one thing or the other.

I had realized something about myself that took some adjusting to. I really had no background as far as the unit was concerned. Nor, in a way, had anyone else. It was almost as if we'd been born at Oswestry. In my case I was no longer my grandfather's grand-daughter, my father's daughter, my brother's sister or 'hor that works in the store'. For indeed, too frequently, on one or other of these counts was how I was identified.

Subconsciously, though, I had given myself an identification. Oswestry hardly mattered. There was so much work to do we had little leisure for anything else. At practice camp, thanks to the drill sergeant, I was a fall guy. And I played up to this, developing a blithe and seemingly light-hearted view of life as the time went on, till it became my identity. There was a spontaneity about this attitude that was almost child-like. It was trusting, too, in a way.

I'd had a penchant for scribbling bits of doggerel on specific subjects while I was in the store, and I started up again in practice camp. There were dozens of them, among which were:

> Yea, Sergeant, I hear reveille,
> I hear it and rejoice,
> My heart leaps up with gladness,
> I sing in happy voice.

> I leap from bed with carefree smile,
> Ignoring storms and gales,
> Dear Sergeant, you must know this if
> You believe in fairy tales.

I will arise and go now, and to the ablutions go,
And the hot tap turn on there from which liquid ice will flow,
And I shall wash in installments and clear up any mess,
Pull out my curlers, clean my teeth and don my battledress.

And after discovering there would be no more marching drill:

> Fear no more the sergeant's shout
> Nor De Silver's furious rages.
> Thou from training hast pass'd out
> And t' army wilt raise thy wages.
> What Gee-ellers must now do
> Is man TX, RX, PU.

After practice camp the monocle and cigarette holder put in an appearance. Dorothy and I developed an archaic–Shakesperean type of speech. We also acquired the knack of talking backwards.

We were sitting in the set doing a spot of maintenance one morning – or to be more exact, we were sitting chatting, one panel off, instruments at the ready, the set swung round in such a way that entry from the outside was impossible, when Vida arrived hot-foot from battery office to tell me the CO wanted me. She gave the 'code' knock so as not to cause undue alarm and precipitate us into any unnecessary, though meaningless, activity. I was soon back, pleased and a little excited, having been told that I was being sent on my number one Junior NCO course. As we were both, Vida and I, entitled to an evening pass we decided to forsake the delights of the

NAAFI in favour of the highlights of the nearby village in celebration. It would be a good opportunity also, Vida said, to collect a pile of magazines that the good soul who dispensed tea and chips at the local forces' canteen had promised her.

As I dressed after tea I reflected that I must conform to rules and regulations now, and my comfortable, civvy shoes were out. Thus I put on my still-new army shoes, unworn since initial-training camp. I was pleasantly surprised to find they were much more comfortable than I had anticipated. By the time we reached the canteen, however, I felt differently. Thankfully I sat down while Vida went to order our sausage, chips and beans and tell the lady in charge that we would take the magazines away with us.

We had been looking forward to these magazines for some days. 'Sure to be the best,' Vida informed us, 'she's that type.' In consequence we were a little surprised when we were presented with a large pile of *Red Letters*, weekly magazines full of lurid, improbable love stories.

Laden with our magazines and clutching a bar of somewhat sandy chocolate, we made our way to the cinema, where a good film was showing. It had started by the time we got there, and after settling my greatcoat, the magazines and my cap on my knees I removed my shoes and, wiggling my toes, sighed with relief.

It was an enjoyable picture. As the end neared we nudged each other and said we'd stay and see the part we'd missed. Hemmed in our seats we idly watched others hasten away as the lights went up and the curtains closed. There was a familiar roll. Those who could escaped through the doors. Those who couldn't stood still. Aghast we realized this was the end of the show: we'd forgotten today was Sunday. There was only one performance! I felt round for my shoes. They'd gone. In any case we were so weighted down we couldn't move and people were beginning to look. Two members of His Majesty's Forces sitting for the National Anthem: we blushed and hung our heads in shame. As we couldn't stand to attention an attitude of reverence seemed the next best thing. I closed my eyes.

When I opened them again I saw that the people nearest us had not moved but were looking in our direction. An usherette was hurrying over. Was our crime then so awful? She touched Vida on the shoulder.

'It's all right,' she said. 'There's someone coming.'

'Good Lord,' Vida gasped after the usherette had gone, 'one of us is supposed to be ill. You'll have to do it. I can't.'

'. . . But my shoes!'

'I'll get them. Go on,' she hissed, 'faint.'

I did my best.

Not far away there were still one or two looking uneasily in our direction, not wanting to dash away without offering help, and yet not wanting to get involved.

The usherette clucked sympathetically as she went round tipping up the seats. 'So far away from home,' she muttered to anyone who cared to listen, 'and so young. They need a mother.'

She turned up the last few chairs, clucked again and looked towards the door. The last bus wouldn't wait for her.

By this time Vida had found my shoes, but my feet, taking advantage of their freedom, had apparently swollen considerably, for it was only with much effort and a great deal of pain that I was able to squeeze them into the offending shoes. My agony was very real. At this point there was a little stir and the usherette said thankfully, 'He's here,' and left our vicinity. A small man hurried down the aisle, his progress in no way impeded by a large framed picture, wrapped in newspaper, under one arm and a box under the other.

'Run all the way,' he panted as he came up. 'A got me sustificate. Haven't got me uniform yet, but A got me sustificate. Brought it so you'd know A was the real thing. Could see there was something wrong. Knew straight away. Trainin', you see, trainin'. Here's me sustificate to prove it.'

As he talked, he removed the newspaper from his parcel and held up a framed first-aid certificate, then he opened up his box and cheerfully uncorked a bottle.

'Now, now,' he said to Vida patting her heaving shoulders. 'There's no need to take on so. She's gonna be all right A know. A know just how to deal with these cases. Knew as soon as A saw. Ran all the way here. Wife had the supper ready. No need for that, Martha, A ses, I'm needed. Didn't wait and here A am.'

Vida snorted.

He extended a small folding cup, poured some liquid in from the bottle and gave it to me.

'Here,' he said, 'drink this. You'll feel better.'

I gulped it down. It was vile. He turned to Vida.

'It would help,' he said, 'if A knew how it took her.' But Vida was incapable of speech.

'It's no good,' I said, as one recovering, 'she doesn't speak English.'

'Foreign, eh!' he fished among his bottles and shook a box of pills tentatively. 'Give up their homes and come here to fight for the old king and country. Makes you think.' He uncorked another bottle. The smell was enough.

'I feel better,' I said. 'Much better. That was wonderful stuff whatever it was.'

'But A've just started.' He sounded hurt. 'They'll not shut this up yet a while. You're all right. A might even be able to get you an ambulance.'

'You're kind,' I told him 'and I do appreciate it . . . but really I *am* much better and we must go.' I turned to Vida.

'Schlatz unbaleg,' I mumbled. 'I'm only saying,' I explained kindly, 'that it's time to go.' I stumbled painfully up the aisle followed by Vida, her lips tightly pressed together, her eyes fixed in a glassy stare.

The little man packed up his box and caught Vida up. 'Your friend,' he shouted at her mouthing his words. 'Care. Tell her take care.' He touched his heart. 'Bed,' laying his head against his palm. 'Bed. Rest. Understand?'

We stumbled out into the friendly blackout and clutching our belongings ran towards the services canteen, in spite of the agonizing pain in my tortured extremities and the dark. Once in the canteen I bent down to tie my shoelaces. My shoes were on the wrong feet!

I returned from Junior NCO's course to find we'd moved to a different site. It appeared to be on top of a slag heap. I could discern no real reason for their having a gun site there.

'We just got here,' Madeleine said. 'You missed the move between.'

'There must be a reason,' I said. 'I mean. All that training we've had. All that training to lead and be of service. All this patriotic fervour, youthful energy and healthful vigour bursting for an outlet

134

and doomed to wandering round Britain's less-populated slag heaps and abandoned fields. Even the people who actually live here, and there are a few, have never heard of it.'

'Perhaps it's a sort of ATS progress. You know, giving the world an opportunity to see so much . . . er . . . so much . . .'

'Yes?'

'The word escapes me.'

'Khaki inertia, perhaps?'

'That's two words.'

'Where's Ellen?'

'Didn't she write? She said she would. I showed her how to address an envelope and we had a whip round for a stamp. She went on a course. She'll be back next week.'

I was coming down from the sets a week later when a tilly drew up in front of battery office and Ellen was thrown out with her kit.

'Howdy stranger,' I said. 'You new to these here parts?'

'Does anyone live here but us?' she asked looking round.

'Hush yo' mouth, chile,' I said. 'There's a prison on one side and an asylum on the other so try and look a bit more intelligent and a little less villainous otherwise if one doesn't get you the other will. Actually, I think we're here to prevent civil disturbance and mob law taking over.'

'O for the Wings of a Dove,' she replied.

'If I were you I'd have wished for the strong arm of a porter. However, neither wish is likely to be granted so I'll help you to cart your kit to the hut and then we'll see about bedding.'

We staggered towards the hut.

'This,' I said as we went through the doorway, 'is where we keep the home fires burning while others fight for our existence. In this landscape, I assure you, no nightingales sing.'

A week or so later, Dorothy and I had just returned from a 24-hour pass, when we'd had a good time. This having a good time was synonymous with returning flat broke. Experience had taught us that there were few hardships greater than having to exist for several days without the leaven of NAAFI rock buns and dough-nuts. Thus we had left behind sufficient cash to provide these commodities in the passless days to follow till next pay day. The reserve fund now lay on the top of my soldier's box. We had not taken the exigencies of the service into our calculations. Instead of coming back to find we were on manning duty as we'd expected, we found we'd been transferred to another team and were 'on maintenance', which meant we were entitled to an evening pass that night – Saturday night.

Unfortunately, it was not only necessary to say we'd had a good time on our 24, we had to be seen to have had one. This entailed arriving back at camp at the last possible minute – and missing dinner. As our money had virtually run out on the Friday night, we'd had nothing but a cup of tea and a paste sandwich since breakfast on the Saturday morning. Mercifully, the YWCA where we'd spent the night demanded payment in full at the time of booking.

I looked away from the soldier's box to Dorothy.

'Which ever way you add it up,' I said, 'it comes to 1/9d [almost 9p].'

Dorothy nodded. 'Yes,' she agreed. 'Deftly using both hands, that's the total I'd come to. Not enough to paint the smallest village the palest pink.'

We fished in our pockets and produced sundry pieces of pasteboard – old railway tickets to be used in an emergency. We shared the colours evenly between us, swept up the money and, doing our best to ignore the void of extreme hunger, changed into fatigues (dungarees) for the labours of the afternoon. Even had we been financially destitute, we could not have endured a Saturday night in camp when a pass was to be had for the asking. Evening passes were due to be taken up at 18.00 hours, but they were usually available in the guard-room by 17.00 hours. As work did not finish till this time, it was amazing the number of personnel who could be out of their appointed place, changed and have picked up their passes by 17.01 hours, scorning the camp tea which was at 17.30 hours. Normally both Dorothy and I would have been among this group, but, on this occasion, our bodies, weakened as they were by lack of nourishment, rebelled. We therefore stayed and ate as much fried bread, baked beans, bread, margarine and slab cake as the cook on duty could be persuaded to give us. We only managed one thick piece of cake each, but Dorothy was given a small extra helping of margarine. She shared this with me and we smeared it over our pieces of cake, putting our jam ration on top of that.

136

'I was going to save this for coming back,' I said. 'But I can't resist it.'

'Nor can I,' said Dorothy, and blissfully unconcerned about the number of calories we had already consumed, we waded into the *pièce de résistance* of the meal.

We were in time for the train which would convey us to the nearest swollen village two stops down the line, the only place near which could mildly approach opportunities for a wild Saturday night.

Before we got to the station proper, we stopped at a vantage point where we could see the train approaching. When it had hissed to a stop, we started running and flung ourselves, panting, through the barrier at the point when the train was about to be waved off. A friendly guard stayed the engine's ardour to be away long enough for us two girls to get into a compartment.

As we drew into our destination, regardless of safety and the rules of the presiding railway authority, doors were flung open along the length of the train and khaki-clad figures jumped off, speeding their way along the platform towards their Arabian Saturday Night's Entertainment.

Dorothy and I made our way along the platform independently. We had already ascertained the colour of the tickets issued that day and we each had a well-rubbed piece of paste board ready to be thrust into the ticket-collector's hand at the height of the rush. As it happened, such strategy was not necessary. The very first man through started an altercation with the factotum on the gate and we were among those who slid behind him to freedom.

'There's a dance on at the Mechanics',' said Dorothy. 'It might be free to the forces.'

'On a Saturday night?' I replied. 'Not a hope.' Nevertheless, it was to the Mechanics' Hall we first made our way. My reasoning proved correct. Dancing 7–11, admission 1/-(5p).

In the entrance hall one or two people were going purposely forward to the table where they paid. We stood at a respectful distance smiling in what we hoped was an appealing way and attempting to assess the gullibility of the man in charge of the basin with the money. Finally, in a lull, we went forward.

'Would you mind very much,' Dorothy said sweetly and with the utmost deference, 'if we just had a teensy peep through the glass doors?' The man grinned, slightly self-consciously. Dorothy wasn't fooled. He belonged to the group that looked a push-over, but was, in fact, mulishly obstinate in sticking to the letter of the rule book. However, we could but try. Under the circumstances we hadn't much choice. At that moment two groups of two arrived and the man's attention was temporarily diverted. We used the opportunity to go to the double doors and look through the glass panels at the scene before us. As it was just after seven, dancing had not yet started. They had just finished laying the French chalk and the band was in the process of tuning up.

'I rather fancy him,' I said, nodding towards a naval petty officer standing on the far side of the room.

'You and the rest,' replied Dorothy. 'You always go for the wrong ones. Anyway, it's better if we can meet two friends.'

We continued to look, each privately assessing the situation. On the face of it, it seemed we would have no lack of partners. There was a lull in customers and the man in charge of the basin looked across and said, 'You haven't paid yet.'

'Well,' said Dorothy, smiling as attractively as she knew how, 'we've been thinking. Seven till eleven is threepence (1¼p) an hour. If I give you a shilling could we have two hours each please? We'll come out of the dance at five-past nine. Promise.'

The man smiled his self-conscious smile.

'It's a shilling each,' he said; 'doesn't matter what time you go in and come out.'

Not all our guile could persuade him otherwise and we retired defeated, but by no means cast down.

Our next call was to the only real 'posh' hotel there was; 'posh' being a relative term. A newly acquired confidence allowed us to walk purposefully past reception to the lounge, where we again peered through glass doors. What we saw met our approval. Quiet, restrained air; one or two groups, well spaced out, drinking coffee or spirits round tables. We made for the powder room which was empty. From our pockets we withdrew a number of shoulder ribbons from which we made a selection. On our left epaulettes we each put a broad band of orange ribbon, a small band of green and a narrower band of orange. Above her left-hand breast pocket

Dorothy pinned a pair of gold wings and I pinned a burnished badge I'd bought for a penny (less than ½p) above my left breast pocket. I slung the monocle round my neck and stuck the long ebony cigarette holder into my mouth complete with Turkish cigarette. We were ready. We chose a table which distanced us as much as possible from those present. Our nearest neighbours were two Norwegian naval officers. We sat absorbing the atmosphere, I taking in as much as I could with one eye – the monocle distorted the vision of the other. I puffed away at my cigarette without inhaling and without coughing (a more recent achievement).

Presently a waiter came up as fast as his ageing person would allow.

'Yes, madam,' he said, impassively, including us both in his greeting. I removed my cigarette holder from my mouth. The monocle fell from my eye and I screwed it back into position. The waiter didn't move a muscle; he had been well trained.

'Ooteck skrind, zeelpeck,' said Dorothy.

'Coffee?' asked the waiter.

We looked at him, not understanding.

'Ooteck skrind, zeelpeck,' Dorothy repeated.

The waiter went away and returned with two price lists, one for each of us. Even with the monocle I quickly saw there was nothing we could afford. I smiled at the waiter and produced the shilling.

'Ooteck,' I said, pointing vaguely to the area of soft drinks.

The waiter could make nothing of it and looked around as he flicked through the smatterings of languages he knew. None fitted.

The two young officers had been watching the scene with interest and finally one came over.

'Can we help?' he asked in very good English. Dorothy almost liquified before him. He was an absolute smasher. But absolutely. 'You spik Engleesh?' He mouthed the words carefully and more loudly than was usual in this rarified atmosphere.

We looked at him blankly and, surfacing from her daze, Dorothy had a brainwave. She produced an old envelope and pencil from her bag and drew a lemon to indicate we would like lemonade, this being the only drawable drink she could think of. By this time, the other officer had joined the group. The two young men looked at the drawing.

'Barrage balloons,' said the newcomer.

I was suddenly overcome with a gurgling snort in my nose which affliction I overcame by staring fixedly at the opposite wall. Dorothy further embellished the drawing with drops falling from the lemon into a glass. This was interpreted as a desire for a fruity drink for which the first young man insisted on paying.

'You not spik Ingleesh,' he said, slowly and deliberately. '*Français, peut-etre?*'

At this, our eyes lit up. After assuring each other that we spoke only school French and that badly, we got round to each other's names. Dorothy introduced herself as Iashta and me as Tolerash. We put a great deal of effort into each trying to demonstrate to each other how our names were pronounced. We followed this with a conversation in French which, being translated, went something like this:

'Since how much you trace here?'

'Yes. Yes. Real. And you? Where is from your country?'

'Excuse.'

'Your country. Is she remote?'

'But no. I am here to hit. You relish?'

'Excuse.'

'But little, Bang. Bang.'

'Ah. The pigeon house. You thief. Like the birds.'

By this time, all eyes were upon us. A senior army officer, who had been sitting unnoticed in a remote corner, got up and made his way towards us. Dorothy saw him first.

'Kooleck Tow!' she said, coughing, put her hand to her chest. I took in the emergency immediately. 'Tnaif. Tnaif,' she said and I did my best to oblige as the elderly officer came up.

'I hope you will forgive the intrusion,' he began, 'but I thought I knew—'

'Mon amie,' put in Dorothy in distress. '*Elle est malade,*' and before anyone could realize what was happening, she seized my limp form, heaved me up and supported me towards the door. Once outside, we lost no time in leaving the hotel and, in the safety of the blackout, we removed the insignia with which we had lately adorned ourselves.

'Idiot,' said Dorothy. 'Stupid idiot! What did he want to come and spoil everything for? I could have gone for that Lars in a big way. Another minute and I would have told him we were only having a bit of fun. Now I'll never get the chance.'

'It's better that way,' I said.

'You may be right,' she answered, 'but I'm not convinced.'

The cashier had gone from the pay-box in the darkened cinema. Cautiously, we made our way to the auditorium and quietly eased the door open. A few people were standing at the back. We joined them unnoticed.

'It's *Flames of Passion*!' whispered Dorothy. 'I've seen it twice already. I didn't like it either time.'

We joined the rush on the last train, back, getting through the barrier without difficulty. In the quiet camp we crept into the cookhouse in the vain hope that a crust of bread might be located somewhere.

'Who's that?' called a voice.

We went to the works part of the cookhouse, where we saw Jake the boilerman stretched out on a form. He was doing his utmost to resemble in colour and build the boiler he tended with such care. The delicious aroma of hot rending fat filled the air.

'We're absolutely famished,' said Dorothy. 'Is there something to eat?'

'By rights I should report you,' said Jake. 'You shouldn't be here.'

'You wouldn't,' I said. 'We just want the teensiest stale crust.'

In the end, we each went out with a thick slice of bread that had been dipped in hot fat and liberally salted.

'Manna,' I said.

'I still wish I'd told him,' sighed Dorothy as she licked her fingers after the last greasy morsel had been disposed of.

'Like I said, it was better you didn't,' I replied.

To my surprise I was sent on another course – NCOs and instructors – and when I returned to the battery it was to find our caravan had been on the move once more. The site was a quiet stretch, not far from the sea. It was early summer and the weather while we were there was warm, even hot, which gave us the feeling that in spite of the presence of the engines of war, we were on holiday. In no way could we be said to rush at life with an open throttle.

Apart from going out to dances, we had no great desire to leave the vicinity of this camp for the few weeks of our stay. We wanted to spend the longer, lighter nights as near as possible to camp itself. We were near a stretch of water and a perfect stretch of sand with no hint of barbed wire anywhere along its length. Many of the others were content to sit on the sand when they could, basking in the warmth of the sun. Delightful though this was, it had a limited appeal for me as it had for both Dorothy and Vida.

One night I got into bed and pulled up the bedclothes, ready to sleep the sleep of the just.

'What is it?' I said, opening my eyes, instantly alert though I had been sound asleep.

'Sh.' It was Vida. 'It's such a beautiful night, it's a shame to waste it in sleep. Come and see for yourself.'

I pulled my slacks over my pyjamas, drew on my battledress top and slipped my feet into my plimsolls. We tiptoed out of the hut and surveyed the silent camp bathed in moonlight. We found a weak spot in the camp's perimeter and went down to the water.

We picked our way to where a small outcrop of rock rose a little above the water and sat comfortably on a ledge, not speaking. Far, far above the sky was dark blue sprinkled with steel bright stars. Through it all the moon rode serenely, silently sending a path of light down the still water. I watched the moon's tranquil progress for some time, enthralled without really thinking, until it occurred to me how puny we were from the moon's distance. Puny people aiming to maim and kill other puny people. Tiny creatures wasting their resources and their lives, their youth and their beauty, in barbaric and cruel conflict while the moon sailed on indifferent.

'It's almost impossible to feel we are at war,' I said. 'How *could* people be so stupid as to squander the thing, which, so far as we know, exists nowhere else in the universe. Life. How can we set in motion the horror, the telegrams, the tears, the empty shops, the . . .'

'Don't think about it,' Vida whispered. 'Just let the beauty of all this dig deep into your soul.'

The high wide sky. A night of majesty. The solitary moon distanced from the stars. Those independent stars. Just as we were independent, our thoughts and feelings making us so. And even though we died together, each one of us would die alone.

142

Dawn, pale and more pale. Pearled and still.

'I wish I were a poet,' I said. 'I wish I could capture this night that it might live for ever. It's a sort of pain that tears at your soul as it soothes and caresses. Something deep. No more war. Please. We are the children of love. The stars out there are dead. They twinkle but have no life. But what are we doing with this life?'

'It's like an orgasm,' said Vida. 'An orgasm of the soul.'

A slight breeze, no more than a caress, stirred.

'I'm going to swim,' Vida said. 'Are you coming?'

'No,' I replied. She took off her clothes and walked out.

'Don't be long,' I said. While I waited I took off my plimsolls and put my feet in the cold water, allowing them to displace the soft sand beneath.

By 4.30 it was almost daylight. We walked back to the sleeping camp and stood for a moment outside the hut door, at one with the dawning day as it gathered strength. I went to bed utterly cleansed and relaxed and when I woke a mere two hours later, it was as though I'd slept a hundred years of deep refreshing sleep.

Two days later our wagons were rolling yet again. Again – we peered at a changing landscape and asked ourselves, 'Whither goeth we?'

11. Take Post

Hardly had we settled into our new camp when we were summoned from our beds for a real alarm. We rushed to the sets and tracked down our first enemy target.

We had begun, in a modest way to start with, to do the job for which we had been trained. By this time we were all qualified tradeswomen (OsFC) and our pay had been raised accordingly to 4/3d (21p) per day. Also, somewhere along the line, I got my promotion to lance-corporal, which meant I was now a number one.

From henceforth (manning) was to be the permanent backdrop to all our activities, our *raison d'être*, the circumstance that took precedence over all others.

The battery, after it left practice camp, was divided into two troops, A and B, but there was a fair amount of interchange between them, and occasionally we were all together.

On this move, I found myself initially in A troop with Joy, Ellen, Betty and Madeleine. Dorothy, Norah and Vida were in B troop. We were, in fact, on the outer London defences, but that we did not know. What we did know was that, in less than an hour, we could be in London.

In the autumn we moved to another practice camp, a firing camp this time. We were housed in what had been a sanatorium. It was built on top of a hill near the sea where unlimited amounts of fresh, bracing, ice-cold breezes were to be had. Our room had originally been a ward.

We seemed to be relatively near a quiet, residential area. There were also an extraordinary number of other troops there, both RAF and army.

Social life was limited and was confined to a sort of village hall where frequent dances were held, a café and a pub.

Of course, no one told us why we moved here but, at a guess, I think it might have been because the gun sites we operated were being modified. New or more advanced guns perhaps, and modifications to the RX at least. At this camp we were learning to use modified, or new, equipment.

'Windows', strips of metal dropped to jam radar screens, had been used by bomber command in July 1943, and it was inevitable that the Germans would retaliate. Their name for 'windows' was *Dueppel*. They were metal strips about 2 ½ feet long (80 cm) and about ¾ inch (1.9 cm) wide. When they were dropped, the radar tubes were jammed by interference: that is, the whole tube became a mass of dazzling white moving snow which totally obliterated the target. At night, without radar, the site was blind. There were, of course, the searchlights which picked up targets and held them in the cross beams while the pilot, blinded by the light, struggled this way and that to get out, a clearly marked target for planes and guns as he did so. Even when he wasn't marked down by one or the other, he was often prevented from completing his mission accurately.

When the tube was jammed, it was the job of the number one to clear it. This needed a modification to the set.

We left the sanatorium in the mornings in thick socks, pullovers, battledress, heavy boots, gaiters, leather jerkins, and sheepskin mittens, and spent the entire day on the practice site tightening up the procedure and (in our case) coping with interference and other hazards, which included low-flying aircraft. During the morning a mobile van arrived with hot cocoa and buns and another later with sandwiches and soup.

On one of these breaks Miss Gaitskill, our junior commander and the senior woman officer in the battery, came up to me as I was sipping cocoa. I liked her tremendously, as did all the other ATS. She was respected and listened to, her words noted, without her ever having to raise her voice or be other than courteous. In fact, she was the model of all I ever hoped to be.

'Good morning, Corporal Summers,' she said. 'Are you enjoying your cocoa?'

'Very much, ma'am.'

'I haven't really had a chance to talk to you since your last course,' she said. 'You got an excellent report. You got a strong recommendation to train as an instructor. Would you like that?'

'Very much, ma'am. But not as an alternative to being an operator on site. I wouldn't want to give that up.'

'You enjoy your work?'

'Very much, ma'am.'

'What part in particular would you say you liked most?'

'I don't think there's any single part. I like operating, of course. The other thing I like is being part of a well-oiled functioning whole.'

'In what way?'

'Well, ma'am, when we move, for instance. A large concourse of people leaves a site. They move out at the right time regardless of weather. They all arrive at the right spot. A train arrives and swallows them up and transports them from one part of the country to another. They're fed. They get out, walk in one piece to another camp and within half an hour they are established and operational. Hut, bedding, food and ready for action. I think it's marvellous.'

'Yes. But it doesn't just happen, you know. An advance party goes ahead to prepare the camp and see that everything is ready when the main body arrives, and a rear party stays behind to clear up. They hand over to the officer in charge of the next advance party. But, as you infer, it all dovetails neatly.'

'Can anyone be on these advance and rear parties, ma'am?'

'In theory, yes. In practice, no. There is a lot of hard work to do in a short time and the officer in charge finds it quicker and better to use people he knows. Why? Are you thinking of volunteering?'

'I'd like to, ma'am.'

'It's very hard and sometimes unpleasant work. I don't think you'd like it.'

'I don't think liking and not liking is important, ma'am. I just like to know how the whole site works. I'd really like to spend time on the guns and the predictors and in the command post, but I know that's not possible.'

The whistle blew for the end of break.

'Well, we'll see,' Miss Gaitskill smiled.

I stood uncertainly with my cup in my hand, wavering. I didn't know whether I was expected to salute or not, always a rather foolish situation.

Our evenings were free, and, like everyone else, at first I made for what passed as night life. Then I made a discovery. There was a sitting-room we could use. It had easy chairs, a fire and a locked bookcase. Naturally, we had thought such luxury would be out of bounds to the rank and file, but no. It had been a well-guarded secret, but now that it was out, it was ATS for the use of.

Also, the ablution facilities were well above par.

One evening, bathed, pyjamas under battledress, I made for this room and settled down with the book I'd been allowed to take from the case.

'Oh, there you are,' said Ellen, coming in dressed for another form of combat in the village hall. 'I've been looking for you everywhere. Aren't you going to the dance?'

'No. I've decided I can no longer live entirely for pleasure. I've given it up for this particular duration. I am intent on seeing how many of these books I can read before we leave.'

'Do they know the risk they're running letting you loose among a group of defenceless books?'

'I am a carer of books. It appals me to see a book harshly treated. I merely save them from a . . .'

146

'I have a mind to give them the inside story. Unless, of course, you change your mind and come to the dance tonight.'

'That is blackmail.'

'I know. I'm willing to stoop to any depth. There's this Pole, you see. . . .'

'Animal or mineral?'

'Funny! You know what I mean, there's a hundred of them here. As I said, there's this Pole and he sticks to me like glue. As soon as I get in the hall, he'll be waiting to pounce. I almost have to come back under escort. Now. There's someone else I've seen. A real smasher. And I know that, given the chance, I'm in with a chance. I'm sure he only keeps away because he thinks this Pole and I have something going. Now what I want you to do in the sacred name of friendship is to prize him off me with all the limited charm at your disposal.'

'Your flattery unwoman's me.'

'The point is, will you do it, or have I to spill the beans?'

I put my hands up. 'I surrender,' I said, 'but you'll have to go on and I'll follow. Don't worry. I have given my word. Our family motto is "Nunquam verbus breakus". Never break your word.'

The hall was packed to suffocation. Responding to the even, steady rhythm of a detached band, an assortment of warm heaving bosoms were being strained to a further assortment of perspiring manly chests. I scanned the room for Ellen. Yes. There she was in the clutches of a Polish RAF sergeant. Looking at him, I couldn't imagine what she was complaining about. I'd seen worse. Still, one woman's meat. . . . I prepared to do my duty in the interests of friendship straight away and forced myself through the crowd. I smiled at Ellen and tapped the young man on the shoulder.

'Dr Livingstone, I presume,' I said. 'You appear to have forgotten in the heat of battle that this is our dance. Excuse me,' I said to Ellen. She stood there with her mouth open, waving her hands. I got hold of the sergeant and, somewhat bewildered, he allowed himself to be barged round the room with me.

'Do you really like dancing this much?' I asked.

He shrugged and smiled.

'Let's go outside for some fresh air,' I said, determined to leave the field absolutely clear for Ellen. I had managed to glimpse her through the throng. She was now clasped in the arms of another Pole. A very tall one.

The sergeant spoke very good English.

'Do you often do things like that?' he asked.

'Well,' I hesitated. 'Not often. Never before as a matter of fact. I . . . er . . . I don't know what came over me. I . . . er . . . thought you were someone else actually. I'm sorry. Forget it happened. Go back to the dance and I'll fade into oblivion. Please.' He laughed.

'No,' he said. 'I felt flattered . . . um . . . pleased. Shall we go somewhere else?'

There was only the pub, which was just as crowded. He seemed quite happy to talk about himself. Unfortunately, the noise in the pub prevented me from hearing most of what she said. He walked me back to the sanatorium.

'Perhaps I'll see you again sometime,' he said.

'I'm quite sure you will,' I answered. 'At the dance.'

Ellen was already in the room when I got there waiting for me.

'You might be a third-rate philosopher,' she said as soon as I came in, 'but you're a ruddy tenth-rate friend.'

It appeared that the sergeant had been the one she'd had her eye on.

On our next trip to the dance hall, matters were apparently put right and all was well. A few nights later I was again tempted to risk being permanently lamed. Almost as soon as I got into the hall the tall Pole whom I'd seen dancing with Ellen came up to claim me as a partner. He certainly stuck like glue. Right through the dance and afterwards. He had never, he said, met anyone like me before. As soon as he set eyes on me he knew I was the one for him. He had been a carefree bachelor till that moment, sailing life's stormy ocean unfettered. But now all that had changed. He had seen at once I was to be the love of his life. Some people took a long time to find these things out. He knew at once. However long we knew each other he would never be more certain than he was at this moment. He stood over me while I got my greatcoat and walked me home like a vulture loath to take his eyes off his prey.

When I'd said for the twenty-second time that I would really have to go he pressed something light and metallic into my hand. 'My old grandmother gave me this,' he said solemnly. 'It's an old family heirloom. She said I was to keep it till I met the girl of my choice, when I was to give it to her as a token of my love. Here, take it. And the next time you leave that dark house I shall be waiting here for you.'

I got away and ran up to the ablutions. By that time the room light was out, the blackout down and the windows opened. We always slept with the windows open, even in the bitterest weather.

There were one or two others in the ablutions getting ready for bed and chatting. I turned my back on them for privacy and looked at the heirloom so recently entrusted to me. It was a bracelet made up of oblongs of grey metal held together by rings of the same metal. For such a heavy-looking object it was remarkably light. I was reminded more of aeroplane bodies than heirlooms.

Somebody else was standing beside me. Ellen. 'May I have a look?' she asked, and took the bracelet.

'It looks to me,' she went on, 'as if it was a Polish heirloom given by some old Polish grandmother to her tall grandson. I can hear her aged voice. "Take this, my child, and give it to the girl of your choice". Wait there,' she said handing me back the bracelet. When she returned she was dangling its fellow. A discreet enquiry round several of our fellow female warriors produced another three.

'We should form a club,' I said. 'The GHS. The Grandmother's Heirloom Society. Gulls for short. I wonder,' I went on, 'where he learned his English?'

On the Saturday night before we were due to leave it was obligatory to go out in search of enjoyment, so once more to the dance. This time it was an RAF corporal who sought me as a partner – and who stuck. Making a choice apparently exhausted them to such a degree that it was all they could do to shuffle round the floor at intervals and give monosyllabic answers to vital burning questions such as 'Do you come here often?', 'Nice band', etc. He took me for a lemonade during the interval and, as a matter of course, walked back with me. Stupidly, I had already said there was no great urgency about getting back that night. We were all on late pass.

He was a little more talkative on the way back, but not much. As we arrived at the entrance to the sanatorium he suddenly became purposeful and when I made to say goodnight he said, 'There's no need whatever for you to go in now. You have plenty of time. Let's walk round to the summerhouse and chat.'

'Summerhouse? I didn't know there was a summerhouse. Oh. I know. That glass place. Surely it's locked?'

'No,' he said. 'It's open and it's sheltered. You can easily chat for another ten minutes.'

'All right,' I said. 'Ten minutes. No more.'

He was right. The door was open. We went in and, as he shut the door, I peered around as best I could in the darkness. The next thing I knew I was down on the floor fighting for my honour. His task was made more difficult by the fact that we were both wearing greatcoats. I kicked and struggled and we rolled over and finally I kicked myself sufficiently free, at least, to get on to my feet. He made towards me, pulling at my legs and I backed off with all my might and went right through a panel of glass, lost my balance and crashed on the other side. Not waiting to find out whether or not I'd been mortally wounded, I scrambled myself up and ran as fast as I could towards the building, flinging myself through the main door. As I got into the light of the entrance hall an officer came racing downstairs, red-faced. Seeing me, he said, 'Have you seen Lance Corporal X anywhere?'

'No, sir,' I replied, startled.

He hesitated, ignoring me, looked this way and that and finally running off in the direction opposite to the one I was going. I looked round cautiously then made my furtive way to the ablutions to examine my person for damage. My face was red, my cap awry, my hair somewhat dishevelled and my coat and stockings covered with dirt and old leaves, but other than that I seemed to have escaped unharmed. One of our number was there. She looked at me uncertainly and said, 'May I ask a personal question? Have you had a . . . a bit of a . . . well . . . trouble?'

'Yes,' I said.

'In the summerhouse?'

'The same. And you?'

'Yes. When I saw you dancing with the corporal I wondered whether I should say anything to you, but then I thought it was me, and you would be all right. Anyway I didn't know what to say.'

Lance-Corporal X came in quickly.

'If they ask for the duty NCO,' she said to me, 'will you take over. Give any excuse you like, but I'm off duty,' and left.

By the time we'd all settled down it was after 01.00 hours and two of our number were still missing. Wondering what could possibly have happened to them we got into bed. Sometime later some of us were wakened by the sound of stones being thrown up against the window. I put on my greatcoat, slunk downstairs with my torch and opened the main door. It was almost 05.00 hours.

'Where on earth have you been?' I asked.

'Tell you tomorrow,' they said.

It appeared that they had decided to go to the café before going to the dance and, while they were waiting to be attended to, Maudie looked down and saw she'd laddered her stocking. She remarked on the fact and the friendly café proprietress said, 'If you come into the back room I'll mend it for you.'

Maudie and her friend followed the woman and after going through a bead curtain, they found themselves in a room where there were one or two army NCOs having a drink. They chatted the two girls up and one of them, a sergeant, offered to mend the ladder if Maudie kept her stockings on. She declined the offer and actually never did get the ladder mended.

Two of the sergeants said they had a vehicle outside and they were going to a decent pub in town ten or so miles distant. Would the girls like to go with them?'

'How long will you be gone?' Maudie asked.

'Not long,' they answered. 'What time have you to be back for?'

'Eleven o'clock,' said Maudie giving herself and her friend a little leeway.

'We'll have you back long before then,' they said.

The vehicle turned out to be a van, fitted out with radio equipment round its three sides. It was here the girls sat with one sergeant while the other drove. Maudie said both men were very pleasant and agreeable. Never having seen a van like this before she asked what it was and what it was being used for. The sergeant said he couldn't say. As far as they were concerned they were to think of it as a van.

Presently, after they'd been travelling about half an hour, the van stopped and the driver came round to join them in the electrical bit.

He said the engine was overheated and they were waiting for it to cool. In fact, it was they who were overheated as it turned out, for the talk soon became personal and over-familiar.

'Just put that hand back where it belongs,' Maudie said. 'Or else.'

'And you,' her friend said to the other chap.

'Aw, come on,' they said. 'You knew what you'd come out for. Don't come the old innocent. We know why you came into the back shop. What do you take us for? Now less of it,' and they got both girls in a clinch.

By this time, Maudie's friend was crying because her sergeant was losing no time in reaching his objective and she could do little to stop him.

'Shut up,' Maudie said. 'That won't help.'

'Atta girl,' her sergeant said. 'Just behave yourself, or don't behave yourself rather, and it'll be all right.'

'Listen, mate,' Maudie replied. 'They're tough where I come from and they don't come any tougher than me. And I'm on radar and I know all about this equipment. I know exactly where to put my foot to put this out of action and to put you out of action. If you go any further that is exactly what I will do on both counts and when you get better you'll have some explaining to do.'

They got up straightaway, opened the door and almost flung the two of them outside. 'Get out,' they said.

'You'll be taking us back to camp?' Maudie asked.

'No bloody fear,' they answered.

'But we don't know where we are!'

'That's your bloody look out,' they said, and getting into the van they started up the engine and left them.

'What I would like to know,' I said, as we discussed the incident afterwards among ourselves, 'is, what did they put in the cocoa? Or is it all this pure fresh air? And if so, what did it do to the patients?'

On the Monday we moved out of camp. I was in the clearing-up party.

I was given the ATS ablutions to clean after first taking all the soiled sanitary towels to the incinerator to be burned. Soiled sanitary towels en masse are not a pretty sight – nor have they an attractive smell. An orderly helped me.

'You get used to it,' she said.

Then we helped in the cookhouse and finally helped generally. The officer in charge said we'd done a good job. Privately, I agreed with him. It was barely 10.00 hours and I'd done a day's work. We handed the sanatorium over, then sat down with the prospective inmates for a very satisfying meal of tea and doorstep sandwiches. The task over, we set off for camp. When we got there it was to find that together with Joy, Betty, Madeleine, Ellen and another girl, Marie McCully, I was to be moved to B site the following day.

Somewhat to our surprise, we were housed in the cooks' and orderlies' hut, extra beds having been put there. Having deposited our kit we re-assembled outside battery office where a staff sergeant marched us through the site beyond the RX to another new-looking piece of equipment also sited on wire. He brought us to a halt.

'This,' he said, 'is the Canadian Mark III. The latest development in radar. The British, Canadians and Americans each decided to develop a new Mark III Radar independently. As it turned out, there is little difference between the Canadian model and the British model, but it is the Canadian model that is available to us here. Some differences may be obvious to you already. The aerials for instance. Smaller. Set in a paraboloid. You have been sent here to learn about this latest development and how to operate it and I have been sent to teach you.'

After we had assimilated this information we learned some very pleasant facts. First, we were excused all duties except the normal hut fatigues. Second, the cooks and orderlies who might well have resented us as cuckoos in their nest were, in fact, very welcoming and friendly indeed. Because of the erratic hours they worked, sometimes starting as early as 03.00 hours and finishing late, their hut was subjected to far less scrutiny than the GL hut and their floor, though swept and polished, never achieved the mirror-like surface the subaltern felt was a necessity as far as GL were concerned. We were wakened to mugs of tea and it was easier to get someone to bring a meal in for you if for some reason you didn't want to go to the cookhouse.

I did note one thing, though I was not aware of its significance, never having heard of either homosexuals or lesbians. Two girls were very friendly with each other. I'll call them Doll and Moll. They went everywhere together and slept in adjacent beds. In the evenings, however, they didn't put their soldier's boxes around the stove to sit and chat as some of us did, they lay on one or other of their beds looking into each other's eyes, stroking each other's hair, cuddling and sometimes kissing. When it got to this stage one or other of their co-workers would yell at them to 'give over' and threaten to throw cold water over them if they didn't. Their answer to this was to smile at each other and go outside hand in hand.

In a raid, only the cook on duty went out: the rest of us stayed in bed. Any activity at this time was light indeed and quickly passed so that apart from jumping at the first note of 'take post' and subsequently realizing it wasn't for us, we simply got on with our interrupted sleep. Doll and Moll however, expressed themselves afraid, and comforting each other they got into one narrow bed.

Kind though they were in the hut, there were drawbacks. Because of the cookhouse floors, the cooks wore clogs. You can't tiptoe round in clogs. The girls were very friendly and chatty, but the room was crowded and privacy was non-existent. The wireless was on all the time so that reading, studying or writing became difficult. There was, of course, the ATS restroom, but this was for the use of all ATS and it wasn't a quiet room.

Naturally, the Canadian Mark III was different from the Mark II. It had a far more solid appearance and it was roomier. And, very important to me, there was no dizzy, fragile-looking ladder to climb to clean the aerials.

The job of number one was very different. The headphone and mouthpiece that kept her in touch with the GPO in the command post were similar, but the tubes before her were different, for now there were two tubes, one of which was the large PPI (Plan Position Indicator). This 'soup plate' gave a plan of the land over a 90-mile radius. Static white dots of varying sizes and brilliance were indications of buildings, high ground, etc. that reflected signals. The moving target was not unlike a small comet. Thus, the number one could report the presence of enemy targets well before they got within range of the guns. In addition, it was possible for her to see the direction in which they (the planes) were travelling. The general situation, then, was monitored till the GPO decided which target was likely to come within the orbit of the guns, when he ordered that it should be tracked. When this happened number one saw the

154

target on her small screen as soon as numbers two, four and five had also homed in on it and were able to read off the angle of sight, bearing and elevation respectively. The system for clearing interference was extremely efficient. Thus 'windows' were rendered comparatively useless. Strangely enough, from the very beginning I had no difficulty whatsoever in reading the PPI and getting a mental picture of the terrain.

On Friday, we were given a test on the week's work. We were not anxious for this time to be over too quickly so we decided amongst ourselves that we would not attempt to excel.

'The results,' the staff sergeant said, 'are poorer than I was led to believe I would get, both from personal observations and from the reports that preceded you here.'

The following Thursday the staff sergeant left us alone in the set while he went off on an errand of his own. 'If I don't get back in time,' he said, 'you are quite capable of dismissing yourselves. Only, for your own sakes, make it later rather than sooner.'

We took this to mean he wasn't coming back.

'Do you know what I've found?' said Marie. 'There are two vacant rooms near battery office. I saw them and had a good look through the windows.'

'I hope nobody saw you,' I said.

'Oh, no,' she said. 'There was no one around.'

'I don't see what difference it makes whether she was seen or not,' said Betty.

'You never know,' I answered, 'and it's best to be on the safe side.'

'I thought,' went on Marie, 'wouldn't it be smashing if we could have those rooms? There'd be somewhere where we could study and be by ourselves. The cooks and orderlies are nice but we're on a bit of a limb.'

'That's what I was thinking,' I said.

'Well, why don't we just ask?' said Joy. 'Why don't we just explain our position and ask if we can have the rooms?'

'I heard,' put in Ellen, 'they used to be the sergeants' quarters till they got new ones.'

'We can't ask,' I said, 'for several reasons. Those rooms were vacant when we came. In spite of that, extra beds were put in the

155

cooks' and orderlies' hut. Why not GL? And if, as Ellen says, they've been sergeants' quarters, then they'll be hallowed and to give them to us would be to elevate us above our station. If we ask, that proves we know they're there. If we're refused then that will be the end of it and we'll have offended the cooks and orderlies into the bargain, and I should think that's the last thing we want to do. So we've got to think of something which will gain us sympathy and understanding, will not offend the C. and O. and will get us those rooms.'

'Illness,' said Madeleine. 'The right sort. That always makes people sympathetic.'

'We can't all be ill,' said Ellen. 'And if we were they'd put us all in the sick bay. In any case what sort of illness would you get from working on radar – softening of the brain? And where would that get you?'

'On an instructor's course,' said Madeleine.

'Just a minute,' I said. 'You might have something there, Ellen. Talking in your sleep. Letting out vital information prejudicial to the conduct of the war. This is supposed to be secret.'

'Oh, yes,' said Marie enthusiastically, 'Yes. That's it! And sleepwalking. That's it. Oh, let me do it.' Her eyes were alight.

'I don't like it,' said Joy. 'I don't like it at all. I think we should do the straightforward thing and put up a case. We've got a good case. We need privacy. It is on the secret list.'

'It's no more than it was when we came,' I said. 'I don't think they'll change their minds. The fact that we're doing something regarded as hush-hush will make it worse – not better. Don't ask me why. I don't know.'

In the end Joy was out-voted, but, after registering their protest, she decided to give us her support.

There was a film in the cookhouse that night. This guaranteed a full attendance. The NAAFI opened after the film was over and stayed open a little later than normal, so that the habitueś could make up for lost time.

'Is everybody going to the film tonight?' they asked as we went into the hut after coming down from the set.

'What's on?' asked Betty.

They weren't sure.

'I think it's Percy Marmont and Clara Bow, the "It Girl", in *Mantrap*. Silent. But better than a lantern lecture,' I said.

'Wait till you see the film before you make such a rash statement,' said Ellen.

'It'll be the Hollywood Esses,' said Madeleine. 'Sex, Sob and Satin.'

'Whatever it is,' said Marie, 'I can't go. I simply must stay in and try to get these facts into my head. And I'm so afraid that in trying to learn them I could give any information away. So I'd better stay in.'

We said that we, too, were staying. The girls thought it was a great shame and said that we worked too hard. Nobody appreciated how hard we worked.

When they'd gone, Joy said, 'I'm still not happy about it all,' but again, after discussion, it was decided we would go on with our plan. Having anything come to the camp gave the evening a festive air and it was likely they would return as from a party. We decided we would all be in bed and asleep when they returned.

When they came back, they got ready for bed, took down the blackouts, opened the windows and got into bed calling 'Good night' to each other. Quiet reigned and over all the pale blue glow of the manning bulb.

Slowly, Marie sat up in her bed, raised her arms aloft, gave a little moan and said, in a deep, 'ghostly' voice, 'Mauve aerials, I see mauve aerials.'

'Ah-ah! A frightened scream from round the room gave testimony to her efforts. Her performance scared the living daylights out of me and I was in on the act.

'Mauve aerials. And pink aerials.'

'Marie, Marie,' I called. 'Stop it. Go back to sleep,' and I meant it in spite of our plan. Moll and Doll had already leapt into each other's arms and were now in the bed farthest away from Marie – legitimately clinging to each other. Marie got up out of bed and, with her arms out, walked towards the aisle saying,

'They rise. The signals go forward. Up, up into the dark night.'

In the blue ghostly light it was a terrifying sight. I got out of bed and put my hand on her shoulders.

'Come on, Marie,' I said. 'Back to bed.' But she was enjoying herself.

'Ah-ah,' she said. 'The target! The light on the screen. I see it. Mauve and pink and —'

'Marie,' I said, 'please', and turning her whispered, 'Stop it. They're terrified.' Aloud I said, 'Get back into bed or you'll put Lady Macbeth out of business.' I said this to try to lighten the atmosphere somewhat. By this time Joy and Ellen were also out of bed and together we tucked Marie up.

'That's enough, right?' Ellen whispered as she patted her head.

'Go and get the duty officer,' one girl said.

'There's no need,' I answered. 'People often sleepwalk. She was dreaming, that's all. We'll sit with her and make sure she doesn't get up again.' Before long the hut settled down and Joy, Ellen and I went back to our beds.

The next thing I knew it was early morning and the orderly NCO was in the hut.

'Private Evans,' she said to Joy, 'the subaltern would like to see you as soon as possible. Could you get up now and dress.'

There was a sort of awed note in her voice not usually present in duty NCOs.

We went across to the empty ablutions after Joy had left the hut. We now knew last night's scene had been reported.

'Why Joy?' Betty asked.

'Probably because they are not sure. If there's been any funny business Joy's the least likely to have been involved. She doesn't dissemble,' Ellen said.

Joy joined us at breakfast.

'The sub wants to see you,' she said to me. 'I didn't give your little scheme away,' she added, 'but I feel I should have.'

I knew exactly how she felt. The sub was concerned. 'What do you make of this, Corporal?' she asked.

'It looked more frightening than it really was, ma'am,' I said. 'Really it was the effect of the manning bulb that made it worse. I think, if I may say so, ma'am, our greatest concern is for the cooks and orderlies and perhaps this concern had preyed on Private McCully's mind. The hut is crowded with us there and we do have work to do at nights. Naturally, they want to chatter and listen to the wireless. It is their hut after all. We have tried the ATS restroom, but it is a recreation room. It's just a pity there had not been a small room somewhere that we could have had. Of course, it's difficult. This is a gunsite not a course centre.'

'Do you think you're being worked too hard?' she asked.

'Oh, no, ma'am,' I replied. 'Certainly not.'

'And Private McCulley, how is she, do you think?'

'Very well, ma'am. It's as if nothing had happened really, ma'am.'

'There's nothing else you can add?'

'No ma'am. Except to say we all appreciate the concern that's been shown. And although we're crowded, the cooks and orderlies have made us most welcome and we enjoy their company.'

'Very well, Corporal. You may go,' she said. 'But have your team stay in the hut till I can come and talk to them.'

We were moved to the vacant rooms later in the morning after the MO had examined us in the medical room. We were given the day off and advised to rest over the weekend. As far as the rooms were concerned we were to sleep in one and the other was to be a second restroom to be open to all ATS. In addition we had our own ablutions, one toilet, one washbasin, one bath.

Bliss. Absolute and utter bliss.

We felt we had to show our appreciation. I decided to start a camp library and went round the area asking for books. I spent the greater part of that day and part of the weekend visiting homes in the area. The others got greenery and jars and polished the room till it shone. When we'd finished I asked the subaltern if she'd care to visit the room and see what we'd done with it. The restroom had chairs, a table and a stove. Now, apart from the greenery, there was a small library on the table.

I put up a notice in the NAAFI to say we now had a camp library – open to all.

On Monday morning we were all crowded into the RX when Staff arrived. He closed the door very carefully and then turned to look at us. He stood thus for some time not speaking, then said, 'Hard work!'

Another pause.

'Mauve aerials!'

Another pause.

'Hard work, mauve aerials or no mauve aerials, is what I expect

159

from the lot of you from this moment on. By next Friday I expect you to have made up for your day and a half's extra holiday. And I expect excellent results in the tests, not only next Friday's but today. And if I don't get them I shall conduct my own enquiry into the mauve aerials. Understood.'

It was.

The course continued thereafter to everyone's satisfaction. Things were quiet until Christmas and winter continued to set in. Last winter had been cold but not actually icy. Nevertheless, it had been cold enough for us to prepare for this one. Most of us did this by 'winning' one way or another extra blankets. These extra blankets were kept out of sight in soldiers' boxes or elsewhere during the day and, in the evening they were brought out to help make a bed which became an envelope-type nest into which we slid.

Except in the very hottest weather I wore something I'd never worn before or since – bedsocks, the thick variety that reached almost to the knee. It saved valuable seconds in a raid as one didn't have to put on socks. I had given up wearing vests at any time, but over my pyjamas I wore a thick pullover with a scarf to cover my curlers. Thus, when I was 'all dressed up to go dreaming' the only possible dream I could have had was a nightmare.

Like everyone else, in winter I learned to dress and undress under the bedclothes and to this end I kept my underwear under the pillow for warmth. Beside the bed, at a strategic point (in common with nearly all other GL) my boots stood, loosely laced, and near them, on the soldiers' box, my slacks ready to slip into. Thus, when the alarm bell rang I shot out of bed, and in a reflex action, with incredible speed, pulled on slacks, slid into boots (in one movement tightening laces and tying them) and put on battledress and leather jerkin as I went out into the bitter cold to join the pairs of running feet already beginning to go past our hut. Behind this automatic response to the alarm bell I knew that every other member of the team had responded in the same way. The icy night air seared the windpipe, but we ran on and jumped on to the catwalk, aware of the jerky searchlight beams already stabbing the sky. There was always the slight feeling of exhilaration as one bounded along the elongated springboard that was the catwalk.

One posting I had with the rest of a new team I cannot place in time at all – and yet it was real. We were sent out as a replacement GL Mark III team. The site was an isolated one, and when we got there it was all male. Did someone blunder? Certainly our arrival caused some consternation, and we waited in the NAAFI till a hut was prepared and we were given sheets, blankets, etc. The hut was quite a small one, just beig enough for us. We were allowed a ration of coke straight away and a girl whom I shall call Bet put herself in charge of the care and maintenance of the stove. After she'd finished lighting it and seeing that it was properly away, she rubbed her hands down her skirt, put on her cap and said, 'That's me ready to find out what I can find out,' although we'd been asked to stay in our rooms till further notice.

'Well, girls,' she beamed when she came back, 'pin back your ears. I've got the inside story from the boiler-man. One of the ablutions is being given over to us at special times. We have a special table at the cookhouse and we can visit the NAAFI if we all go together. No manning or fatigues or inspections and the fire on all the time.'

'Long may it last,' I said. We were undergoing a very cold spell at the time, which would have meant that back at camp I would have taken my turn at keeping the sets in working order.

Bet had organized the morning brew and had made arrangements for three of us to bring breakfast back for the other three. The ablutions differed vastly from the ones we knew. The wash basins were in the centre of the room, two sets of stone bowls facing each other with a flat piece of wood between them on which to place soap and other toiletries. The plugs used were captive plugs at the end of a rod which could be raised or lowered as required.

The waste pipes were open-ended right-angled pipes that fed into an open floor channel, along which the water flowed into a sink. There was only one tap per basin – a cold-water tap. The flush toilets we used were set in little cubicles, without doors and with sides that did not touch the ground and reached to a height of about three feet. The other thing I learned at this camp was that the men in the army did not sleep in sheets but grey blankets and that, unlike us, they were not issued with pyjamas unless they had to spend time in hospital.

Our hut was snug all the time, for Bet so organized the stove that it never actually went out, and she declinkered as she went along.

We wrote, read, played cards, lay on our beds and chatted and for exercise walked to the cookhouse or the NAAFI at prescribed hours. Occasionally, just so that we could savour the more this little bit of good fortune that had fallen into our laps, we watched the men going about their lawful toil.

'They're a friendly lot,' one girl remarked, 'but I get the feeling we're untouchables.'

'Me too,' I said. 'As if we're up in those rooms above the perfumed gardens where the sultan or whatever he was called walked with his favourites and the women were allowed to look down on them but no man, except the sultan, was allowed to look up to them.'

'Yes,' she said. 'I get your meaning. The only thing is I can't really see anyone I'd cast in the role of sultan.'

'No word of complaint shall pass my lips on that score,' I said. 'I do not wish to be transported to Siberia, the inevitable next stop. I take no sadistic pleasure in enduring cold and privation. Let us then lie low and hope there will be no uprising civil or otherwise. Peaceful days and pleasant nights is my aim.'

At the end of a week they sent us back again. For what reason had we gone in the first place? Who shall say? It wasn't only God who moved in mysterious ways.

Back in camp action became commonplace once Christmas had passed. London and its environs was subjected to another wave of bombing. Once on the set, I'd hardly have fixed my headpiece in place when the voice of the number three came over from the TX saying they were ready for action. Before this could have happened the number six would have started up the power unit without which neither TX or RX could operate. There was always one REME (Royal Electrical and Mechanical Engineers) on duty. The three we had whom I remember most clearly were John Izard, Bill Cooper and Cyril whose last name escapes me. Usually they went to the power unit first to see that, in fact, it had started, then checked at the TX before coming in to the RX.

Seconds after the number three had reported I would be able to report that the entire team was ready for action, and not long after this the REME bod would fling himself in through the door to be on hand should anything go wrong.

During these raids in the early part of 1944, wave after wave of targets came over and one was entirely impersonal about them. They were dots on the screen to be deflected, to be fired at so that our fighters knew where the planes were, or to be fired at and brought down. In a big raid the concentration required was such that we were totally unaware of what was going on. When the raid was not a heavy one in our area, and when one lone plane appeared on the screen, in spite of my trained automatic response, I was always apprehensive. What if it was one of ours limping home off course with his IFF shot away or out of action?

And then there would be the sudden sickening realization, kept at bay during heavy raids, that those dots were really planes full of young lives.

Take post – TX and PU

After a raid, when the tube began to clear till all that remained were static signals, the order 'Stand easy' was usually given. That meant we had to stay in the sets but could stop searching, probing the sky for possible targets. This was the trying time, when fatigue set in and one had to try various ploys to keep awake and alert. Finally came the last order, 'Stand down'. The raid was officially over.

It was then that we would step out into what was possibly the

163

beginnings of another dawn. Around us, at a distance, we would see fires burning and the question we tried to answer was who had 'got it'. The smell of cordite was like a physical assault; the searchlights darkened, snapped off.

Most personnel walked to the cookhouse where the cook on duty had made hot cocoa. This cocoa was like nothing else. It comforted, substained, fed. She poured it from the stove where it had been keeping warm, her greatcoat only partially covering her night attire, the scarf on her head reticent about covering her curlers.

'It's been a terrible night,' she would say, and for her it must have been: indeed, not only her but all those who were not involved and who could do no more than wait till it was over. Those of us who had the energy nodded in agreement. Speech required too much effort. We sipped our cocoa waiting for the CO's pronouncement about reveille. Had we been on duty long enough to qualify for an extra half-hour in bed?

In fact, one really didn't notice the extra half-hour. It was just as difficult to wake at 07.00 hours as it was to wake at 06.30 hours.

We grumbled among ourselves as a matter of course after a raid, the 'I never want to see another dawn as long as I live after this lot's over' being the most frequent. In fact I think this was merely to cover up the feeling of satisfaction one had at being involved and actually doing something tangible, making use of the training we had been given. We survived broken nights and diminished sleep as we also survived the noise and shrugged off any thought of danger, but underneath it all we became more starkly aware how precious were some of the things we had previously taken for granted. On occasions we were called out twice, and even three times, in one night. I used to feel that never again would I take anything for granted.

Also, early in 1944 we were told that, till further notice, all leave would stop and that although 24-hour passes would continue, they were, as ever, subject to the exigencies of the service. In addition, all letters would be censored, and ordinary letters put in the camp post-box would be censored by the officers on site. Those who did not wish to have their letters censored on site could ask for 'green' envelopes, of which we were allowed a limited number. These letters were not censored 'regimentally', but they were liable to be censored at base. They also had a printed certificate which had to be signed: 'I certify on my honour that the contents of this envelope refer to nothing but private and family affairs.'

It would seem, then, that we had a full complement of personnel for manning and other duties (the manning, of course, taking precedence) but this was not so. A full complement of number ones was four, but often, for various reasons (a course, temporary transfer elsewhere, etc.), our numbers were depleted and this meant those of us on site manned much more frequently than once every four days. Also, although we had an 'official' team, in practice we could work with any group of operators.

These raids and their subsequent call-outs lasted throughout the first three months of the year, tailed off a bit in April and petered out in May. As we 'saw' over a fairly wide area, we were sometimes called out when the raiders were simply passing over our area either going towards a target further afield or coming back therefrom.

I am going to stick my neck out and give a date. On Monday or Tuesday, 20 or 21 March 1944, we of 625 Battery 'B' Troop shot down a plane. I had seen it as it came in on the edge of the PPI pursuing a direct course which would bring it well within the orbit of our guns, and I watched it die on both the PPI and the small screen. It appeared as if we were responsible, but it could have been the fighters. We were credited with the direct hit, however, and congratulated from both Captain Wright, our CO, and the Major, our OC.

After endless talk about the second front, the mounting restrictions placed on us led us to believe the actuality could not be far away and indeed, early on the morning of D-Day we were assembled on the parade ground and given the momentous news. Once again, news bulletins became paramount and we were avid for all information from the BLA (British Liberation Army).

Some days later I went up to London for some reason or other, I forget what. It must have been official, however, because I stayed in Warwickshire House, an ATS transit camp. I was awakened early and told that a signal had come in asking me to report back for duty as soon as possible.

When I arrived at the station nearest our camp a tilly was waiting there and in it a REME officer (REME were less aware of the differences between ranks among their fraternity than were most other branches of the army). 'Jump in,' he said, 'and we'll give you a lift back.'

After we'd started he said, 'What was it like in London last night?'

'Quiet,' I replied.

'Hear anything at all? About anything unusual that dropped, I mean? Well, a strange specimen dropped' (I am sure he said in the south-east) 'last night. We think it's the secret weapon there's been talk of. Anyway we're on full alert and all available personnel are being called in. That's what you're doing here at this minute. There's an emergency meeting of all personnel in the cookhouse this morning.

'And so,' Captain Wright said, 'we must prepare to meet the emergency. We do not know what to expect but we must be ready for an onslaught when it does happen. From now till further notice there will be no need to barrack your beds. There will be no further hut inspections, but we shall expect you to keep your huts as tidy as possible. Other than that, the work of the camp will go on. Meals today are being prepared as normal, but it may be that we won't be able to follow the normal pattern. It may well mean that we are on continuous duty, in which case there will be a supply of hot cocoa and sandwiches always available in the cookhouse for those on duty to eat when they can. Any questions? Right. Go to your huts, make up your beds then go to your normal duties. Dismiss them, Sergeant.'

We walked silently and thoughtfully out of the cookhouse. Nothing further happened that day, but in the early hours of the following day the awaited secret weapon arrived in numbers – in great numbers. This was the V1, revenge weapon number one – the doodlebug, and we were in what came to be known as doodlebug alley. It looked like a small aeroplane and it made a noise like an old and noisy motorbike. Flames belched from its rear. When the flames went out, the noise stopped and it dropped – a flying bomb.

At first we followed the drill as for piloted planes. 'Take post' sounded, we ran like the wind, reported 'on target' and the guns fired – when it was possible. Unfortunately, the V1s flew in below the radar screen. When we actually picked them up they were almost overhead. As far as the guns were concerned they could not depress low enough to fire at them from a distance. When we had tracked the target till it dropped and exploded or had been hit we were given the 'Stand down'.

I took over as number one at 14.00 hours that day. At first we just stayed on the set, but later, we made (or tried to make) dashes to the cookhouse for corned-beef sandwiches and cocoa.

This went on for about three days, I think, when the order came that there was to be no more firing. Once the doodlebug crossed the coast it was going to come down anyway. Firing at it only meant there was an added danger, that of shrapnel from the shells of the gun as well as the effects of the bomb exploding.

We did not realize as we mustered to hear the order read out that this marked the end of the useful life of this particular gunsite. Two days later we learned that our 'other half', A Troop, had packed up their equipment like the Arabs and silently stolen away to Foulness Island, there to live in tents. Everything had been moved, kit, cookhouse equipment, PU, TX, RX, netting, predictors, guns, furnishings of the command post. Incredible.

There A Troop continued to have a very active existence for the rest of the natural life of the gunsite. Sometime previously Ellen, and later Joy, Madeleine and Betty, had been transferred back to A Troop. I missed them at the time. Now, even more, I wished that I, too, could have been where the action was.

Shooting the doodlebug down over land might not have been such a good idea, but shooting them down over the sea was a different matter. A great many were disposed of this way, but there were still those that 'got through' and exploded on land.

In September there was a new menace – the V2. They could not be tracked down because they travelled so fast. Indeed, as they were faster than sound, the noise of their coming followed the explosion. Often, it seemed that both the V1 and the V2 had been aimed at no specific target, just at London and its environs generally. Many targets had no military significance. A shower of bricks and other articles would suddenly spout up into the air to descend as rubble. Only seconds earlier this had been a home. It had sheltered people and their household goods – the collection of a lifetime. The only answer to the V2s was to nullify them at source.

Being so near London and visiting it fairly frequently, it was not surprising that one had an occasional less-than-pleasant experience.

Once when this new wave of bombing in the early part of 1944 was at its height I went up to London on an errand, then found my way to an unfamiliar area of the city to pay a promised visit. I was actually on a 24 pass and I decided at the last minute not to stay overnight but to make my way back to camp. As I walked towards a station the air-raid siren went and I redoubled my efforts to reach the station.

I had just passed the end of a wall when there was a whistle. 'Down!' a voice shouted, and I dropped to the ground. When the after-effects of the bomb had subsided I got to my feet, shaken.

'Get under cover!' shouted the voice that had ordered me down. It was a warden.

'But—'

'Run. There,' he said pointing me in the direction of a dark blob. I did as he ordered and fell up against the door which opened easily. I got in, and more to keep up my courage than anything else, I took up my shaded torch and made myself look around to take my mind off the tumult outside. Air raids are very, very noisy affairs full of thunder and whistles and bright flashes stronger and more awful than lightning.

The hut was fairly small with a tiny window. It seemed to be a store house of some sort with boxes and drums stacked about and shapes on, or hanging from the rafters. The hut itself was eerie. There was no one else there. I moved to the farthest end and stood against the wall under the beams. Snapping out my torch, I prayed inwardly that the raid would soon be over.

There was a loud whistle, the earth shook, toppled and crumbled. Bricks, it seemed, were raining down. I stood still, panting slightly. The place had caved in and, miraculously, I stood in a little protected pocket. I felt my body all over and my face. I was all right. There was another sound of falling masonry and of something heavy settling. When I thought it safe, still panting with my mouth open, I allowed the fingers of one hand to probe the area around. A brick wall at the back. Nothing in the immediate area at one side. Cautiously I stretched my arm out. A beam lying at an angle. 'Use your torch, you idiot,' I said to myself aloud. This effort to give myself an order also gave me greater courage. I looked around as far as I could without moving. Above me, a beam also at an angle. I hardly dared move or breathe. I was hemmed in. But I was all right. Habits of economy made me switch off the torch because of the battery. I started to count.

One two, three, four, five and so on silently, hardly moving my lips. When I got to a hundred I said: 'My tea is nearly ready and the sun has left the sky and it's time to take the window to see Leary going by.' As I neared the end, my mind was trying to think of another poem so that I wouldn't have to stop . . . 'I too will something make and joy in the making though tomorrow it seem like the empty wards of a dream tell it not in Gath publish it not in the streets of Aschelon lest the daughters of the Philistines rejoice lest of Jonathan very pleasant hast thou been unto me thy love to me was wonderful passing the love of woman my heart aches and a drowsy numbness pains my sense as though of hemlock I had drunk ye daughters of Jerusalem the Lord is my shepherd I shall not want he maketh me to lie down in the still water he annointeth my soul yea though I walk in the valley of the shadow no Mary had a little lamb she also had a watch and swallowed it one day now she's taking Beecham's pills to pass the time away where was I Oh yes swiftly walk over the western wave spirit of night come in to the garden Maud I wandered lonely as a cloud – that's a noise.' There were voices. *Keep calm keep still keep calm keep still help is coming. It is.* Breathe deeply. Movement and more movement nearer and nearer. Cold air coming from a hole a light in my eyes so that I have to blink and put my hand up.

'She's alive. My God, she's alive.'

They pulled me out and I stood on my own feet. I breathed in and closed my eyes. I felt gritty and dirty and giddy and I wanted to pass out.

'Are you all right, love?'

It was the warden, he put his hands on my shoulders and held me to him briefly.

'I thought . . .' he said.

I patted his shoulder. Speech was a luxury.

An angel disguised as a WVS lady gave me some hot sweet tea. It helped. They kept saying what a miraculous escape I'd had. I could hardly take it in. I had not thought I was in danger. Shaken and frightened, but not in danger. The raid was over and I wanted to get away, to get back to camp. A man, a priest, came forward and asked if I'd far to go. I told him my intention and he said, 'You'd much better rest for a while and make your journey later. You may stay at my house if you wish. You can have a bath. It'll help.'

It was a largish house, the house of a Catholic Father. Their hospitality towards me was all part of the unreality of the night. They gave me a room. I had a bath. I went to bed. I slept. I awoke, got up, washed and dressed and went down to breakfast. The Father had a meal with me, he at one end of a rectangular table, I at the other. The housekeeper brought in the food. He asked a few questions and I answered them, briefly, still feeling subdued. I did my best to thank him.

It was the housekeeper who set me off on my journey back to camp. I didn't mention the episode, neither to talk of it nor write of it. To have been in it was enough.

It was true that the best place to be in a raid was on radar. You never knew the bomb that hit you. You did, however, know the thing that put you out of action. Not long after the episode in London we were put out of action. It was a busy night. We were tracking one target and the PPI was alive with others from which to choose after this one passed out of the orbit of the guns, when suddenly the set shuddered slightly and went dead. A large, heavy inert mass in the sudden blackness.

The next instant the REME on duty (I'll call him Jim) switched on his powerful inspection lamp and we went through a quick series of drills to try to get the set back working. Nothing doing. Jim took off a front panel and peered into the neat bright entrails. There was a hammering on the door. The light was switched off and I opened the door. Another REME shouted from the outside.

'We're starting up the Mark II. Send the box over, then give it another few minutes. If you still can't locate the trouble come over to Mark II,' and he slammed the door and was gone. As he talked Jim had already begun unscrewing the box that was located above the place where the number one stood. It connected her with the command post.

'Here,' he said, 'take it over. Quick.'

He switched off the light. I opened the door and jumped down. He handed me the box and closed the door. I hesitated just a moment. All hell was let loose. The noise was deafening. The searchlight stilts criss-crossed the sky. The lights from the tracer shells. The planes overhead and the bursts of flame. The fires. The flares. It wasn't the thought of a bomb that frightened me. What terrified me was the thought that I wore no hat and any second now a small piece of shrapnel might come down and pierce my skull ending the life I knew. I ran as quickly and carefully as I could, panting not from exertion but from the effect of the raid. As I was about to get up on to the Mark II catwalk John Izard came running along and took the box from me. I turned and stumbled back to the Mark III. They hauled me in.

The Raid

171

'It's no good,' Jim said after a short time. 'I can't raise a spark. It'll have to wait till the raid's over,' and he left for the Mark II.

Inside the set it was very, very dark except that occasionally a flash could be seen through what were obviously small gaps in the floor boards.

We sat silent for a time, then: 'I'm trying to think of the words of a song,' the number two said. 'But it escapes me.'

'What was it about?' her friend asked.

'I don't know. I can't think,' number two replied.

'Try poetry,' I said. 'Something we all know. Each take a turn and come in straight away. Nursery rhymes. All nursery rhymes. Jack and Jill went up the hi . . . hill . . .'

After a time it grew quieter and we stopped talking. Presently we opened the door cautiously. The air was thick with the quiet smell of cordite.

'We'll wait till we hear footsteps,' I said, 'then go to the cookhouse and report.' Without any further talk we did just that.

The last small incident of this nature happened as the second 'day of the doodlebug' dawned. Lacking any other order we followed the drill for piloted planes. Alarm. Search. On target. Stand down. They followed relentlessly one after the other. We'd been relieved at tea-time for a meal and we'd had a snack half-way through the evening. It was now 01.00 hours or thereabouts and the camp was silent if not sleeping. Time after time, after stand down, we'd attempted to run to the cookhouse with our mugs to grab some sandwiches and get some cocoa and time and time again before we got to the cookhouse the alarm went and we had to double back to the set.

On this occasion I was the front runner and very near the cookhouse when the alarm went. I decided to get a handful of sandwiches at least before I turned back. Accordingly I ran on, grabbed the sandwiches, dipped my mug into the cocoa pail and returned towards the set. I ran evenly to keep my mug steady and not spill any liquid. As I reached the road leading to the set the camp became lighter and noisier as the now-familiar belching flames and death rattle of the doodlebug began its passage over the camp just above set height. I ran harder keeping my eye on it. They were ugly, wicked-looking things, those V1s. It had passed over the

Doodlebug

far perimeter of the RX wire when the flames went out and the engine cut off. I had leapt on to the catwalk and was making for the RX with all speed. I heard a voice cry, 'Oh, Mother' as I suddenly felt something hit me and I sailed up into the air to utter darkness. *This is it*, I thought.

The first thing I became aware of was the noise, the darkness and the fact that I was chained by the nose.

I haven't made it, I thought. *It must be those library books*. Then I became aware that I wasn't so much chained as embedded. My nose was stuck in the wire. And the noise belonged to one voice. A familiar voice. It was shouting, 'Where the hell's the number one.' Hell wasn't the operative word after all. I was still alive. I picked myself up *sans* mug, *sans* cocoa, *sans* sandwiches and made my way to the set.

What had happened was that the number five was behind me in my dash to the cookhouse. When I didn't turn back when the alarm sounded, neither did she. However, before she got into the cookhouse she heard the approaching doodlebug and made back to the set. When she got to the catwalk and it was directly overhead she got down on her knees presumably to pray that it continued its journey a little while longer. When the engine cut out I, not knowing she was there, cannoned into her at the moment the engine shut off. The springy catwalk gave me a good send off. When I hit her she thought it was the bomb and her end had come, so she called to her mother. The bomb came down harmlessly in some marshy ground beyond the camp.

And with that slightly farcical incident my active service came to an end. From thenceforth we could only do as defenceless civilians did, listen for the engine and drop down if it cut out in our vicinity.

As far as my personal involvement was concerned, we had shot down one enemy plane. But that wasn't really the point. It wasn't what we'd actually done that was important. What was important was the consideration of what could have been accomplished by the enemy had there been no gunsites.

12. Letters

A highlight of the day on camp was the advent of the post corporal sergeant. His was a Jekyll-and-Hyde existence as far as the rank and file were concerned – Jekyll if he had a letter to give out, Hyde if he hadn't. At morning break it was definitely a case of 'haves and have-nots' – the 'haves' were those with letters, the 'have-nots' those without.

Not only had we a wide selection of friends on site, we had an even wider one whom we'd never seen.

'The kid next door, you know, the one I told you about, Lynette Louise, what a name, she started school last week. I suppose the next letter I get she'll be teaching.'

'This is from me friend, Penny. Guess what. She's sending me some shoes she's finished with. They'll be smashing. Joyce shoes. She only wears the best. She has some lovely clothes. She's a prostitute, you know, but she's a really nice girl.'

'What,' I asked one day as we sat in the RX waiting for the 'Stand down', would life on site be without letters?'

'Wait for it. Keep calm,' said Ellen. 'A "Summers" observation is about to be given birth to. The announcement will come any second.'

'Giving that ignorant and jealous remark the lack of recognition it merits, I will continue. Much thought, I might add, has gone into the profound statement I am about to utter. To get letters you must first of all write them. So that . . .'

'Just a minute. Just a minute,' put in Joy. 'Give the grey matter a chance.'

Eventually I was allowed to get my point across and the letter club got under way, the idea being that it was reasonable to suppose that if we liked getting letters, so would other members of the forces. And the further likelihood was that they'd like to get letters from members of the opposite sex.

To join the group you had to supply the names and addresses of one, or more, young men willing to take upon themselves extra correspondence. For every name you supplied you were allowed one in return. When all the names were in we each wrote a brief description of ourselves, and each copied the list out. These lists were sent to the young men who then had to make their choices, first, second and third. I cannot remember whose names I personally put in the kitty but there were three and, as a result, I wrote out three lists and sent them off. I was then entitled to three new correspondents. As I already had a fairly wide correspondence I was about to settle for only two new additions, both serving abroad, when this letter arrived for the club.

I have only one choice. Number six. Linda. May I have further details please.

> Signed – Robert. A dour Scot.

I replied:

Dear signed dour Scot Robert,

I shall do my best to supply the details for which you ask as if I were a sensible person.

My teeth, hair and sight are reasonably preserved considering my advanced years. I'm over 18 years of age. My figure also is reasonably preserved considering the army ginger pud, which is our staple diet.

With regard to legible writing and spelling, I live in a glass house. Thus you have a fair amount of licence in this respect. I am a fairly proficient reader and have mastered all the *Radiant Way Readers* from books one to two.

In music, I am very happy if I can stumble through *The Bluebells of Scotland* (with variations) well enough for Mr Ezra Reid to recognize the tune as coming from his *Easy Pieces for the Pianoforte*.

For the rest, the harsh reality is that I am a Geordie at present requested by the military authorities to reside in khaki oblivion in the south. For me, Merrie England is a mud-bespattered gunsite about which my lips (and my pen) are sealed.

In conclusion, I must beg of you, do not address me as 'hen'; not even as 'ma bonnie wee hen' which, I believe, is the highest compliment one can be paid north of the border.

So far, paper Xs have not been rationed. However, I have a cautious, thrifty nature. I shall append one. If it burns your lips, so be it.

Yours,
Linda. X

And thus began a correspondence which was to last through the war and into the first year of peace. In fact, from D-Day till some time after the end of the war, I wrote him every day. I also collected books which I sent regularly for him and his friends as they fought their way across Europe.

At this time, I had upwards of forty people to whom I wrote regularly. Not everyone, however, was overjoyed to have me as a correspondent. As one person said when I was home on leave. 'You're always on my conscience. I keep thinking, *I must write to Linda*, and finally I get the letter finished and off and I think that's that, and two days later there's a reply from you and I'm back where I started.'

Often when we wrote letters we were making bricks without straw. Virtually the only thing we could say was that it had rained or it looked like rain or it had just stopped raining or we hadn't had any rain, so I devised another plan. I put up extracts from the prototype letter which I would use for all later models until I'd gone through that particular round of correspondence. I suggested it was only fair that others did likewise – that we each put up our little gems. A sample selection of mine was as follows:

A. There are three kinds of tea in Britain: India, China and army. At the insistance of the War Office the only tea I have any knowledge of at the present time is the army variety. Like our celebrated brands of whisky it improves with age, growing in strength and drawing from the vessel in which it has been made. Army tea, unlike the China and India varieties which are made in a vessel called a teapot possessed of a lid, a handle and a thing for pouring called a spout, is made in a pail and, generally speaking, it draws an added flavour from whatever might have been in the pail beforehand. In the cookhouse proper, there are special pails kept purely for the use of tea and similar liquids, but the same cannot be said for the pail in which the boilerman brings round the early morning brew for his favoured colleagues (of both sexes). Nothing braces the constitution like a mugful of this tepid, dark brown liquid with the faint aroma of engine oil and other fragrances difficult to put a name to. In extreme circumstances tea has been brewed in an old tin that has done previous long and sterling service as a container for screws, nails, bits of wire, insulation tape and string, the hairy offshoots of the latter being difficult to get rid of completely. The containers from which the tea is actually drunk also vary with circumstances. Jars, little tins and sundry containers, once the property of the sick bay, are emptied of their contents to accommodate the brew that does not inebriate but might well give the stomach a turn. When this war is over it may well be that we shall eschew the comfort of the dining room and its fine bone china and brew a tinful in some cheerless spot, pour it into an old discarded pot and drink it in a welter of sentimental nostalgia.

B. I was this day on guard duty and did repair joyfully to the guardhouse which is a stone edifice of great interest visited as it is frequently by the highest and the lowest in the camp and beyond. The house itself has a somnolent atmosphere engendered by the perfumes of, if not Arabia, then certainly its Ack-ack equivalent. Thus the leisurely hours are spent in sleeping, interspersed with an hour's refreshing meditation in a spot where even the mildest breeze grows angry and aggressive; a worthy challenge to mind and body. Old Omar had the right idea. A book of verse (unread), a mug of cocoa, a NAAFI bun and 'Thou beside me sweating it out in the guardhouse makes fatigues seem Paradise ennow.' (Whatever ennow means).

C. The spirit is willing but the flesh is helpless. It neither gives nor receives ought of interest. So – to the weather. What would we do without it? Ice is everywhere. It crackles beneath the feet. Breath steams the windows opaque with crystal covering. The landscape is beautiful and changed, its harsh contours obliterated. All roads have disappeared, levelled so that they have no significance. The ablutions are chilled enough to delight even a Wackford Squeers. The warmest day is icy. The pain in fingers' ends brings unwanted tears to the eyes. The hourly turning of the equipment to keep it mobile keeps tepid its mechanical innards while it leaves the operator frozen. Heat from the cookhouse stove dissipates as soon as it leaves the cylindrical belly. Water stands frozen in buckets and the ink has frozen in my pen. . . .

To avoid duplication each paragraph had a code number and, on the back, the name of the person to whom the effusion was written and the date. We were all supposed to contribute. Madeleine's rare contributions were always good, being both witty and informative. Ellen's were more frequent and they were also good. Joy refused to contribute. Letters, she said (rightly), were highly personal things. They took on the personality of the writer. To copy what another had written and pass it off as your own smacked of dishonesty.

'I don't see that,' I said. 'You don't have to use the same words. It's only a guideline. It's only to give you ideas. I see no difference between me putting up these things and answering questions to people who sit chewing their pens and asking, "What can I possibly write about?" '

'Sometimes,' Joy said, 'you exasperate me. There's a flaw in your argument but it escapes me at the moment.'

'Mine is a debased mind,' said Madeleine. 'I copy them word for word and am happy so to do. After all, what they want is communication. And what is there to write about most of the time?'

'Me too,' said Ellen, 'though I'm thinking of curtailing my letter writing. But these – whatever you call them – make a change from a list of menus, which is the only other thing I write about, food being of such importance to the growing ATS.'

'I thought we were all slimming,' I put in.

'Don't quibble,' she rebuked. 'I'm on your side.'

As I've already said, our letters were censored. One day the subaltern came to me and said, 'I can't talk to Private Gunn myself because what I know I know as I censored the letter she wrote, but she's broken-hearted. Her fiancé has been killed and she's carrying that grief around with her. Do you think you could have a quiet word with her and offer her sympathy?'

179

'I could try, ma'am, if you think it would help. But I'm not a particular friend of Private Gunn. Perhaps it would be much better if one of her special friends spoke to her?' I said.

'Possibly. But there's the question of confidentiality. I'm sure you could somehow talk to her without ever letting her know I had spoken to you.'

'I'll do my best, ma'am, but I don't know that I'll succeed,' I replied.

The next morning when we came down from the sets I saw her walking by herself ahead. I caught up with her.

'Now for the much needed NAAFI rock buns,' I said, 'not to mention coffee. And, perchance, the mail. I haven't had a letter from Geoffrey in aeons. It worries me. How is your boy friend?'

'All right,' she shrugged. We continued our journey in silence.

'I'm afraid, ma'am,' I said later to the sub, 'I got nowhere with Private Gunn. I don't really think she wants to talk about it and I think I understand. There are things I find easier to get over when I don't talk about them and maybe she feels the same way and, with respect, I think she should be left alone. Perhaps work is her solace. You see, people mean well but often they make things worse. They tell you about other people that have had to suffer far more than you. It's true very often, but it doesn't help. In fact it sometimes makes things worse as I said. Sometimes what's happened to you fills your thoughts and you have to listen to somebody else going on and on telling of their or someone else's sufferings which were much worse than yours – and they bore up. With respect, ma'am, I think that when she's ready to talk she will and she'll choose for herself.'

'Perhaps you're right,' the sub said.

Later she spoke to Dorothy, this time on my behalf. I'd written a poem, a copy of which I'd enclosed in a letter. It read:

If (with apologies to Rudyard Kipling)
If you can sweep your floor when those about you
Have strewn it with their kitbags, plates and shoes.
If you can hear the orderly sergeant shout you
While the wireless blazes forth *Limehouse Blues*.
If you can dust the locker tops with an old stocking

That has served its purpose nearly thirty years,
And stand by while the officer murmurs, 'Shocking',
And firmly hold in check impending tears.

If you can search for cobwebs with a broomstick
Or look aloft for dust, the merest speck,
Balanced on a bed and chair erratic
And fall, and still not break your ruddy neck.
If you can polish all there is to polish
An empty Mansion tin your ration for the floor,
With the state of th' lino absolutely hellish
And know that, in the stores, there is no more.

If you can rush around and not be late
When the sergeant looks at you in great disdain
And says, 'Your blanket labels are not straight,
Stoop down and barrack the blue pencil lot again.'
If you can shine your buttons till they glitter
And scrub your plimsolls hard, inside and out
And hear them say, 'It's your turn to empty litter',
And do it – not once hinting at your doubt.

If you can scrub your chin strap till it's whitened
And never, never in the process whine.
If you can have every toecap brightened
And every bed correctly lined by nine.
If you can hear the first note of reveille
After being up half the ruddy night
And rise without further shilly shally,
You're a better man than I am – Captain Wright.

'I'm speaking to you as a tactful, understanding person,' Dorothy
said to me. 'The sub censored your letter. I wouldn't be surprised if
she handed it round the officer's mess. Anyway, Captain Wright
happened to see it and he'd like a copy. I don't think they're going to
put you in the glass house or similar. I think he was quite chuffed.'

I had to take my turn as orderly NCO from time to time and this
meant seeing that they got out of bed as soon as reveille sounded, a
Herculean task for me.

'I wonder what would happen,' I said to Ellen as I prepared to tell the orderly officer that the lights were out in the ATS ablutions and all was correct, 'if I reported . . . orgy in the ablutions. Floors awash with water. Six ATS and three gunners out for the count. Otherwise, all correct. . . .'

'It's an interesting proposition,' she said. 'Try it. But I think they're only listening for the end bit and that's all they'll hear.'

Apart from writing letters, make-do-and-mend nights, and performing any necessary duties, another camp recreation was toy making and leather craft. For David, my nephew, I made a series of unlikely looking animals from the felt available. Having some dark brown felt I made him what I regarded as a gollywog. He would not look at it. I think it frightened him, and my mother, quite rightly, put it away and it was lost to posterity. The dolls I made for my niece Fiona had cloth-stuffed bodies with a moulded and painted face sewn on.

I had greater success with my leather work, and the stout ration book cover I made is still serviceable, as are the purses. These are now housed in a shoe box for the benefit of posterity. Posterity, so far, has shown not the slightest interest.

13. Love and Love

We were allowed to stay in our two rooms with all mod cons for several months, and how marvellous it was.

One night shortly after midnight I was awakened by a drunken hand, part of a drunken body controlled by a drunken mind who, in a drunken voice ordered me to take part in an alcoholic whimsey and sing *Auld Lang Syne* with her outside the officers' mess. When I refused, she threw all my clothes on top of the lavatory cistern. Those that fell off she attempted to flush away, saying in drunken tones verging on alcoholic tears, 'You're a bugger, Linda. A real bugger. Not sing *Auld Lang Syne* to Captain Wright. He's a bugger too. Two buggers together. Oops, up she goes again.'

The girl concerned had been celebrating a birthday, whose I do not know.

Grateful for the fact that we were well away from the ear of authority, we finally persuaded her to go to bed and prepared to see what could be done for her in the morning to combat what would undoubtedly be a hangover of fair proportions.

Although the restroom adjoining our sleeping quarters was open to all ATS and the library was open to all personnel, few disturbed us in our haven. One or two intrepid souls did come to view the library, but most often I was simply asked to bring a book to the NAAFI. The choice was not wide and frankly what there was met few tastes.

In the evenings, a favourite pastime for those of us who remained in camp was to sit in unprecedented comfort on chairs set around the stove in this restroom when we talked. Tea, the drinking of which does so much for sociability and friendship, was replaced by cookhouse cocoa or NAAFI coffee. Our field of discussion was relatively wide: life, death, reincarnation, after the war, children, poetry, music and God, among other subjects. God and anything with a religious background were dealt with very gingerly. Joy did not take part. Her views on religion were her own. I, personally, did not have the courage to say I questioned the existence of God. I had not yet had the strength of mind to throw out the childhood images and work out my own doctrine, except to say that it was a pity that the Christian view of life was that we were all sinners regardless. The main subjects, the ones which came into almost every discussion, were boyfriends and love and what was meant by love.

Those with individual problems they felt they could talk about, did so. These problems most often were concerned with whether he loved her or not. We heard of how he had looked, what he had said, the tone of voice in which he said it, whether he'd appeared to look at any other girl with interest, whether he ever spoke of any other girl, how often he wrote, and the length of the letter. And there the line was drawn. Anything further that happened between them was not to be spoken of. It was intimate.

Other discussions on the subject were objective. 'To be in love,' said Ellen, 'to be very much in love does take up an awful lot of time. When you think of one person and of one person only you must, of necessity, miss a good deal of what else is going on. And when the only thing you have to talk about is what he says on any given subject, frankly you're hardly worth listening to.'

'Yes, but when you love someone like that,' I said, 'the rest doesn't matter. You carry your sunshine with you in a way. The thought of him, the being with him casts a warm glow over everything you do.'

'Yes,' replied Ellen, 'you do. That's just the point. The rest of the world doesn't seem to exist. And they don't only bring sunshine. What about the shadows?'

'I think you really only fall in love like that, wholeheartedly I mean, once. I think it's only that first time that you give everything without regard for the consequences. After that you wonder and doubt and only give part of yourself and compromise,' I replied.

'You sound a bit jaded,' said Madeleine. 'You surprise me. When we were talking about the differences between living and existing, you were all for living at any cost. "Throw yourself into life whether you want to or not" was what you said. With the boyfriends you're running at the moment I would expect you to speak of the sacred name of love with a little more enthusiasm.'

'Perhaps it's because I'm not in love that I'm disillusioned. Perhaps that's why I'm able to run boyfriends in the plural. Anyway, it depends upon what you mean by boyfriend.' This last remark injected a fair amount of animated discussion into our hitherto rather detached talk.

As I have already said, the discussions, however animated, did not go beyond a certain point. Our intimate life, if it existed, was our affair. We did not speak of it, nor did we expect anyone else to speak of theirs. This was about to change, however. Marie McCully, she of the mauve aerials, got married and moved out of our orbit. She was replaced by a very attractive girl with a lively bubble cut, large light brown eyes to go with it and a golden skin. I shall call her Jan. Jan had celebrated her eighteenth birthday a few months earlier. In her eighteen and a bit years she herself had amassed more wordly wisdom and experience than we had collectively. She had been with us scarcely two days when sex, even if we hadn't so far used the word, was part of our vocabulary.

Her mother and father were living apart and before they had split up Jan had been made fully aware of their frequent and loudly expressed differences of opinion. After the separation they apparently spent their time getting back at each other. Not having a wife to supply him with the solace of a shared bed, the deserted husband had turned to his daughter to make good the omission and Jan had to develop a fair amount of cunning to make sure that she didn't comply. Her mother had not been a great deal of help other than saying she had to learn the harsh facts of life sometime and if ever she was in any trouble (i.e. if she became pregnant) she was to go to her and she would see that she was all right.

'And I can tell you now,' Jan said to our astonished ears, 'she would do the same for any of you. Any of my friends. She's a real nice woman, my Mum. She would go out of her way to help anyone. So don't forget. If any of you get into trouble just say the word and I'll take you to see my Mum.'

On her very first 24 she came back with a box of candies.

'Been with a Yank?' we asked as she generously handed them round.

'Yes,' she said. 'I went up to London and met him there. We had smashing time and then he took me to this place. It's not actually in London. A bit nearer here as a matter of fact. The woman that has the house doesn't ask questions. Of course, you've got to pay in advance. But Homer – that's his name, Homer – he knew all about it. Of course, she doesn't give you anything to eat but Homer had brought a snack with him so it wasn't too bad. I hardly got a wink of sleep. Honest. We no sooner got into the room than he started. And then after the second time I fell asleep and he woke me up. His hands were all over the place. He said sleeping was a waste of time, I could sleep when I got back to camp. Go on. Have some more sweets. I'm seeing him the next time I get a pass and I'll get some more. We'll be going back to the house.'

'But you can't,' said Ellen. 'You can't stay out all night on a pass.'

'Don't have to,' said Jan. 'You can go to the house for an hour. She doesn't mind. I think she pretends you're not there. I'll give you the address. And I'll give you my mum's address, too, just in case I'm not around when you need her.'

When we could, which wasn't easy, we got together to discuss this new interest in our lives. Opinion was divided. One or two said it was frankly disgusting and others said they didn't believe her. But they didn't say this with conviction. I, myself, thought her recitals had the ring of truth about them. She was a likeable, lively soul even though she was given to asking some questions we'd rather not have been asked. As a result she thought we were a puritanical lot.

'That's a sweeping statement,' said Ellen. 'Because we don't talk the way you do it doesn't mean we don't know anything at all about love and sex. I do know some girls sleep with their boyfriends. The others will know some as well. We just don't talk about it. It's their affair.'

'What concerns me,' Dorothy said, 'is that the word "love" doesn't seem to exist for you. You don't know if your Yank's married or not and you don't seem to care.'

'What difference does it make?' replied Jan. 'I'm not going to marry him. Or anyone else. I don't believe in love. It's a confidence trick and marriage is a mug's game. All men want is a permanent mistress and a permanent servant. And you've got to be one or the other at their bidding. No, thanks.'

This sort of topic made our little gatherings more of a discussion than the monologue they had become since Jan's arrival. Once this had started one or two of the girls were a little critical of her lifestyle, but Jan good-naturedly pointed out it was none of their business.

'In any case,' she said, 'I'm not the only one on this camp having a fling. I keep my eyes open and there's more than one dark horse stalking this government property.'

'Don't mix your metaphors,' said Dorothy. 'It's very bad for the GL image. Now you've cast suspicion in our midst. We're all wondering who the dark horses are. I only wish I was one. Or I think I do.'

'Not me,' I said. 'Every woman her own enjoyment. Spending every available moment in doubtful accommodation with somebody I neither know – and I don't mean this in the Biblical sense, obviously – or want to know doesn't appeal to me. Dull I may be, but I haven't quite given up the idea of Romance with a capital R. Just look what it's done for that stringy girl, whose hair is forever escaping from the bootlace she scraped it into, who spends her off-duty time in the NAAFI holding hands and gazing into the eyes of that gunner, a much-married man if all stories are true. Romance that uplifts the soul and gladdens the heart. That's the thing to aim for.'

'You read too many stupid magazines,' Jan said. 'Love is a snare. An illusion. It stops you from seeing the awful truth. If you must get yourself battened down it would be far better if you forgot all about all this love idea and sit back and think about the men you know and, sensibly, pick the one you're most likely to get along best with.'

It was true that, at that time, late 1943, early 1944, I did have a number of boyfriends, so my limited off-duty time presented me with certain problems. Not surprisingly, they were each serious to a greater or lesser degree. This, of course, was largely because of the war and the knowledge that they were preparing for something, and the impending second front was ever with us. Many of them were going to be in that second front and some of those many wanted to feel they had a girl, or even a wife, of their own to come back to – if they came back. I tried to make myself believe I thought more of at least one of them than I did. But which one?

Then I met Geoff. I nearly didn't. It came about because I was a sort of stand-in for a gooseberry. The girl who asked me, Joan, was not a particular friend of mine so that it might well be that she'd asked three or four others before she got down to me. It happened that I had an evening pass that night but had elected to stay in and read. I still had not got over the luxury of our room and intended to make the most of it before it was taken from us, as it assuredly would.

Joan, it appeared, had a cousin, a lieutenant, at present on a course, in our vicinity. Her mother had written suggesting that Joan and her cousin met.

'He's completely wet,' she had told her friends. (Perhaps that's why she had such difficulty in getting her foursome together.) 'They must be desperate for officers. Heaven help us if we have to rely on him. Thank goodness for Ack-ack, surely the backbone of the British Army.'

'Perhaps you are prejudiced,' suggested one of her friends. 'He must have some worthwhile qualities or he'd never have got this far. They are pretty shrewd at OCTU.'

At first, Joan had pleaded extreme pressure of work, which didn't allow for family reunions as they did not further the war effort. But it's a small world, as they say. A little later, she had gone to a dance and met a smashing officer. Time and circumstances had not allowed her to make much of the encounter and she feared he might be lost to her forever until she realized he was on the very same course as her cousin. A little ingenuity, one pound and a tactfully worded letter to her cousin about having been given four dance tickets for the following Saturday and her first date with this smashing new acquaintance was in the bag.

Unfortunately, the friend with whom she was going dropped out at the last minute. I had just begun to think of settling in front of the stove, now turning a very pale red at the bottom, when Joan appeared dramatically.

'Thank heaven you're in,' she said. 'It is the work of providence. Everything set for us to have the time of our lives and D. can't come. You must come in her stead. Please. I beg of you. In the sacred name of Ack-ack, whose motto is stick together through thick and thin—'

'*Ubique*,' I put in. 'The motto is "*ubique*". Everywhere.'

'That's right. Stick together absolutely everywhere. Now do hurry. We're going to be terribly late. Do you think we could go shares in a taxi? I would pay it myself but the price of those tickets just about cleaned me out.'

'That last 24 in London cleaned me out. Joan, don't you think you'd be better going yourself? Couldn't you just tell your cousin what's happened and ask him to buzz off and leave you two on your own?'

'I couldn't. You've no idea what he's like. He's so dim he wouldn't take a plain hint. No, I'd be stuck with him and have to sit there watching some blonde floating round with Peter. I know I'll make the grade given the slightest fraction of a chance. You must come. Think of all the trouble I've taken.'

'If all you say is true, the outlook is grim I must say. However, once a girl guide, always a girl guide. We can't live entirely for pleasure. Give my buttons a rub and I'll be ready in two shakes,' I said.

We met our escorts in the foyer and went straight to the ballroom.

It was something of a shock. I had become used to plain no-nonsense dance halls of the church hall/hut variety. It set me back a little to see all this plush richness and padded seats and a dance band in tails and a somewhat restrained atmosphere. There was going to be neither heavy boots nor heavy breathing. I wasn't prepared for it. My all-purpose uniform did not seem to fit the occasion. Neither had I spent ages in a perfumed bath emerging into a cloud of talc, Evening in Paris and a carefully applied make-up.

There was a bar at one end and thither Joan's cousin steered us. I hardly looked at the hoped-for boyfriend. I gazed at Joan's cousin with what I trusted looked like the utmost devotion as per instructions. I attempted also to hang on to his every word, but this was difficult as his word output was limited and consisted mostly of 'Same again, please,' which was not evocative of great emotion, at least, not the right kind of emotion. He was a solid morose young man with a seemingly insatiable thirst and a fear that the bar would run dry before it was quenched. I tried several conversational forays but as they seemed to be interpreted as the babblings of an idiot I felt too discouraged to continue, and presently there was no need, for Peter took Joan on to the floor. When they were dancing their second consecutive dance I felt that I could relax. The strife, as far as Joan was concerned, was over and the battle won. I looked around. It was then that I saw Geoffrey. He was a pilot officer and stood there looking so debonair, so handsome and so obviously unattainable that I felt I could gaze at him in open admiration. He was tall and slim with thick black hair and dark eyes. He looked in my direction and I smiled. He smiled back and I had just time to notice his strong white teeth and the dimple in his chin before I looked away, blushing slightly, and turned my attention once again to the unresponsive cousin.

'Excuse me, ma'am.' I turned and saw the RAF officer smiling at me. He bowed.

'May I have the pleasure of this dance?'

'Certainly, sir, with pleasure,' I added and turning to my escort said: 'Excuse me.'

He danced very well and neither of us spoke till it was over.

'Thank you,' he said. 'I enjoyed that tremendously.'

'So did I,' I answered.

'Is that your boyfriend?' he asked.

'Oh, no! I'm a sort of mongrel as far as he is concerned. A cross between a partner, a gooseberry, a wallflower, a chaperone and a very present help in time of need.'

'I'll settle for the flower and ignore all the rest. Shall we go back to him or shall we stay here while I acquire sundry pieces of information, such as your name and are you a native of these-here parts?'

'We may as well stay here. I don't suppose he even realizes I've gone yet,' I said. I could hardly believe my luck. One dance possibly, but for him to want to talk to me, to dance with me again seemed almost incredible. He must, I thought to myself, be doing his good turn for the day, and there being no little old ladies handy to guide across roads, he had chosen to bring an oasis of glamour and heady delight into the desert of my evening.

'Now for the inquisition. Name, please?'

'Linda Summers, spinster, temporarily of this parish or at least its environs, to wit, a gun-site some leagues hence. I say, I hope you're not a spy.'

'Honourable Eenglesh gentleman, I assure you.' He put his hands in the cuffs of his jacket, Mandarin-fashion, and bowed.

'Geoffrey Grenville, bachelor, also very very temporarily of this parish.'

I felt a little disappointed at this information but shook myself mentally. He was an interlude, I told myself. However long he stayed here I wasn't likely to see him again after tonight.

The music started up again.

'Shall we dance?' he asked; and again we gave ourselves up to the music.

When the dance was over, he suggested we had a drink and offered his arm with old-world courtesy.

'I know a better place in the hotel than this bar,' he said.

I hesitated and looked towards the cousin who had not changed his position since I left him. Joan and Peter were nowhere to be seen.

'Do you think I should?' I demurred.

'Of course,' he answered. 'It's his own fault. The man must be blind. You said yourself you didn't think he'd missed you.'

He took me to a quiet room where the carpet was thick, the lighting subdued and the low table which he chose overshadowed by potted palms. He smiled.

'Tell me what you're doing here and why you smiled at me. It was such a beautiful smile I couldn't resist it.'

'I smiled at you because you looked so handsome standing there. I wouldn't have been surprised to have seen movie cameras trained on you. You looked more like a film star playing the part, extremely well I might add, of an airman, than a real live airman in the flesh.'

He laughed, but he was clearly pleased.

'I am a real live airman, I assure you.'

We talked about the lighter side of our respective jobs for some time till I looked at my watch.

'Good Heavens,' I said, 'is that the time? I must go back to my partner and then run for all I'm worth if I'm to be back in time.'

'Why?' he asked.

'I forgot to tell you: Cinderella is my middle name. I have to be back by twelve.'

'And so you shall. May I take you back, please?' he asked. 'I'll make it all right with your partner. Just give me a few minutes, and I'll come back and we'll have the last waltz before we go.'

The lights were low, the music slow and tender and there were fewer couples on the floor. I had never known anything so romantic. It was like a dream. 'I'll wake up in a minute,' I thought. But the ride back in the taxi was real enough. Geoff held my hand and asked if he could see me the following day.

'I'm sorry,' I said with real regret. 'I can't, I'm on manning duty tomorrow. I can get an evening pass till 23.00 hours on Tuesday but I just can't get out tomorrow.'

'Couldn't you change with somebody?' he wheedled.

'Not a chance,' I said, hoping he'd suggest Tuesday instead; but he didn't and we arrived at the camp gates just in time for me to bid him a hasty goodnight and be in the guardroom by a minute to 12.

'Got yourself a Yank or a millionaire, not that there's any difference,' observed the guard commander, a corporal, who followed me into the guardroom. I felt too dispirited to think of a rejoinder and went quickly to the hut. The blackouts were down, the blue pilot light glowing and everyone was asleep.

The next day at break Joan sought me out. She was decidedly aggrieved.

'Where on earth did you get to? We looked everywhere for you. My cousin was quite upset,' she said.

'He couldn't have been. Geoff spoke to him about taking me home. And I can't see him being upset,' I countered. 'I don't think he even realized I was there.'

'Oh, yes, he did,' Joan replied. 'In fact,' she went on, 'I think he quite took a fancy to you. He hinted as much.'

'He what! He's a master at the art of concealment then. I'd never have guessed. Never in a million years. Why this sudden change of heart towards him?' I wanted to know.

'Well,' demurred Joan, 'he is family. And perhaps I was a bit hard on him. You know how it is. He never mentioned anyone speaking to him about you and I don't see how he could have forgotten in so short a time. Anyway, I was saddled with both of them all the way back here.'

'Oh, I *am* sorry, I really am,' I said. 'Didn't Peter make another date then?'

'Oh, yes,' Joan answered happily. 'Tuesday. But their course finishes in a fortnight. Just my luck.'

'You can do a lot in a fortnight,' I answered.

And as things turned out, so could I, apparently, for, at the end of that time we were head over heels in love, Geoff and I. He wrote to me, beautiful romantic letters, and our few dates were in keeping with our first meeting. We dined in hotels, visited a theatre and I returned to camp in a taxi. I wrote two 'Dear John' letters and Geoff proposed. He told me he was going to and asked me in which particular spot I'd like to hear his proposal most and would not be satisfied when I said the spot was immaterial, it was what he had to say that mattered. In the end we chose the room in the hotel where we'd had our first drink together. We would choose the ring, he said, after we'd informed our parents. He spoke to his parents on the telephone and wrote to mine. His parents, it appeared, had a house near London which they had closed for the time being. They were now living some distance away in a quiet country retreat – also theirs. The immediate result of Geoff's news was to bring them back to London for a short while, long enough to meet me.

'I can hardly believe it all,' I said to Ellen. 'There was I saying I wanted romance and it's dropped into my lap just like that. It just shows, you never know what's round the corner.'

'Ye-es,' she replied and, strangely enough for her, she said no more.

I was more than happy to fill any gaps in the conversation with Geoff's many many perfections, and yet, somewhere in the dim recesses of my mind, there was a little niggling doubt. It had first made its presence felt for a fleeting moment after the wheels had been set in motion regarding our marriage. Geoff was standing at the pay desk getting tickets for the theatre when I looked at the back of his neck and in that second I found myself thinking, *What have I done?*

It went as suddenly as it came and I was easily able to explain this vague thought away. It was because I found it difficult to cope with this new heady happiness fate had thrown in my direction; because I really felt a fraud and unworthy of someone like Geoff being interested in me. I could understand Maddy shooting down males at sight, but not me. I didn't think of myself as attractive and I thought looks were very important.

Ellen did manage to chip in with one observation as I listed Geoff's plusses: 'It's not a very Gaitskill-like choice.' This was anent something I had said in an earlier discussion concerning the fact that I admired our senior officer very much. 'If you admire somebody and you want to be like them, surely that gives you an indication of the sort of person you really are,' I'd said. This considered, I felt I had to admit, in all honesty, Ellen had a point; but I couldn't say why.

Came the day when I went to meet Geoff's parents. It was a beautiful house and they were a united family. Geoff had an older married sister whose husband was in the forces. She came in with an aunt to join the family party. From the beginning, I felt I got on well with all those present except his mother. I also had a sneaking feeling that everyone was being so nice and kind because their opinion of me didn't matter. I don't even think they thought Geoff's mattered. It was Mrs Grenville who was the important one. There was obviously a very close relationship between mother and son. Little half-smiles, glances of mutual understanding and in-jokes passed between them, shutting the rest of us out during the moments they happened.

We arrived in time for afternoon tea. I was surprised to find we had fingers of toast dripping with melting butter and pieces of a cake that owed nothing whatever to Lord Woolton's recipes. Later, at dinner, we had reached the coffee stage when Mrs Grenville said to me, 'And does your father own one coal mine or a group of mines? I'm not very clear as to what exactly happens in these mining areas.'

I looked at her and at Geoff who was busy with his coffee cup.

'My father doesn't own a mine,' I said in wide surprise. 'He works in a mine. Not underground. My brother too. He's just been given his first appointment as a manager.'

'Oh.' She put a great deal of unexpressed meaning into the word. 'I'm sure Geoffrey told me—'

'Nonsense, Mother,' Geoff smiled. 'I'm sure I simply said Linda came from a mining area.'

'Perhaps you did, dear,' she smiled back. 'It was I who made a natural mistake. I had assumed that that would be the case. Any more coffee anyone?'

Everyone started talking at once and were more interested in the state of my coffee cup than they were in their own.

I didn't take much part in the conversation during the remainder of the evening but, before we left, Mrs Grenville was able to say emphatically, apropos nothing at all, 'Of course there can be no question of Geoffrey getting married till this war's over and he goes up to Cambridge and gets his degree.'

Not surprisingly, I was very despondent as we made our way back to camp. 'You must admit,' I said, 'your mother doesn't want you to get married.'

He laughed. 'I'm quite sure she doesn't,' he said. 'I'm her blue-eyed boy. You must have seen that. You should also have seen it didn't affect me. She'll come round to it and she'll love you as everyone else does. Nothing has changed.'

Eventually, I was won over.

Naturally, the girls were interested in him and I wanted to show him off. On one occasion, we all attended a dance.

We had arranged that we should be married as soon as we could get leave together and I had asked for a compassionate twelve hours to be added to my normal 24 so that I might go home and make what preparation I could for this happening. To this end I left the camp at midday and, after spending most of the journey in the corridor of a packed train, arrived at home at about 10.30 in the evening. I had brought with me pages of things to see to, ask about and make tentative arrangements about, and having had something to eat, I sat down to talk things over with my mother.

'You don't seem very interested in what I'm saying,' I said.

'No,' she replied, 'because I know there's not going to be any wedding. You're not really ready for marriage.'

Now my mother wasn't psychic by any stretch of imagination, but I knew she was speaking the truth. My body suddenly felt as though it were made of lead. I felt weary and defeated.

'If I were you I'd go to bed,' my mother said. 'You look tired out.'

The next day we did not discuss Geoff at all and my mother, who was a very bad traveller, took the unprecedented step of travelling back as far as Newcastle with me.

I got back to camp shortly before 23.00 hours. My bed was made up and there was a hot water bottle in. A mug of tepid cocoa stood on top of the still faintly warm stove. I went into the ablutions to prepare for bed and, as I did so, I heard someone getting up. It was Jan. She stood at the door.

'I've something to tell you,' she said. 'I went out with Geoff last night. We didn't go to the house. But. . . . Never mind. The point is we spent the evening together. I should really charge you a box of candies but I'll let you off. Goodnight,' and she went back to bed.

I stood mute and drained. The dull, dead leaden end to a dull, grey leaden day. They had seen more than I did. No. They had seen what I would not admit to seeing. I saw Romance because he had the aura of Romance and Romance was what I wanted. I felt ashamed. At least bed and darkness would hide me till Reveille.

The girls did not mention the subject of Geoff again and neither did I. The ability to carry on despite the rubble of our relationship was made easier because we were so busy at this time. Also about this time, one of our number who slept in the GL hut proper was suddenly withdrawn from duty and packed off without the usual kit inspection. Rumour had it that she was pregnant, an unlikely state of affairs we thought, a) because she was on GL and b) because she'd passed her free-from-pregnancy test the previous month. However, the infallibility of this last had already been called to question because a cook on A site who had also passed had later been found to be four months pregnant by a gunner, and their nuptials were already under way.

Nothing was said to us re. our departed colleague and finally we decided to ask the GL sergeant outright.

'Yes,' she said. 'It is true. I was disgusted when I heard. I could hardly credit it. The dirty beast. No one knows who the father is.'

I was taken aback by the sergeant's attitude and felt extremely sorry for the girl. I thought of her travelling to her home in Scotland and her probable reception once she got there.

In the case of the cook everyone had seen the need for as speedy a wedding as possible, and as circumstances would not allow the gunner more than a 48-hour leave and each lived a distance from the camp in different directions, it was decided the wedding would take place from the camp to which the couple would return for a modest wedding breakfast before going off to enjoy what was left of their time together.

It did not seem fair that the two girls should be treated so differently.

Later, for some reason, never ever revealed to me, I spent a week or two in a largish house in the country. Why it had been taken over by the army I was never destined to learn. My job was to sit at a switchboard arrangement, take down certain messages and pass them on. While I was there I became very friendly with a girl whom I shall call Freda. She was a most natural person, devoid of any form of guile or artifice. Magazines dealing with how to make the most of yourself in dress and make up would have gone out of business, had they to rely on her custom.

She was engaged to be married to a young man in the army who was stationed near enough to come and see her fairly regularly. Theirs was a beautiful, secure love. It reminded me of the tale that the gods were angry at the happiness they saw on earth where each person was a complete whole, so they had everyone cut in two, parted them and condemned them to roam the world, each looking for the half that would, once again, make up the complete whole. Freda and her fiancé looked like two halves that had found each other and they were now a perfect whole. Although their love for each other was so deep, they did not resent the intrusion of a third person; rather did they make others welcome.

Freda was painfully thin although she had a good appetite. Also she tired easily. However, her medical examinations showed up no abnormality. Then one day a bruise for which there was no cause appeared on her leg. It became very sore and stiff and she was obliged to see the MO who sent her to hospital. Detailed examination there brought to light the fact that she was suffering from TB (of the bones), by that time so far advanced that, at the time I left, they could offer up very little hope.

Before I went, I sought the young man out and asked him to deliver a letter and small parcel to Freda. I tried to express the feeling of great sadness I had for them both.

'I'm not here much any more,' he said. 'I'm up at the sanatorium helping her to pull through. She knows that. She knows that, whatever happens, we'll never really be separated. Anyway, we had more happiness together than any two people can be expected to have in a lifetime.'

14. Entertainment

In an effort to entertain us troops and keep up morale, we had weekly dances, an occasional film, the odd camp concert, a rare visit from the Voluntary Entertainment Service, and one visit from Ann Shelton, bless her.

The films were not always regarded in the way that Hollywood intended, and were often a vehicle for the camp wits to yell out their not very subtle repartee to the accompaniment of the loud appreciation of their friends.

I have already mentioned the camp concerts we sometimes gave. Sergeant Smith was one of the outstanding performers and there were at least two singers of note who contributed regularly. I was one of the appreciative spectators.

Then I went on a course. My first, I think. A junior NCO's. Inevitably, we had to give a lecture that they might discover instructor potential. The newest, the latest thing about these lectures, was we had to provide visual aids. The officer commanding the course was one Clifford Craddock, and the second in command was George Carpenter whose favourite expression you shall learn later. Among the other officers on the course was a Mr Morgan, who frequently illustrated his lectures with 'I remember when. . . .' Also, a weekly talk on British Way and Purpose (BW and P) was compulsory throughout the service.

One day we had a visit from a high-ranking officer who came into the set I was on and watched the team at work. Of course we played up and snapped out information as we smartly got 'on target'. The officer was impressed by this efficiency and general bearing and said so to the camp CO as he went out of the set. We just caught the CO's reply: 'Yes. They are very intellectual girls.'

This tickled us mightily and the story quickly went round the course. Under normal circumstances I would have written a piece of doggerel about the incident but the course was near its end and they were asking for volunteers to take part in the concert that marked the finale. I said I thought those of us who had been on the set the day of the visit would do a turn and I wrote a sketch after the fashion of a Salvation Army meeting.

We straightened our hair with a multitude of kirby grips, put flour on our faces and wore uniforms either too big or too small and came on with a makeshift banner on which was written THE INTELLECTUAL GIRLS. As we came on and made a sort of half circle on the stage we sang, to the tune of 'We are the Ovaltinees':

> 'We are the GL wallahs,
> Intellectual girls.
> F'you want a date we must refuse you,
> Our grave chatter won't amuse you,
> We never go to films or dances,
> We never bother boys,
> No happier life we've ever led,
> By half-past eight we're all in bed,
> No painful curlers in our head,
> We're intellectual girls.
>
> We are the GL wallahs,
> Intellectual girls,

We can answer all you ask us,
Greek or Latin, Jove or Bacchus.
We don't want t'be someone's darling,
No romantic whirls,
The only books we ever see
Are Macaulay's *Ancient History*,
BWP 'nd Philosophy,
We're intellectual girls.'

Then I went to a make-shift lectern and took from behind a large suitcase with VISUAL AID in white lettering. I held it up so that all could see before opening it and taking out the monocle, after which I read:

'The lesson is taken from the Epistle of St Waroffus to the Gee-Ellites.

'And it came to pass that there were gathered together tribes from all lands round about. Yea from the north and from the south thereof and even from the heathen lands of Lancashire and Yorkshire and the wilds of darkest London and the wastelands of Scotland.

'And, lo! There were among them men from the hosts of anti-aircraft who dwelt in great comfort and peace in camps which are called sites. That is to say places flowing with mud and water where they toil not, neither do they spin.

'And there appeared unto them one who was leader of all the scribes and the prophets and learned men of divers tongues, who was called Clifford, and he bore upon his mighty shoulders stars which are called pips because of the effect they have on they that are of lower rank.

'And he spake unto them that were gathered together, saying, 'Be strong. Fear not. You will be possessed of great wisdom.'

'And they that were gathered together were exceeding glad for they were Other Ranks of Above Average Intelligence.

'And there were with Clifford the Craddock many of his followers, George the Carpenter, Morgan the Historian, Benjamin who worked with figures, Matthew skilled in the lute and the harp and Wallace the man learned in many things which remained unknown to they that heard him.

'And George the Carpenter saith unto them, Behold, these are a few points of admin. There shall be detailed among you several to serve as fire picquet that ye may be skilled for the life hereafter.

'And they murmured amongst themselves, saying, 'What manner of course is this?'

'And there was muttering and cursing and gnashing of teeth.

'Here endeth the lesson. Now I call upon Sister Charity to come forth and give her Testament,' I went on.

Sister Charity was more obviously gifted in physical attributes than the rest of us, and she wore a very tight skirt and shirt that strained (sometimes in vain) to cover her person. She had been known, she said, in her wild dissipated days as the Jezebel of Little Mudpuddle and sometimes Hetty of the Haystacks, so called because of the number of times she had tumbled therein and fallen. 'Oh, Sister, Sister' we intoned shaking our heads at each pronouncement and soon the entire room was joining in. There were no depths, she said, to which she had not sunk when a letter came from on high summoning her to pastures new where she met a kindly missionary called a drill sergeant who pointed out the error of her ways.

'And now,' she said, 'I intend to do good in this world. I have joined GL and, in thinking of Higher and more Intellectual Things, I deplore the gaudy drunken night life in our ancient strongholds, our cookhouses and NAAFIs. I wish to protest to the US Legation about the unfair distribution of GIs whose conduct surely indicates that the tracts I have with me, the lesson I wish to teach, will be as welcome to their ears as it is to yours. For I wish to speak to those who need to hear my message most. The virile young men of handsome physique and noble mien. No man is too handsome or too virile to be led to the path of Virtue (who unfortunately cannot be with us tonight). So, if any of you young men listening care to speak to me after the meeting, I shall be in my usual spot in the NAAFI, third housey-housey table down. I'm afraid that is the only venue I can give. King's Regs and blackout restrictions do not allow me to put a guttering candle in my window to guide the wavering footsteps of those wishing to be saved.'

'Halellujah!' we shouted. 'Halellujah. Bless you Sister,' and lifting up our hands clapped and sang:

> 'Come and join us, come and join us,
> Join our intellectual niche.
> Come and join us, come and join us,
> Learn the lesson we would teach.
> Come and join us, come and join us,
> Join our intellectual few.
> Come and join us, come and join us,
> Join our movement, do, please do.'

And picking up the banner we marched round the stage and off singing to the tune of *Onward Christian Soldiers*:

> 'Onward, GL wallahs,
> Onward to your task,
> We will give you lectures,
> Answer all you ask,
> We'll give demonstrations,
> We're not faded jades,
> We'll show you life and living,
> With our visual aids.
> Onward then, brave women,
> You must not despair,
> Grab your bump of knowledge
> And throw it in the air.

It was unexpected. It was topical. The applause was music.

As luck would have it, at the follow-on course I went on I met up with someone who'd been on the first course, as a result of which I was pressed into service to provide another sketch for the end-of-course party.

This one I called 'Gee-Ella'. It was built round one of the officer's idosyncrasies and the fact that on Ack-ack we were supposed to dubbin our boots, for reasons of safety, I think. The only GL who actually did this was Joy. Dubbin made the boots look very dull indeed, so most of us rubbed polish into our boots in the morning to make them appear to be dubbined then we buffed the polish after the day's duties were over. On the course there was one senior officer whose boots were shone to mirror perfection so that they glinted at the merest hint of sunshine.

The playlet was a hotchpotch – part dialogue, part singing, part narrative. I tried to make the singing appear at the most awkward times.

It began with the sergeant major bringing a small group (principals also doubling as chorus) to attention. The captain arrived and said, 'Right Sar-major. Bring them to attention. As you were. They *are* at attention. Stand them at ease. Right chaps and chapesses. Words for your ears. Orders for the day. No further volunteers are required for pickato potting. As you were. Potato picking. GL team C will go on a course. As you were. Team D. Right. Dismiss them Sar-major.'

The gist of the playlet was as follows: Gee-Ella wished to go on a course. She was a number six who for various reasons had been transferred from team to team and had always missed out. She had heard much about the idyllic life of those who went on courses. No reveille till seven o'clock. No fatigues. Jolly, handsome lecturers. Long breaks. NAAFI rock buns of exemplary standard. Off duty every night and every weekend and no air raids. And so she wanted to go on this course. Her heart had leapt when she heard Team C was to go, only to plummet when it was changed to Team D. Ree Mee tried to comfort her telling her how miserable he would be if she went, but Gee-Ella would not be comforted. Then kind Sergeant Magna Tron (GL) appeared and said, 'Gee-Ella, you *shall* go on the course. I shall transfer you to that team. Just bring me your kit and lay it out as per King's Regs and your place in the Tilly at six hundred hours tomorrow is assured.'

The ugly (and wicked) sisters Cath and Ann Ode overheard this and determined on a dastardly plot. They appropriated one of Gee-Ella's wellingtons so that she was deficient of one wellington for kit inspection, and as she could not explain this wanton carelessness with government property she paid the penalty. No course and seven days confined to barracks with fatigues.

Now Ree Mee was a boffin possessed of much wisdom (as were all Ree Mees). His heart was filled with love for the fair Gee-Ella but she was even less able to see this than normal because of her present affliction. A brass hat arrived to inspect the camp. He wore the finest pair of shiney brown boots ever seen. As he walked towards the catwalk leading to the RX, he kept to the roadway to keep his boots clean and leapt the short distance to the catwalk steps to avoid besmirching his beautiful boots. Alas. His foot slipped and he would have sunk ankle deep in the mud, but his foot rested on something which prevented the catastrophe. His boots had been saved by a wellington.

He summoned his aide and asked him to find out whose boot it was. Ree Mee, who was on the periphery, recognized it and told the corporal who told the sergeant who told the sergeant major who told the second lieutenant who told the lieutenant who told the captain who cleared his throat and told the Great Man. For presence of mind and services rendered in the field Ree Mee was immediately promoted to the rank of lance corporal, acting, unpaid. Further he was allowed to restore the wellington boot so fortuitously placed. When Ree Mee returned the article and Gee-Ella learned how he'd been distinguished and promoted and had been instrumental in getting her off CB, her heart beat with joy and they fell into each other's arms and everybody said, 'Ah'.

Not many miles away from us there was a fairly large American camp. They were very generous, and as Christmas 1943 neared they invited the entire camp to a Christmas party. Naturally, not all the camp could go. A skeleton manning team had to stay behind. Volunteers were asked for on an individual basis and I volunteered straightaway, as did the others in the rooms in which we were still housed. We felt it was the least we could do because of our having this accommodation.

A special supper was to be laid on for those staying in camp. I had an idea a few days beforehand and asked the sub if I could leave camp early one day to go up to London to borrow several copies of a play. 'I thought,' I said, 'we might have a play reading in the sitting room on party night.'

'What a splendid idea,' she said. 'Do you mind if I join you? I'm the duty officer.'

Of course, I said we didn't. She would be most welcome.

The one-act play I came back with was Philip Johnson's *World Without Men*. It is a very funny play. We read it through once and then tried acting it out and altogether had a great deal of fun. The next day the sub said to me, 'Do you think you could put that play on for the camp on Christmas Day?'

'I should think so,' I said. 'But, if I may suggest, 'ma'am, let's keep it a secret so that if anything goes wrong or it doesn't happen no one will be any the wiser.'

We asked both the entertainment officer and Sergeant Smith if we could borrow items from either of their messes as props, but we drew a blank. So I went to the headmaster of a nearby school, with whom I'd become acquainted, and asked if he'd help. He and his wife were more than willing to do so. We, in the cast, each sent home for civvies. We were able to rehearse undisturbed in the sitting room and managed to have a dress rehearsal in the cookhouse one evening completely undetected. Because of sundry noises off and the need to douse the lights at a certain time we had to have helpers in the wings also.

The play required a dog and we decided against a real one, even could we have got it, and eventually made a most unlikely-looking stuffed creation from some blue material.

From the beginning the play was set to be a success. Things went wrong. The gramophone didn't play when it should have and then suddenly started up at the wrong time. The doused lights did not produce a full blackout so that it was possible to see a bit of activity going on where none should have been seen. Madeleine was a rich and pampered woman who doted on her pampered dog. In the blackout the dog, being male, had to disappear as all males were supposed to do so at the touch of the female scientist's switch. When the lights went up again and Madeleine had hysterics because her dog had vanished, the dog itself was visible for all to see in the waste paper basket into which it had been thrown.

To say the evening was a success is to put it mildly. First of all, we had been well fed and a free issue of beer had already been consumed. And we'd managed to keep the impending performance secret. Madeleine, glamorous in a silk dress, pearls, high heels and a fur was a knockout. She was definitely the heroine of the hour.

'I've seen more glamour just looking at you,' one gunner said, 'than all the film shows and concerts I've seen since I joined up.'

Miss Gaitskill asked if we'd perform the play for A troop and we did. It was another gala night.

Everyone was anxious that this success should be followed up with another. It took many years for me to find out that in situations similar to this one, you should estimate that your volunteers will be reduced by seventy-five per cent, at least, by the time you're well under way. I wanted a play with an all-woman cast, which I got, *Ladies in Waiting* by Cyril Campion. It was a mystery thriller. To take up the slack of volunteers and to provide a contrast I prefaced the three-act play with a short comedy.

The opening night in the cookhouse was to be quite an affair. There were more armchairs than usual in the front row as we had quite a number of visiting officers from A troop and from GHQ.

I was in the midst of the last-minute preparations, the bustle, the continuous recounting of things to be done, the answering of numerous questions from others doing their last preparations and the calming of those who felt the whole thing was going to be an unmitigated disaster, when there was a knock at the door. It opened and the head of Junior Commander Gaitskill appeared tentatively through the narrow opening.

I stopped what I was doing and went outside. She had gone into the sitting room. With her was another officer, Junior Commander Judy Montagu.

'It's all right, Summers,' Miss Gaitskill said, 'we're not going to stay long. We don't wish to disturb you at what must be a very busy and anxious time for you. We only want to wish you well and say how much we're looking forward to the evening. It's quite a gala occasion. The officers are having a little get-together beforehand.'

'Yes. Good show. Jolly good show,' put in Miss Montagu. 'I don't know how you do it.'

This coming from Miss Montagu, that she should consider putting on a play required unusual effort, was quite a surprise. Although we had never been told officially, we knew who she was – the niece of the Great Man himself, Mr Winston Churchill. She stood with her hands behind her back, the person she was more important than the uniform she wore, which she appeared to have put on as an afterthought. Miss Gaitskill I had liked and admired from the very beginning, not with any juvenile schoolgirl-type crush but with an admiration for all the things I saw her as being, a person of authority whose integrity, sincerity and bearing was such that she commanded respect and esteem. She was no jumped-up officer. Neither was Miss Montagu, but in a different way. She had that instant rapport which made you think of her as a staunch friend rather than a superior officer.

Friendships in the army were sometimes quickly made, to be enjoyed while they lasted, because there was no telling for how long they would be allowed to flourish. Posting came quite suddenly. Ellen's posting when it came was one such move. I missed her sorely, but that was the army. Thus it was possible for this feeling of friendship to be engendered in very few meetings and those of short duration. Later, I talked with others who had met Miss Montagu and they said they had the same feeling. She was a friend.

'All I want to say,' Miss Gaitskill told me, 'is that I do congratulate you most heartily. You have done an excellent job in difficult conditions.'

'Thank you, ma'am. I do appreciate what you have said. But would you say that to the rest of the cast, please. They too have worked hard. Any success we have is due to them as much as me. I wouldn't like to be separately distinguished.'

'How wise. How very wise. We will do exactly that after the show,' and while Miss Gaitskill talked Miss Montagu vigorously nodded approval.

Next day I wrote to my parents.

Dear Mother and Father,

Sorry not to have written earlier, but as you most probably remember we gave the play, yesterday, Saturday. As it is the major topic of the moment I will give you a brief account of same.

It was an undreamed-of success. Congratulations have showered down from all quarters and verbal bouquets were handed out unstintingly.

Twenty-two programmes (written and designed by self) were sent out beforehand. We had about 10 visiting officers from the heights, our own officers and site personnel together with others from nearby establishments military and otherwise. Everyone played splendidly. The noises off noised off with all their might and main. The applause at the end was thunderous – Major Walton made a speech – we were cheered which was over-whelming – I said 'a few words' – and then after the show our junior commander – our Miss Gaitskill – shook hands with me and congratulated us all. The senior commander also spoke to me, as did nearly all the visiting officers, but the crowning glory, the real climax came this morning in a handwritten letter from Miss Gaitskill which read as follows.

Dear Summers,
Although I was able to see you after the play yesterday, I feel I must write as well as to say how very much I enjoyed the evening and what an extraordinarily fine performance I think you all put up.

Believe me I am basking in your reflected glory. I know very little about producing plays but quite a lot about the finished article so though I can only guess at the amount of time and effort you put in I know how good the production was.

I go on a six-day course this evening but hope to see you perform when I return. In the meantime perhaps we shall be able to arrange for you to go to other batteries.

Again, warmest congratulations to yourself and to all members of the cast.

Yours,

With thoughts of a new production I became more ambitious. So far our props and stage settings had been simple. Now, I wanted a better setting. Also, I thought it would be good to have a play with a mixed cast and fewer characters. There would also be a curtain-raiser as usual. For this last we turned again to Philip Johnson for his one-act play *Matrimonial*, and for the main attraction I chose *Gaslight* by Patrick Hamilton. REME did the stage management. I wanted a set which could fold up for easy transportation because I felt that so much work went into each production it should reach a wider audience and we should travel further afield. Many gun sites were now under canvas and I felt we should at least visit those in the brigade. Also, regulations forbade that there should be civilians on site and I felt we'd had a great deal of help and encouragement from the people around. Why could we not hire a hall and give a show to civilians? At the very least I thought it would make us part of the community.

There was such things as auditioning for parts. Everyone who was interested was given a part. As with the previous play, so with this one. It's one thing in a welter of euphoria to say you'd like to become part of the drama group; it was quite another to have to turn up for rehearsals. Things were made more difficult because we'd been moved out of our rooms into the GL hut. I slept with the other NCOs in a small room at the top. In the reshuffle Joy, Madeleine, Betty and Ellen had left for A Troop.

I had to take rehearsals in the cookhouse, which I did every night it wasn't needed for a dance or a film show. I took most players individually at first till they were fairly conversant with their parts. Sometimes, I'm afraid, I had to bring them away from the NAAFI. They came most reluctantly, feeling that it wasn't necessary to spend so much time on something which was being done for fun.

On one occasion when I went out of camp to see if I could borrow some props, I was walking past a row of houses fronted by small gardens when a door suddenly opened and a woman came out waving a piece of paper and shouting, 'He's a prisoner of war! He's a prisoner of war!'

There was no one else in the vicinity. She rushed down the tiny garden, took me by the shoulders, and, tears running down her face, said, 'Thank God. Thank God. He's a prisoner of war,' and we danced round in a small circle as a spontaneous expression of joy. A nearby neighbour came out to see what was going on and when she heard the news she kissed her friend and took her into her house for a cup of tea. They invited me in but I pleaded the prior command of duty. Who the 'he' was I never discovered.

On another occasion, with one of the cast, I set off to go to the nearby town on some business to do with the play. We waited hopefully for the bus that, if we were lucky, might take us to our destination, cost 3d (1½p). On the horizon there appeared an ancient cart drawn by a slow horse. When it finally drew abreast the wizened, ageless driver said, 'Wannalif?'

It seemed a good idea at the time. The horse was urged to stop while we got on and then encouraged to move off again, which it did after some thought. It was a painfully slow journey, pain being the operative word as we were bumped along. Needless to say, the bus passed before we'd gone very far. An hour later, stiff and sore, we arrived at our destination and prepared to thank the old man. He got in first.

'That'll be one and six,' he said (7 ½p).

As this new show neared its first night the members of the cast were myself as Bella, Bill Cooper as Mr Manningham, Jim Waud as Sergeant Rough, Dorothy Alter as Elizabeth, Grace Smith as Nancy, and two gunners, W. Tasker and F. Reynolds. These last two characters were changed umpteen times before the day. Costumes came from ENSA, Drury Lane, London.

There was a gala opening night in the cookhouse.

It must be remembered when evaluating the rather fulsome praise we were given, that there were not a great deal of amateur theatricals and the like done at this time. We were some years away from being able to watch professionals at the flick of a switch. Also, considering all the circumstances, that these shows were put on at all was praiseworthy. Perhaps it will be best, at this point, to describe the happenings as I saw them when I wrote to my parents.

Dearest Mother and Father,

I would not care to assess the number of miles I have travelled since my last letter to you – miles covered in open trucks, covered cars and tillys.

Our show from the beginning has been a success. This past week we have been on a requested brief tour. But, to begin at the beginning if it is possible for me to reflect calmly at the moment.

The dress rehearsal was shocking. The lights, a most necessary part of the show, flickered, died and failed. Sergeant Rough forgot his part and just couldn't bring it back to memory. The second act dragged abominably. Even the curtains refused to work properly. When the person concerned pulled them at the end of the act, one half stayed out, the other shot across the stage to keep it company. But, two days after, we gave the opening performance. The applause at the end was sweet music to our ears. I made my speech, put in a topical self-manufactured crack, got my share of appreciation. The officers entertained us afterwards.

Since then we have given several shows elsewhere. Perhaps our greatest triumph came when the Brigadier attended one show and came behind the scenes to congratulate us.

We gave a show yesterday. We only give shows on our non-manning days. We have to have the 3-tonner loaded by 09.00 hours, because first we have the journey there, and then we have to assemble our flats and props, a mass of art-pot stands, aspidistras, over-mantles, fire irons, etc. Yesterday, unfortunately, the transport was not forthcoming till 11.00 hours. When it did arrive, it was not what I asked for. However, I took what I could and with three helpers departed for our destination. When we arrived (at a camp under canvas) *the stage was still in process of construction*. I went to see about additional transport for the rest of the cast and our effects. At 16.00 hours we began setting up on a semi-completed stage. Thus, we had no time to give the necessary lighting, exit and entrance rehearsals. We were due to start at 19.45. At 19.00 hours I hadn't begun to dress. But we made it on time.

The audience was marvellous. *Matrimonial* had a wonderful reception. Then came *Gaslight*, with its elaborate setting. Just as the entertainments officer had completed his introduction, the scenery, over-mantle, fireplace, bric-à-brac, candlesticks, vases, pictures came toppling down about us as we sat waiting for the curtains to part. Considerably shaken, we re-organized the confusion, hammered a few more nails in place and started again. The curtain wavered and stuck half-way. And the lights went out. Total darkness. A voice was heard throughout the tent: 'The bloody lights have fused!' Time was pressing so we started off in darkness hoping that before we'd got very far we would be seen. The audience was with us, fortunately. We rose above the creaking floorboards, the unco-operative curtain, the precarious scenery and the extreme smallness of the stage which could not quite take four of us among all the scenery, to receive the verdict: 'A magnificent show.'

This letter saga takes up the story a month later.

Dearest Mother and Father,

I have just returned from the *final* tour of *Gaslight* [I think we'd had more than one 'final show']. Today the company has been disbanded and I feel a little sad.

We gave our public performance on Wednesday and though I think the audience enjoyed it, myself, I prefer to play to six of the most outlandish Forces' posts to one civvy audience. We had difficulties with the cast. The leading man had had to go home on leave and had to rush back late for the performance. The curtains wouldn't work and had to be kept permanently open. The man who worked the lights had never seen the play and wouldn't attend a rehearsal. 'A one-word cue is all I need,' he said. Of course the lights went out at the wrong time.

We have played several times since then. The cast think the best performance of all was given last Thursday, but, in my opinion, last night's was. We had the biggest audience ever – 500 troops in a tent miles from anywhere in Doodlebug Alley.

Coming back we travelled in an open 15-hundredweight. About five miles on our journey the van broke down. It was pouring from the heavens and we were soaked to the skin. Four hours later we were towed back to camp.

Domestic matters followed as usual.

I had said I was a little sad that the company was now disbanded. 'Sad' was really not the word. I was confused. There had been mutterings on camp for the last two weeks and I was at a loss to know why. I had a feeling that the fault was mine but I could not put my finger on the reason.

Major Walton, Miss Gaitskill and Miss Montagu had been supportive of our efforts throughout, so I had no clues from that quarter. Other than that we had worked as a unit within the camp.

I was told that the sergeants had complained en masse and had asked for the drama group to be disbanded. This was a gun site, they were reported to have said, not an amateur dramatic society. I was confused about this because no sergeant had anything to do with the shows given outside camp, nor were they in any way inconvenienced. We only gave shows in our own off-duty time. Added to which we on B Troop were now no longer operational unless piloted planes came over, which they had not done for some months past.

On the evening of our official disbanding we'd had a visit from

Major Walton, who had sent for me while I was sorting out the grease-paint-soiled costumes and the props we had borrowed preparatory to returning them from whence they came. His words were pleasing to the ear and I went back to my job with a light heart. It was late when I finished. I felt grubby but elated. Although it was after lights out I decided to have a bath, even if the water was cold.

My euphoria was such that I didn't feel at all sleepy. The cold bath made me feel even more wide awake. I had a half-written letter to a friend and I decided to finish off writing it in the ablutions. I did this and posted it in the camp postbox.

As I walked back I felt that the only thing that was wrong as far as the cast was concerned was the fact that we'd worked hard for a long time. For some weeks past we'd given up our free off-duty time to travelling with the show. Well. It was over. I felt a tremendous sense of well-being. I felt sure they did too.

I went to bed and fell asleep. I had not slept long when I awoke with a start realizing that I'd said more in the letter I'd written earlier than I meant to, or would have done in different circumstances. I had forgotten it would be censored in battery office. I got up, dressed and walked down to battery office to wait for the postbox to be emptied.

I leant against the wall of the, as yet, deserted office. Signs of life in the camp were quickening and presently, the familiar figure of the post sergeant issued from the sergeant's quarters. He came, making the last adjustments to his uniform and altering the set of his cap. I watched his approach with affection and, as he neared, smiled in greeting and in anticipation of the back chat we would no doubt have. He did not, however, return my smile or my greeting. He did not even look at me. Incredibly, he appeared to be in a bad mood, a thing which in him I had thought to be impossible. I changed the smile for a look of contrition.

'I'm sorry to be a nuisance,' I said, 'but I've been waiting for you. I wrote a letter and posted it last night and I've changed my mind about sending it. Could I trouble you to give it back to me, please? It's addressed to the army post office.'

As I spoke he unlocked the box and took the letters out one at a time. Suddenly he turned on me. I saw that he was very angry.

'You think,' he said, 'you can bloody well do as you like. Every bugger runs after you from the colonel down. Well, this bugger doesn't. You can't have your bloody letter. You posted it. It doesn't belong to you any more. It gets sent off like the rest. You're no bloody different from them.'

I was completely shaken. 'But . . .' I stammered, 'I thought . . . I. . . .'

'You never bloody thought,' he said. 'Never about anything except what you bloody want.'

'Look,' I said, 'I'm sorry. I didn't know. I didn't know this was regarded as an official post box. If I can't have the letter, I can't. It's not that important. Please don't get upset about it.'

'I'm not bloody upset,' he almost shouted. 'What the hell do your letters matter to me? Or you either, for that matter?'

There weren't many letters in the box. Mine was easily distinguished: it was the fattest one there, and he knew my handwriting.

'Is this it?' He held up a letter in his clenched hand.

'Yes.' I answered. 'But. . . .'

'There's your bloody letter,' he said and flung it angrily on the ground.

I picked it up. 'Thanks,' I said. 'I'm grateful. I really am.'

He ignored me, shutting the box and locking it with as much force and noise as he could muster. I walked away, puzzled and concerned. What could have got into him? He was the most likeable, the most friendly and even-tempered of men. I did not, however, dwell on his problem, whatever it was, very long; I had much more pleasant things on my mind. I walked the long way round the camp, savouring the fact that all the hassle of the last weeks was over and the outcome had been successful. I meant to enjoy the day to the full. Coming towards me on his way to battery office I saw the lieutenant. I grinned as we were about to pass and put up my hand in friendly salute.

'The top of the mornin' to ye, sorr,' I said.

He saluted smartly and stopped.

'Corporal,' he said, 'come here.' His tone was icy and formal. 'When you pass an officer, you turn your head smartly in his or her direction and salute smartly. Never in that slovenly way. Stand to attention while I'm speaking to you! If you feel a comment is necessary, and it rarely is, a simple "Good morning, sir" is more than adequate. Do I make myself clear?'

I stood, my whole body rigid. 'Yes, sir. Perfectly sir,' I replied in a small voice.

'That will be all. You may dismiss.'

'Thank you, sir.'

In a reflex action, I saluted with precision, turned in the approved military fashion and marched off, my cheeks burning.

It wasn't the sergeant. It was me. The sergeant had been angry because of me. The lieutenant had been frigid and disciplinarian because of me. What had happened? It didn't make sense. Was there something I didn't know? Had I been so wrapped up in the show that some chilling war news had not reached my understanding? I walked back to the hut, apprehensive and cautious, determined to wait for someone to speak first, so that I might get some clue. I might be being over-sensitive. What affected the lieutenant and the sergeant need not affect the others. It might have nothing at all to do with me and everything to do with the war. Had there been some terrible set-back?

Walking through the hut, I might have been invisible for all the notice anyone took of me, except that, perhaps, they spoke to each other in louder voices than usual, talking of trivialities as though they were important. No one asked me why I'd been up so early.

It is *me*, I thought. *Why?!*

I delayed going in to breakfast (in any case, I had little appetite) so that I could eat the meal hurriedly and sit by myself. I wanted to try and work things out, but in spite of all my endeavours, I could find no clue. All I knew was that I had been sent to Coventry.

The morning presented no great difficulty. I confined my remarks to routine work on the set and the programme before us. To ease the situation I did not go into NAAFI break and adopted the same tactics for midday dinner as I had for breakfast. As we were short of number ones, I took over another team of manning duties in the afternoon. Hoping the situation would somehow clarify itself, I was careful not to offend and to be present only when it was essential. There was no friendly discussion, as was usual, to relieve the tedium of searching the barren skies for evidence of enemy activity other than the doodlebugs.

214

I missed Ellen more than I could say. Had she been there I would have asked her outright what had happened, but I felt I couldn't ask any of the others, not even Dorothy. I tried to bide my time but the feeling of isolation grew, as did the feeling that they knew something which I didn't. I was becoming more and more unnerved, and even frightened. During the evening I kept myself busy with routine tasks, washing my smalls slowly, ironing them with care, tidying my soldier's box.

The following day, as we walked down from the sets at teatime, Dorothy came up to me.

'Listen,' she said. 'I'm not supposed to tell you this, but I don't approve of what they're doing, so I will. The colonel left £10 behind to be spent on the cast and everyone who had anything to do with the show, in appreciation, I think. The sub collected us together yesterday afternoon. It's been decided to give a party in the ATS rest room. You weren't to be told about it till the last minute. As I said, I didn't agree. I feel the whole thing should be left in abeyance for a while, at least. I think we're all on edge.'

As soon as she'd spoken she walked off and I was too taken aback to stop her. Party? What sort of party? Why couldn't I be told? Was it a secret to surprise me? Had I only imagined I'd been ignored? Was it just that I'd been over-occupied with everything that had led up to the show?

Well, if surprise was what they wanted from me, surprise was what they would get. I felt hurt to think I had not been told about the £10, nor had I been consulted about how it should be spent. Nevertheless, tonight I would smile, be friendly, be pleased and take part in everything, no matter what.

It was Dorothy who came to fetch me so that I was not immediately called upon to act out emotions I did not feel. In the ATS rest room all the females seemed to be determinedly occupied in doing something, although what was not quite clear. At one end of the room were trestle tables covered with cloths, the outlines of which suggested there was food underneath. At one side, looking decidedly ill at ease, were the two gunners. They sat, hands on knees, looking as if they'd been coerced into the room with difficulty (as indeed they had). There was no sign of the REME bods. It appeared they had suddenly found themselves confronted with a job on the sets that had to be done there and then and required all three. I smiled round the room, not looking at anyone.

'What a lovely surprise,' I said.

There was a dangerous lull in the conversation and one girl immediately filled the gap by saying, rather too brightly, to one of the gunners, 'I just heard you got engaged. Isn't it smashin'? You kept quiet about it, didn't you?' The girl concerned was a cook in A Company who had not been in the least reticent about her conquest. The topic had been one of camp speculation for months and the actual engagement had made camp news about three weeks previously.

Nevertheless, they all now turned to the uncomfortable and bashful gunner and showered him with congratulations and asked when the happy day was to be. All he could do was what he had done when the announcement was first made public, i.e. grin, blush and say he didn't rightly know, although everyone knew the date had been fixed and his compassionate leave granted. By this time he was the focal point of the room. Felicitations for him and his fiancée were taken to the point of exhaustion. Inspiration of further interest was lacking and there was nothing left for anyone to do except look towards the sub who was obviously mistress of ceremonies. That lady could think of nothing other than suggest we ate the food prepared for us and everyone agreed that, yes, we were ready to eat, although it was scarcely one and a half hours since we'd finished high tea. We busied ourselves round the table till someone asked what about coffee and other drinks. These, it appeared, were not due to be sent from the NAAFI for at least another hour. What should be done? Should we eat now and accept the liquid refreshment when it came, or wait and eat when the said refreshments arrived? Most had no fixed ideas on the subject, not even the girl who had raised the issue. Once again we looked towards the sub who said, after consideration, that those who wanted could eat now and those who wanted to wait for coffee etc. could do so; there was plenty for everyone and we had the evening before us, raids permitting. We gathered round the table and proclaimed at the excellence of the food, but took little and what we did take we ate slowly. Even so, twenty-five minutes later we were looking towards the sub yet again for guidance. This time she said she thought it would be a good idea if we opened the presents before the drinks came. This was agreed and a box of parcels that had been secreted under the table was brought out and placed on the table. Everyone who was standing sat down while the sub stood up.

'As you know,' she said, 'the Colonel very kindly left £10 to be spent on all those who have taken part in the shows. He felt, as we all felt, that everyone, and I mean *everyone*, had an equal share in making these both possible and successful from the captain and the officers and NCOs down to the last gunner or private, although this might not always have appeared obvious. However, after discussion, it was decided that the money should be spent on a party for those who actually took part in the show and this includes all those who worked backstage. I was put in charge. Three pounds ten went on food and drinks. The cooks prepared the food and I think you will all agree they did a first-class job.' She paused to allow some hand clapping. 'The drinks, of course, are still to come,' she went on. 'The remainder of the money we decided should be spent on presents, an equal amount to be spent on each person. As you know, you were asked to say what you would like and write this, with your name, on a piece of paper. We drew the pieces out of a hat, and again, as you know each of you took a share of the money and went out and bought the gift you'd drawn. Those who wished to add money of their own to get a better present, were allowed to do so. I hope I've made everything perfectly clear. Well, that's it in a nutshell.' She looked in the box. One girl clapped her hands once then, looking around, blushed as no one else had clapped. However, one or two belatedly followed her lead, so she did not feel so bad.

I struggled with the lump in my throat. No one had told me of this. Indeed, the sub's rather long explanation was for my benefit. I had been deliberately excluded. I felt terribly hurt, but I determined not to show it.

'Now,' said the sub as she stood with the first, loosely wrapped, parcel in her hand. 'Lance Corporal Summers. We had no difficulty whatsoever in deciding what you would like.' I got up, grinning fixedly and forced the whispered 'Thank you' out from somewhere in the pit of my stomach. I opened the parcel in front of them all. It was a book. I nodded as a sign that a book was what I would have chosen. I neither heard nor saw what the others got. I clenched my back teeth and continued to smile, ignoring as best I could, my aching jaws. Finally, there was only one parcel left.

'And now,' said the sub, 'the last one. This is a special present. Another one for Lance Corporal Summers.' I stood up. The parcel the sub held out was carefully wrapped and fairly large. Tears welled up in my eyes. I took the gift from my superior and, holding it in one hand, ran the fingers of the other gently over the outside of the parcel to give myself a little time to settle my emotions. Then I looked at them all and said, 'Thank you. Thank you all very much.' My sincerity was total. 'I . . . I cannot hide from you that I felt a little hurt that no one had told me about the party, but I should have known better and I'm sorry. I can see now that you meant it as a wonderful surprise . . . and . . . this special gift touches. . . .' I swallowed finding it difficult to go on. In the silence somebody whispered 'For God's sake shut up and open the parcel' was distinctly audible.

'Of course.' The words motivated me to action and I took off the wrapping. Inside the box was another box, and inside that yet another, and so it went on. The atmosphere was absolutely still. I could no longer even pretend to smile. At last, a small object wrapped in newspaper emerged. I took off the newspaper and stared at the object in my hand. It was a china basket with a broken handle. I stood transfixed. The message got through. The price was still on the basket – 1d. Slowly I raised my head and looked steadily round them all and, without saying anything, I walked out of the room. When they returned to the hut I was in bed, determinedly asleep.

The next night, I was not on duty and there was no reason why I should not have had a pass. I was even entitled to a late one. I had not used my full quota of passes for some weeks and what time off I had taken was to get props, or do something for the show. This evening, as soon as I finished work, I went to the ablutions, had a bath, dressed and walked out of camp, *sans* pass, *sans* explanation, *sans* any real idea of where I was going.

In the end I took the train to Tilbury, crossed the ferry to Gravesend, walked along the quayside and there, for some time, gazed into the quiet water.

I arrived back at the camp station at 11.35 with three miles still to walk. Even if I'd been given a late pass, I could not now get to camp on time. From midnight, pass or no pass, I was officially absent without leave. It would mean a possible court martial, the loss of my stripe and my position as number one. It would also probably mean fourteen days confined to barracks and a stint of unpleasant extra fatigues, such as scrubbing the cookhouse floor. I had realized all this before I set out, but I was past caring. I could understand the punishment for flouting the rules, but not for the other thing.

I walked along the darkened and deserted platform and gave up my ticket at the other end. As I did so, a man stepped out of the shadow into the feeble light surrounding the ticket collector. It was an officer from GHQ. I saluted him.

'Good evening, corporal,' he said. 'You're late. Been detained? There's a tilly going to camp if you'd care for a lift. You won't get back in time otherwise.'

'Why, yes, sir. Thank you, sir,' I acknowledged.

'Just wait here a second. I won't be long.' He disappeared on to the platform and I wondered vaguely what had brought him here at such a time. He returned after a few minutes and said, 'Sorry to keep you waiting.'

'That's all right, sir,' I replied. We walked to the waiting utility van.

'We have a passenger,' he told the driver and, turning to me, he said,

'I'm afraid I'll have to ask you to pop into the back. I'll keep you company there. I'm delivering a special container and I don't want anything to happen to it.'

There was some equipment in the back, but I couldn't tell what it was. When he reached the camp he said, 'Your pass has been taken care of. You have to report to Miss Moore (the subaltern) tomorrow at 09.00 hours.'

The room the sub interviewed me in had been temporarily denuded of all other personnel except ourselves.

'I'll come straight to the point,' she said. 'You're having a bad time, aren't you?'

'Yes, ma'am,' I answered.

'And you don't know why?'

'I have no idea. I was asked to do something and I did it. I just thought it was expected of me. I had no idea it was as good as all that till the colonel said what he did.'

'It was good. That is really the trouble. Before that they hardly took you seriously. They looked upon you as a buffoon. You played up to that and now they think that all the time you were laughing at them. Perhaps they should have had some idea that you were capable of other things, but most people don't think below the surface. Do you understand what I am saying?'

'I'm trying to.' I was shocked. Buffoon! Surely I wasn't as bad as that!

'I wasn't laughing at anybody,' I said. 'I don't laugh at people. I laugh with them.'

'Yes. Yes. Perhaps. We knew there was a serious side to your nature, but then, we had access to your course reports. Things other people wouldn't see or know about. Tell me what happened from the beginning.'

'But I thought you knew, ma'am. You asked me to put on that play for Christmas.'

'Yes. I know. I just want to hear what you have to say.'

'I was asked to put the play on for Christmas. After that everyone was keen. The trouble was no one really wanted the fag of rehearsals. I think they thought they should just be allowed to read their lines any old how. They didn't much like it when I suggested they did it another way.'

'Suggested?'

'Well, told. I was producing the play. But I did try to make some of the parts easier. Private Alter and I each took extra work. Some just thought it wasn't turning out to be the lark they thought it was going to be and they opted out and I just accepted what they said and got someone else. And in the end we put on *Ladies in Waiting* and it was wonderful. Everyone was thrilled and they asked for another play so of course I got one.'

'Had you ever done any play-producing before?'

'Never.'

'You behaved like a veteran. And you decided on a mixed cast?'

'Yes. The REME bods were different. They were marvellous all through. I don't know what I'd have done without them. But I had to get two men – gunners – to take small parts. I can't remember how many different men we had. I did ask for help with the props and scenery, but no one would risk giving me stuff to do things by myself and they said they were too busy to help. In the end, I got help from the headmaster of the junior school not far away. He was marvellous.'

'So I heard. And you don't know what went wrong?'

'Well, obviously I put up a back somewhere along the line.'

'Any idea where?'

'None. I feel a bit hurt about it, to tell the truth, and I just want to forget the whole thing.'

'That would be a pity. There was a lot in it worth remembering.'

'Why do the others feel so different then, ma'am?'

'I can only hazard a guess, but I think I won't be far out. In the first place, you gave the impression that you took a very lighthearted and irreverent view of life. The only other similar entertainments we have had are the camp concerts which were always impromptu affairs with very little, if any, rehearsal and everyone knew what to expect. You changed things rather. Everyone enjoyed the first play tremendously. I don't really think anyone was aware that it was you who put it on. Again, with *Ladies in Waiting* you were a group of young girls in pretty dresses who did a very good and entertaining job. After so much khaki you were pleasing to the eye and again, no one was really aware of what had gone on behind the scenes. Later, one thing began to stand out apart from the content of the shows, and that was the terrific organization that must have gone into them, and your determination to put them on, come hell or high water. You did it in spite of every obstacle that was put in your path. In fact, you seemed not to notice obstacles and carried on regardless. And then you organized help for costumes and other things from outside, without telling anyone.'

'Only after I couldn't get what I needed in camp and no one seemed interested in what I did anyway.'

'I know. But they think you went over their heads. And now they think you've been laughing at them all the time. None of the NCOs and few of the officers, I guess, would have been capable of such organization, especially as it was carried out while you went on doing your other work efficiently. Now are you beginning to see?'

'I don't know. And I don't particularly like myself, the way you

221

put it. I assure you I didn't feel big-headed.'

'I'm not trying to make you feel worse than you do already; I'm merely trying to clarify the situation. Very few people have your sense of dedication. Their enthusiasm soon wears thin. They want the kudos, but not the work that goes with it. It's not that people are not capable of greater things, it's just that they feel they don't want to spend the time putting in all the energy it takes. There's a point beyond which they will not go for a thing like this. In an air raid it's different, and fighting is different, but dragging them away from housey-housey in the NAAFI at night to attend a rehearsal in the cookhouse just isn't on. I don't know how you did it.'

'With the utmost difficulty,' I put in.

'You seemed popular. But you cannot do what you have done and not expect some sort of reaction. Though don't let this stop you from putting all you've got into something else. If you want to be popular you'll have to sacrifice your personality. If you must always have everyone's approval you will certainly lose control of your life, because the crowd, the fickle crowd, will control your actions. Not, I might add, that I think for one moment you do want to be popular.'

'No. Oh, no.' I protested. 'I didn't know I was popular. I just thought how friendly everyone was. I like that. I like laughter. I love to see people having a good time.'

'But you did go out of your way sometimes to create an impression? To be, as I said, a buffoon?'

Buffoon. That word again. My throat was so tight speaking was painful. I was terrified I was going to burst into tears. *Not here*, I thought, even as I spoke.

'I . . .er . . . I had no idea it was a bad as that.' The words came with an effort. 'I've never really agreed with Robbie Burns. I think we want people to see us as *we* think we are. I certainly didn't want to be seen as . . .' and I couldn't go on, my mouth was so dry.

'Summers,' she said, 'if you take my advice, you'll fight the desire to say something interesting at all costs. And if you're going on to a position of higher authority, and I think you are, don't make your intense devotion to the job in hand too difficult for others. Try to be in tune with them. Try to find how much each can cope with.'

There was a finality and a slight tetchiness in her tone that made

222

me think the interview was over and that, somehow, I'd annoyed her when she had set herself out to help. But I couldn't cope with her feelings (if, indeed, I had jarred them); it was all I could do to cope with my own. I wanted to get outside.

'Thank you, ma'am,' I said. 'I'm most grateful that you've given me so much of your time.'

'Possibly I think it needed saying. You need to be brought down to earth. I understand too that Miss Montagu is getting some information for you regarding your possible transfer to the Education Corps.'

'Yes, ma'am. She's seeing about a correspondence course.'

'Good. Your application to transfer to education has gone forward. In the meantime, you are free till break. Anything more you'd like to ask?'

'No, ma'am. Thank you, ma'am.'

She nodded and the interview was over.

Outside, the air was refreshing but there was no solitary place to which I could go. I desperately wanted release from the tension that locked my being. In the end, I chose a spot at the outer edge of the fuel store. Here I was out of sight of battery office, while at the same time I had the rest of the camp in view. Somehow I had to compose myself for after-break duty. Buffoon! They thought of me as a buffoon! Tears were very near the surface. I tried to think of something bright and cheerful so that I could suppress my other thoughts till I was alone in bed, the rest of the hut asleep.

'The trouble with you,' said a male voice which startled me so much that I jumped visibly, 'is you're a dreamer. You live in a dream world. You're out of touch with reality. The things going on round you. You need some man to take you in hand and show you what's what. God help him whoever he is. You don't even know what time it is. When I came up to you just now you weren't even here. You were up in the clouds. What are you supposed to be doing anyhow?'

'I'm free till break, sergeant.'

He looked me up and down without speaking and, with a little verbal explosion of disgust, turned and walked away.

In the NAAFI no bright voice called out to say, 'Your coffee's over here.' I got into the depleted queue and drank the liquid slowly, making it last till the whistle blew to mark the end of break.

A girl, who had been at the party, fell into step with me as we made our way to the parade ground.

'It's a great pity you didn't laugh the night before last when you opened that parcel. It would have made all the difference. Cleared the air,' she said.

'Yes,' I replied. 'Yes. You're right. You're absolutely right. I see that. But at the time I didn't see it as a joke.'

'Pity,' she answered. 'You should have done. You've played plenty on other people.'

The courses came from the correspondence college. It was some parcel. Because there was so little time I could not do the work week by week. I had to do it as I could and hope for the best. The grounding I'd had in English language at Bothal and Bedlington Schools had been so good I had very little extra work to do in English grammar. Indeed, the only subjects which presented me with real difficulty were French and algebra. The latter I just could not understand.

What I had to find was somewhere to work, and somewhere with privacy, because just to pick up a book was a signal for all kinds of activity and interruptions to start. To start reading, however engrossed you were in the book, was to invite attention. If you were reading you were 'doing nothing'.

I had recently been put more or less in charge of the information room. The orderly responsible for its cleanliness was very proud of the dust-free state of the room and the gleaming shine on the floor. I was requested not to walk on the polished lino if I could avoid it, but just in case I couldn't, would I mind putting on the duster-shoes she'd made to cover the feet of any who might have to enter the room.

I was pretty sure the information room only ever saw me and the orderly, so thither one evening I walked with my papers. As I got into the room I was met with the combined icy stares of one of the sergeants and the orderly. They were sitting decorously holding germ-free hands at the far end of the room, their feet encased in duster shoes. I slunk out.

Finally, I found my haven – the drying-room. It was warm and humid. Suspended from the ceiling were lines of khaki issue at varying stages of fading, creased and not the least attractive, interspersed with wizened lisle stockings, grey socks, khaki shirts and here and there, to add a dash of subdued colour, issue pyjamas. The whole resembled drab bunting put out to depress, not raise, the spirits. A dirge rather than a paean. There was an all-pervading hot alkaline smell about the place that made breathing difficult. The only seat available was the upper part of the huge, black hot pipes that ran along three sides of the room. The lighting was poor in the extreme but here, in a neglected corner, I did my work. Not being very well upholstered I found the floor exceedingly hard. The pipes were hot to warm to tepid depending upon the hour of night. Whatever the temperature they didn't make for comfort. I tried sitting on a folded greatcoat. I tried a folded greatcoat and a backrest of my fatigues. In the end I figured I spent too much time trying to make myself comfortable and decided to alternate between the floor and the pipes, sitting on each for as long as possible.

By this time the monocle, cigarette holder and cigarettes had disappeared for good.

Christmas was approaching and still the war raged.

'What about one of your shows?' they said. 'One you write yourself.'

I tried. I tried very hard. I got out a clean sheet of paper, which is how I usually start, and waited for inspiration. 'Dear Mother, this NAAFI's a terrible sight,' I wrote and could get no further. The wells of inspiration had dried within me. They were arid.

I have no recollection whatever of my third army Christmas.

15. No Fixed Abode

After D-Day we were, once more, avid for news. At 21.00 hours that night we stayed in our rooms and listened to the King's broadcast, when he asked the nation to join him in prayer.

On camp we had a feeling that things were happening in a big way at last and we were useless. The information room had become my responsibility. I procured a large map of the world and a quantity of coloured tapes, ribbons, markers and drawing pins. I read as many papers as I could get and from each one I extracted news about the Second Front and pinned it on the wall, attaching a piece of coloured tape that led from the news to the area on the map where it had happened.

In spite of the doodlebugs there was a feeling, once D-Day was established, that we were advancing on a tide of victory and the war would be over by Christmas.

As it happened, I had my own front-line correspondent. Bob was in the British Liberation Army, the BLA, also known as Burma Looms Ahead. As I have already said, I wrote daily and sent regular parcels of books across: 'They are being eagerly devoured – to say read would be an understatement – by a group of fiction-starved soldiery,' wrote Bob.

I feel I cannot do better than devote this chapter to extracts from Bob's letters as he fought his way – with others – across Europe to victory. For some time I addressed his letters to the Army PO when he was actually abroad. The following gives an idea of the situation.

I should apologize, at the outset, for failing to write you recently, but when I claim that another military upheaval has taken place I know you will interpret the circumstances correctly. I have not had a letter from you for some time, but this is understandable and when I do get mail I know there will be two or three or more from you.

I am, therefore, at a disadvantage. I have no personal news and everything else is strictly verboten.

October 1944
Last night I devoured a large glassful of ice-cream. Nothing ersatz about it. Fruit, too, is plentiful.

4/11 Seen action in Belgium and are now in Holland, where going has been rough. However we are now more or less in control at this stage and the unit [1st Glasgow Highlanders] has won very high praise and generally distinguished itself. For me a wonderful sight was a mass of 2,000 to 3,000 Nazi prisoners being led to captivity after having capitulated to our lads. Sights like this make me feel that I am doing something tangible to win and end this doggone war and as the prisoners marched off I was happy in the knowledge that another batch of Germans had ceased to exist in fighting form and consequently our folks at home and our armies overseas would benefit, however slightly, from it. Life has not been easy or comfortable but I do not mind the hardship if such results are obtained. I think that is the opinion of every other man in the Army.

The devastation and wreckage in many places is appalling and when you think there is German sabotage on top of that you may have a rough idea of the general position.

Holland is surprisingly like the picture book representations – clogs, patched trousers, queer head dresses, canals, queer pipes.

15/11 I visited my first movie for umpteen weeks. In cinemas in Holland and Belgium smoking is not allowed and it is surprising how cool and clean the air is.

While on this subject, it is hard to believe how much the Dutch and Belgians will give or do for a British cigarette – the best and most profitable currency in Europe at present. In every town and village you have small children lisping anxiously, 'Cigarette for Papa.' Fortunately, we are supplied regularly and generously with cigarettes.

How I long to catch a glimpse of a hill, a mountain or even a glen, glade or grove. There is nothing here but the flat, undulating, canal-sunk land, monotonous and never-ending, stretching as far as the eye can see and completely free from variety or change of contour. The towns, too, are all so similar, similar even in ruins, shattered houses, beheaded steeples and glassless windows.

(undated) In Holland and Belgium folks are eager to do soldiers' washing, mending and darning.

19/11 I have been in the slight fracas which took place at Walcheren and assisted in minor affrays and have come out unscathed, nominally resting, although this last is not possible.

(undated) We are having a very active time at the moment and there is no mail. I have no idea where I shall spend Christmas or whether or not I'll be able to get cards and presents. I hope I am not too far forward. Christmas Day under fire is not a pleasing prospect. Still some will have to 'man the line'.

10/12 In spite of your desire to do a little more towards the war effort I feel you are serving to the fullest possible extent. I should hate to think of you being at, or near, the front line. This idea of women guerrillas, female snipers and so forth is repulsive to me and though I agree that women can help I think there is a limit. It has been said that this is a man's world and I should hate to think that the only way to true equality of the sexes is through women shouldering arms and manning the trenches – literally in the front line. Fortunately, we haven't reached that stage yet, but in forty years' time it might be possible, and God forbid, actual practice. I gather all troops are to have English beer at Christmas.

This is my second night in the same spot – a pleasant and unusual break.

16/12 I am still giving all my time to King and country (roll of drums). To my tired eyes this war is going to run till summer. I am writing in a house devastated by shelling but it is a protection from the stormy blast.

26/12 Hope you have a happy time ushering 1945 into its place in history as I am sure it will be eventful and historic. Sorry, all I could send you was a 'Hobson's choice' Christmas card. My sole aim over these past weeks, getting you a present, was deplorably unsuccessful. Militarily we are extremely active – perhaps too much so: socially – I remember the word. The German offensive has not made life easier, but it did not deprive me of my traditional Christmas dinner and although it was not on the Home Service lavish scale it was a damn sight better than usual and I enjoyed it down to the last dreg of English beer that followed the repast. Otherwise Christmas Day was only one day nearer victory, let it be hoped.

6/1/45 My writing hand is bandaged and still painful. Things over the past ten days have been grim and I can hardly realize yet that I have passed another Christmas, and New Year in this brave old world. At one time the prospect of this happening was not rosy so I guess I should be thankful I am still able to write 'Dear Linda'. The 'fun' started on Christmas Day and from then till New Year I experienced incidents, events and thoughts which I sincerely hope I shall never experience again. But I shall not weep on your shoulder. It is over and done – successfully thank the Lord, and my only scar of this particular battle is my painful right hand.

I shall always remember Christmas 1944 and New Year 1945. I remember shaking hands with a fellow under a stout oak table in a cellar which merited the description 'open unto the fields and to the sky' and my only toast to the New Year a glass of rum was drunk with the feeling that my life was being saved by its warm effects.

11/1 I do not think of leave. I have no yearning to spend seven days at home and return to this other world. I would prefer to get this gruesome war finished and done with and know that when I do go home my soldiering days were over. I have left the land of the tulips (I never saw one). Incidentally, I can appreciate why the Dutch still wear clogs.

19/1 It's a long time since I managed to write you a spontaneous letter – even to find time to write a little note. By a twist of circumstances I am isolated in a lonely spot and there will almost certainly be a lapse of four to five hours before I begin my wanderings – an advantage I would be foolish to waste. There is a great deal of activity here at present and verily you are receiving a letter from the front of the Western Front. It is difficult to concentrate due to immediate effects and noises off but I am in good spirits although the going is rough and tough.

Jan. '45 Disturbing letters arrive here and the going is tough – very tough. Some cleric in England has said the morals of soldiers' wives are lousy. This is a far from comforting thing for soldiers to read. The majority of desertions are made because soldiers are afraid of what their wives are doing. They return to shoot their unfaithful wives. Are they justified?

23/2 From various people I have spoken to who have recently returned from England I understand that the general impression there is that the war in Germany is as good as finished. Nothing could be further from the truth. 'Jerry' has still plenty of resistance and though it is hard to fathom what he can actually gain at this late stage he is not giving away one inch of territory without a stiff fight. It is rather annoying to us over here to read the newspapers and hear reports from home which show that the general attitude is 'It's all over bar the shouting!' I wish it was true but it is not. So far as I can judge I would say it will be summer before Germany is completely licked and I don't give a damn what Roosevelt, Churchill or the Daily Express wiseacres say. Perhaps if they were fighting out this affair they would not be so prophetic or complacent. Do not get the notion that I think Germany is strong – she isn't – but there is a good deal of fighting ahead and the war is by no means over. I am not haranguing you, far from it, but if you ever hear one of the many amateur war prophets spouting perhaps you will intervene softly with some good sense – and a little fact.

28/2 There is a good deal of activity on all parts of the Front now, and that holds good in this sector. It is pitiful to see the younger members of each nation here. They have suffered more than any class from the direct and indirect effects of this world war. Undernourished and under-sized, it will take years to bring them to normal health. I hate to think how they have been affected mentally.

I am not, however, in favour of whipping them over to Merrie England as is being done. It disproves the old adage 'Charity begins at home'.

4/3 The past week has been successful but not without personal loss to me. It is heartening to see the Wehrmacht on the run and I guess sacrifices must be made if victory is to be gained. Many of the villages and towns I have passed through are beyond description, believable only if seen and the stream of prisoners and captured materials is on a large scale. I have survived without loss and feel fit and cheerful.

10/3 Once upon a time I enjoyed 24-hour passes but did not appreciate it. The glory and appeal of an endless, carefree day. One day at my own selfish disposal.

I move quickly and frequently so time passes quickly. I do not get much sleep. The progress of the war is promising but it is no 'cake-walk'.

18/3 I had two eggs for tea. I am staying on a farm where there is a plentiful supply of milk, eggs and butter. The Rhine valley appears to have suffered no food shortage.

2/4 There is still some stiff fighting ahead but the end is in sight.

8/4 To the newspapers the war might be over after a series of headlong, dashing victories, but, where I am, it's no pushover. The past week has been grim and although the outcome was successful it has not been achieved without an almost inhuman effort of arms and energy. I feel rather bitter when every letter we get says the war is nearly over. Of course, I do realize my own view is narrow. It cannot continue much longer – but caution is still necessary.

(undated) It is anticipated that large numbers of ATS will be sent to Germany when the war is over so that the eyes of soldiers are kept away from Frauleins. Keep Britain British. Do you see Whitehall as a matrimonial agency?

(undated) The road to victory seems never-ending.

11/4 It has been suggested that the members of the coming peace conference should sit through a film show before opening the discussion. The film would bring home to them the magnitude of the problem they were dealing with and the awful consequences which Germany has brought about by her actions. Your friend (more anon) need have no worry about retribution to the German people. It has become a common sight to pass through cities and towns which look like graveyards, to see weeping women, despairing refugees and the dead. The whole thing is tragic and no matter what nationality or creed is involved one cannot help deploring the fact that there has been such a war which has shattered the entire life of Europe and caused devastation of life and property on all sides. The post-war plans are feeble and compromised.

12/4 After our recent sticky period it is now hell for leather across Germany. The war cannot last more than a month or so.

28/4 I am in a house at present. Oddly enough it is almost intact. You would have to be here to appreciate how odd that is. In its time this house has been a masterpiece. I have gained a host of ideas from its interior. German thoroughness is almost a byword and this house is standing proof of it. After seeing parts of

Germany I wonder why, in Heaven's name, they started this war.

4/5 It has just been announced that the German army in Holland, Denmark and north-west Germany etc. has surrendered unconditionally. There was a terrific roof-lifting cheer. I cannot convince myself the war is over and keep saying, 'It must be true, it is true, and yet I dunno.' It's a wonderful feeling.

Everyone here is acting as if the Christmas dinner was on the table. Bottles have appeared from nowhere and have been emptied, smiles and laughter are the order of the day and I sit here writing to you. The skirl of the pipes is heard in the street and there is 'hooching' and wild laughter. What a day! What a night! We kept a bottle for this day, a rare old French brandy 'won' some time ago – nectar, wasn't it?

I have not been in action since Bremen. The people here are friendly on the surface. They, too, must be glad the war is over.

Goodnight my fair one, I certainly will never be able to convey just how much you have helped me in the past by your courage, your cheerfulness and perpetual interest. Have happy dreams tonight. I will at least sleep peacefully – and if I dream of lovely things perhaps you will step in just as you are.

6/5 The weather is more like March than May. I feel flat and lacking in inspiration.

8/5 VE Day. Two letters from you and a celebration of the end of the war to the fullest possible extent. Night of nights and I am on duty but well on the way to being mortally 'soaked'.

15/5 After the excitement of D-Day affairs have been humdrum. We have moved around – can't tell you where. The security blackout continues but I am destined to serve as an occupying force. Where? Don't know.

Now I shall toddle to my wee pickle straw. In the morning I shall be wakened by the unholy skirl of the bagpipes – the 'doodlesax' to the Belgians. The Belgian for drunks is – 'Ah. Jock zeeg-zag' (with a corresponding movement of the hand) and perhaps if I could zeeg-zag tonight I would.

Yours always,

Love,

Bob.

16. Elysium

All troops were supposed to get at least one half-hour period a week on current affairs. There were two such programmes, BW and P (British Way and Purpose) and ABCA (Army Bureau of Current Affairs). At that time I was becoming increasingly fired with enthusiasm regarding education and in spite of the fact that I was not sufficiently well qualified, the goal of my life was to be accepted into the Army Educational Corps. In camp, however, 'education' raised only feelings of keen apathy. The word 'lecture' caused personnel to disappear almost before your eyes. Chameleon-like, they became indistinguishable from their surroundings. Few were interested in any form of current affairs and those who were roped in sabotaged any lecture with all their aggrieved might. Those whom the sergeant had managed to dragoon into the cook-house, where he left them to the mercy of the speaker, might well look for release ere long as one or other of those who had escaped would appear noisily at the door, come even more noisily to attention breaking across whatever was being said and bawl out,

'Gunner Bloggs wanted in the implacements at the double,' and Gunner Bloggs, brushing into, kicking and falling up against as many of his less fortunate colleagues as possible made his exit with the maximum amount of disruption and ill-disguised glee. It was uphill work being an instructor. Generally speaking, officers and civilians were called lecturers, NCOs instructors.

After the New Year, on B site, we could no longer pretend we were an active unit. Our equipment was dismantled and taken away while still the V1s and V2s wrought havoc although in lesser numbers. The wire which had surrounded the RX had to be cut in strips and rolled. It was like seeing a good set of teeth being prematurely extracted. One by one, my friends were interviewed and, in quick succession, left the camp to remuster. Dorothy became a Don R (Despatch Rider). Familiar faces gone; the corner stone crumbled.

I had three selection boards to attend for AEC, another for university entrance and a further one for teacher training college at intervals during the next months.

I cannot actually remember saying farewell to 625 Battery and the familiar haunts, nor can I remember the journey to Sinah Camp where even as I arrived, personnel were leaving in droves.

It was a very damp place and it was suffering at that time from a plague of lizards or newts. My clothes and my person seemed to be damp all the time and however gingerly I walked about the place I could not avoid stepping on these lizards/newts. In all the corridors and the rooms the floors were bespattered with their squashed carcasses – a horrible sight. My job was to look after a number of girls who had been sent from another camp, for a few days. Apparently the Brigadier was about to descend on this camp for an inspection and it was considered that they would offend his noble Brigadiership. Actually I had great sympathy for the camp authorities who had dispensed with their company for this time. Certainly they had proved an embarrassment to the service since the day they were first admitted.

After keeping these girls for some days in my passive care, I was really quite sorry to see them go. In fact, I was definitely sorry to see them go, because by this time, the equipment had left the camp and the men with it and we were left with the chicken wire to cut up and put into rolls. For the second time I gave myself up to the wire-cutters and the blistered hands.

I went on to help dismantle a third site and there I stayed with those who, like me, had nowhere else to go. One morning, while we were still in the process of cutting up the wire netting we were summoned to a special muster on the parade ground, now far too big for our needs. There we were told that Princess Elizabeth had joined the ATS and that she had cast her lot with us, a tremendous boost to the service. It was felt that something special was called for and we gave three rather self-conscious cheers. To be really rousing, cheers need a male voice to give them impetus and volume.

The wire netting and everything else disposed of, we settled down into a routine. Although there was barely enough work to go round, my day was full. In the mornings I was NCO in charge of ablutions. At break and lunchtime I read as many papers as I could, cut out little bits of interest, wrote out the part of Bob's letter dealing with the conduct of the war at the front and repaired to the Information Room to bring it up to date. The room was no more widely used than were other Information Rooms with which I'd been acquainted. Very often, in the afternoons, I was asked to give a lecture to the other ranks on site. Sometimes this was an imposition, especially when I was given very little notice, but I always complied, even though on occasion I had no real idea what I was going to talk about till the words came out of my mouth.

My job in the ablutions wasn't at all bad. We had the entire morning to do what could have easily been accomplished in an hour, and I was at liberty to do a fair amount of my own work sitting on the floor in one of the bathrooms.

We still kept up the old eight-day cycle and, one morning, when I handed in my request for my 24 from Wednesday to Thursday, the clerk said, 'A signal came in about you today. They've asked for you specially for the next education conference and there's a report in on what you're doing. So you won't be able to go on your next 24 Thursday to Friday, but don't say I told you.'

I waited. Day followed day and no one gave me the official news. I became more and more depressed, unsettled and 'washed up'. I was being swept under the carpet. No one but me read the notices I put up in the Information Room, no one cared what I talked about so long as I helped to preserve the idea that work was being done. This lack of interest began to affect me. To say that I was out of ardour was to put it mildly. Only once had I risen to a slightly lighter frame of mind when Bob had written in one of his letters 'I still feel that Sinah ought to be the signal for a limerick but I can't think of one' and I wrote in reply:

> There was a young AT of Sinah
> Who on fatigues was a top-linah
> As Ablution Lil
> She topped the bill
> When cleaning lavat'ry Chinah

Not having heard anything to prevent my doing so, I put in for my next 24 hours, 14.00 hours Thursday till the same time Friday.

'You can't have it,' said the staff sergeant on the Wednesday.

'You are being detailed to go on an education conference.'

'But it's important to me that I go on my 24,' I said. 'I knew there was going to be some doubt about this conference, so last time I asked and I was told you would get at least ten days' notice. When no one told me, I presumed you were going to send someone else.'

'You presumed wrong. In any case it is not for you to presume. And your 24 is not a right – it's a privilege. You have no choice in the matter.'

'In that case, I request to see my commanding officer as is my right,' I said, hardly aware of what I had said.

The staff sergeant pursed her lips and went away. Not long after, the subaltern appeared. 'Oh, Summers,' she said. 'You were right. What are you doing on ablutions? Surely someone else could do this?'

I couldn't think of a suitable reply.

'As I said there has been an error,' the sub went on after a pause. 'I can't imagine how it happened. A signal did come through and you should have been told. However, I'm sure you understand and I'm quite sure that, being the person you are, you'll go to the conference without any fuss.'

'But, ma'am, as I told staff, this 24 is important to me.'

'Very well. I'll tell you what we'll do. We're not inhuman, you know. Take your 24 from Saturday to Sunday and go on the conference but don't come back to camp. That way you'll be effectively getting almost a 48, certainly a 36.'

As a matter of fact it was a very tempting offer, but it also tended towards blackmail. Also, her remark about the ablutions nettled me a bit. She had inspected them several times with me standing to attention while she did so.

'I'll go to the conference, of course, ma'am,' I said. 'Because I have no choice. But my application to see the CO still stands.'

On the Thursday morning I stood before Major N.S. Sampson.

'You see, sir,' I finished my recital, 'I feel that my going as a representative is unnecessary. Anyone could go. I send in reports, but as far as I know, no one reads them and certainly no one acts on any suggestions I might make. And a Saturday to Sunday 24 is really of little use to me because I spend most of my 24s at the university library because of my course.'

'Which course?' he asked.

I told him. At the end he said, 'Bring your papers here and let me have a look at them.'

I took them and he turned them over.

'What would you say were your greatest problems?' he asked.

'Algebra and French,' I replied. 'You'll see a crowded graveyard of crosses on the things I've got wrong and I've no idea why or how to put them right. It looks as if I'm going to fail in those two subjects and, as you know, that means I won't matriculate.'

'Go and have some coffee,' he said, 'and come back in half an hour. I can spare you an hour during which time we'll see if we can make algebra any clearer to you. I'm afraid I can't help with the French but we might be able to locate someone who can.'

As a result of that interview and Major Sampson's interest I spent the next three and a half weeks at Brighton Polytechnic. This was luxury in the extreme. Hitherto, since leaving school, all the work I'd done had been after I'd done my normal job. Now I worked at the course during the day and went to the theatre, the cinema, the ice skating rink or sat talking in a group at night. I was billeted in a small hotel (which might, in fact, have been commandeered by the army) on the sea front. Billeted with me was a very self-contained, quiet, dark-haired girl. One day I noticed that underneath her shirt she was wearing pearls. They weren't like any I'd ever seen before.

'Are they real?' I asked her, almost before I could help myself.

'Yes,' she answered.

'They're beautiful,' I said. 'I'm not surprised you wear them. They must make you feel good.'

'You do not know what you say,' she spoke in the careful accentless way people do whose first language is not English. Suddenly, I found myself the target of a torrent of anger and near abuse. She was a Jewess. Her family had lived in one of the occupied countries from which finally they'd had to flee. At first they tried to keep together but when the going became difficult, the father had gathered them all to him and said, in effect, that it was each for himself or herself. They had a duty to survive if they could. They'd had to jettison almost everything but the clothes they stood up in. The pearls were her only wealth, the things she would use to begin life again when the war was over. She'd been smuggled from one place to another till she arrived here. As far as she knew only three of her family had survived the holocaust. She was afire with an anger that almost consumed her at what the Germans had done. At the way her family had been hounded from their home and hunted like animals. At the hunger and cold they'd suffered. At the way her mother had tried to keep up though she was ill and near to death. And she feared the Germans were going to get away with it. That they were going to be treated leniently.

'You have no idea,' she said vehemently. 'No one has. Churchill hasn't. The Germans will get away with it. I know.'

I told this to Bob in a letter and I read out his reply, but I doubt whether she really thought it was retribution enough for the loss of most of her family.

Her story haunted me. It haunts me still. Even today when I'm out walking in the Cheviot Hills, or rambling in the Lake District or the Yorkshire Dales or walking over moors, I think of that family on the run and wonder how I would survive in similar circumstances. And where, I wonder, would I run to?

The Brighton stint over, I became a sort of refugee sent from khaki fold to khaki fold. Summers fargo, Bob called it. He thought his signature tune should be 'Where is my wandering girl tonight?'

And where were the paths of glory that should have led to education actually leading? Apart from my skill in the ablutions I became a telephonist on a switch board. As soon as I had learned to put those springing snakes with their fangs into the right holes I was sent elsewhere.

I also became a medical orderly. The medical room is not my delight and I have a minus vocation when it comes to ministering to the sick. Had I not seen mention of it in some of the letters still extant I would not have believed it happened because I've forgotten all about it. There's Freud for you.

I also seem to have compiled crosswords at this time but no scrap of even one exists. Nor does the plot of a play concerned with the perfect murder. (Whom had I in mind?)

So, like a hot potato, I was passed quickly from one spot to another. Some of these spots were pleasant. I spent some time in a large house with nine other ATS. The surrounding gardens were neglected and there was a huge orchard which promised well for the autumn. Two of us shared the room which had once been a nursery and was so placed that it attracted every bit of sun there was. We had our own bathroom, too, with a built-in bath. In that neglected garden I spent many a happy hour reading.

On one marvellous spring day when Peter, a boyfriend, came to spend a 24 pass with me we walked in the glorious Surrey country-side, eventually coming to a garden alive with colour and a fairytale cottage with a charming thatched roof and tiny bottle-glass-paned, bow windows. In that same window was a discreet notice to the effect that bed and breakfast was to be had there. We had intended looking for a place in town but I found this so enchanting I felt we had to stay there if we could. We rang the bell and waited for the rosy-cheeked motherly woman to make an appearance.

A small thin woman wearing pince-nez came to the door. Her staple diet appeared to be lemons soaked in vinegar.

'Yes?' she asked as she looked us up and down taking in every detail and, obviously, not liking what she saw.

'We're looking for rooms,' my friend said. 'Two. For one night.'

'Are you married?'

'No.'

'Engaged?'

'No.'

She continued to stand at the door sucking her lemon and vinegar.

'I don't like it,' she said at last, 'but as long as it's understood there's to be no hanky-panky and no sitting up till all hours burning the electricity, you can come in. It's bed and breakfast only and the door shuts at half-past ten and after that you don't get in. And if you want the rooms I'll need your emergency ration coupons and you'll have to pay in advance. You can have the room next to me,' she said to me, 'and you can have the little one in the attic. It'll have to be a bed on the floor because I don't usually use it.'

The breakfast, I am happy to say, was reasonable and well cooked.

During this time I went up to London for the examinations and stayed at Warwickshire House, an ATS transit camp, the best possible place to be because it fed and sheltered me – and left me alone to concentrate on the examination.

There was a vast concourse of people taking the examination. Well over two thousand. The majority were men and some were in the services. Among the men were two naval officers, an army captain, four RAF aircrew, one airman, four REME staff sergeants and two sailors. There were also a number of clerics and two nuns. I was the only girl in the services there.

I met a sixteen-year-old girl on the first morning. She had a plethora of good luck charms given her by one person or another, a small American doll, a threepenny piece with the Lord's prayer on it, a chain with a charm on, a silver horseshoe, a card, a telegram and a letter of good wishes. By the time she'd set these up on the desk she hardly had room to write. Like a number of others, she had been privately tutored at home.

VE Day I spent somewhat quietly at home attending the thanksgiving service in church with my parents and later going to visit one or two of the street parties.

And back to the wanderings, and being given sergeant's stripes. I can't remember where I was given these or who gave them to me. Perhaps this is because it was made plain I was only an acting sergeant and merely given this status to mark me off as an instructor still attached to the artillery.

I was sent to a camp where I was received with some suspicion. I was allocated a small office, with the word 'Education' painted above the door, and I was left to get on with it.

Bright and early next morning, I went to my office. As I opened the door, a man stood up. He had been rubbing the plinth on which the stove stood. I stared at him. He was a POW. A German POW. The first member of the master race I had ever encountered. He looked to be slightly older than my father, his greying hair was close-cropped and his uniform hung about him. He nodded without speaking. I returned the nod, and came into the office. He left.

I looked around after he'd gone. The place was spick and span, shining with cleanliness.

I spent the day wandering round the camp gleaning what information I could. There was a fairly fluid ATS population, some awaiting early demobilization, some awaiting another posting.

The following morning I was again at my post bright and early.

'Good morning, Fraulein,' the POW said as I came in.

'Guten Morgen,' I replied.

'Ah,' he said, 'you speak German.'

I shook my head. 'No, but you speak good English.'

'I see you are a teacher,' he went on.

'No. You're wrong again. I have not yet qualified.'

'I am a teacher,' he said.

It turned out that he was a teacher of English in a school in Leipzig and over the next few mornings we discussed what I might do to justify my existence as an education instructor and together worked out that the girls would be more interested in clothes etc. than current affairs.

Having got together a tentative programme, I prepared a poster.

'It will never be seen,' he said, 'among all the other notices. It must attract the eye. Give me materials and I will write your notice.'

It was a work of art and, after that, he did all my notices.

One morning, as we talked, a junior officer came into the room. I stood to attention and said, 'Can I do anything for you, ma'am?'

She looked at each of us in turn before making some non-committal remark and going back out. A short while later I was summoned before the senior commander.

'I have sent for you,' she said frigidly, 'because of a very serious matter that has been brought to my attention. You are fraternizing.'

'I, ma'am?' I said in disbelief. I thought at first she meant that I was having an affair with one of the male officers on camp and I wondered how on earth she had got hold of such erroneous information.

'Yes, you,' she said. 'It has come to my attention that you have been seen and heard fraternizing with a German POW. How could you! It disgusts me. Have you forgotten so soon? Belsen? Auschwitz? The devastation? The misery?'

'I most strenuously deny, ma'am, that I have been fraternizing,' I said aghast. 'Such a thought never entered my head. With respect, ma'am, I have not forgotten Belsen or Hitler or the Gestapo, the SS or the brushes I, and others, had with death. Nor could I. It's just that I discovered that this particular POW is a teacher. I hope one day to teach and I felt I could learn something from him in that respect and it would help with my work here.'

'He is a POW,' she said. 'You had no right even to speak to him, nor he to you. He is here to do menial tasks only. It does not matter what his job was in civilian life. Do I make myself clear?'

'Yes, ma'am, perfectly, ma'am. But I would like to be permitted to say one more thing. You say because he is a prisoner he may only do menial tasks. The tasks I have seen him do are the ones many of the women I love have to do every day of their lives and they are not prisoners. I did not think of the work he was doing as menial. I only saw it as a job that had to be done. I equated it with my own job. He could help me to be a better teacher. A better instructor. He has much to teach in that respect and I have much to learn.'

'The order, Sergeant Summers, is no fraternization. What you have said, whatever may be your personal views, means that you have been fraternizing with the enemy.' (*But the war is over*, I thought.) 'Take this as a warning. Another complaint and you may be reduced to the ranks. You may dismiss.'

I spent VJ Day in London with my then boyfriend. We joined in the crowds chanting in front of the Palace, we laughed, we sang, we danced and, when we were tired, we lay down on the grass in Hyde Park as did hundreds of others, to sleep. We slept fitfully till it was light then picked our way over sleeping bodies to a station to see when the trains would be running. It seemed we could rely on getting one later in the morning so we retraced our steps daintily (there were people sleeping on the steps) and began looking for breakfast and somewhere to have a wash and brush up. It was late when I finally made it back to camp.

At last the summons for which I had waited so long and sometimes despaired of ever getting arrived – the AEC course.

Of the many, many courses I have taken throughout a varied career, this one stands paramount. We were assumed to have the background knowledge required.

The course was concerned with the best methods of putting our material across, i.e. lectures, lessons and discussions and how excellence in these areas might be striven for and, even, achieved. What I learned there has stood me in good stead ever since.

I was sent with five others to the Notts, Derby and Leicester group. These others were all graduates who had gone straight from university to the army – the intelligence corps. We were also given to understand that we were earmarked for commissions, although in my case I had to serve a much longer probationary period because of my not having a degree. One of our number went up for her commission after a month.

From there I was posted to a huge camp sprawling in a sea of mud. Twice a day the mud was churned up when a fleet of 3-tonners took almost the entire personnel to a depot some miles away at 07.30 hours. At 17.00 hours the fleet brought them all back when they poured into their various messes for the hot meal, after which they made what toilet they thought fit for the evening's entertainment – mostly drinking. About once a week in the sergeant's mess at least, they had an all-night session, drinking through the night, taking it in turns to keep the fire going and turning out for morning parade as spry as ever and with a healthier than normal flush. They had come straight here from a lengthy stay in India where, it seems, such thirsts were developed.

On the second day I presented my credentials, such as they were, to the CO and he was not in the least impressed. But he was a man of metal used to doing a difficult job to perfection in spite of the obstacles the War Office saw fit to place in his way every now and again. He would much rather have had an extra ablution orderly (a job for which I was well qualified) but was resigned to providing me with food and shelter as long as I kept out of the way. The interview should have been over but a thin, timid, weedy voice – which must have been mine, there was no one else there, said, 'But, sir, they don't even get the statutory British Way and Purpose.' This BW and P was to the army what Religious Education is now to schools and it was administered in much the same way.

He looked as if he was going to explode but this interesting phenomenon didn't occur. Instead, so thorough had been his training and so great his personal control, he said, 'I'll look into that. Any more observations you might have on the subject should be said to the officer in charge of education. You may dismiss.'

I sought out the officer in charge of education. It was a woman. She had been given education as a job lot which also included entertainment. As I have already said, the camp entertainment was more or less taken care of, and as far as education was concerned, whatever the War Office said, this was a busy and serious camp with no time for frills. Also, the education officer had more on her mind. She was engaged to be married. Her fiancé was expected home from abroad any time when they were going to get married after which, she hoped, she would be demobbed. She was not, therefore, greatly concerned about my crusade and she more or less gave me carte blanche.

The CO had seen to it that the other ranks should have their just ration of BW and P. The following Monday at 06.00 hours one-fifth of the camp were roused from their slumbers half an hour early for the pleasure of listening to me. A sergeant marched them smartly into an unheated nissen hut at 07.00 hours, told them they were to pay attention to what was said and be on the 3-tonners at 07.30 hours sharp.

I looked across the khaki sea of incredulous faces: incredulous that such a thing was actually happening to them. But the Crimean spirit was not yet dead and if there was no bloodshed on this particular Surge of the Ordnance Brigade as they went to the waiting 3-tonners, it was, perhaps, because I gave to the Beveridge Report a little more than Sir William originally intended.

I stayed behind for a little while after they'd gone straightening chairs in a sort of automatic reflex action to recover as much of my composure as possible. This performance was to be repeated every morning that week and beyond.

Finally, I went to the mess for breakfast.

'Breakfasts are finished,' the cook in charge said.

When I'd gone earlier, before I tried unsuccessfully to light the fire in the hut, I was told I was too soon, breakfast hadn't started. Recognizing the situation, I drank some tepid tea and ate the remains of the bread and butter.

I had some money for outside lecturers and for craft and other materials at my disposal. I spent two days making enquiries about possible lecturers/instructors in the area. I had already made arrangements about the materials.

On the Friday morning, I went down to the depot and cautiously entered the building where I met two agreeable young men.

'This is my lucky day,' I said. 'Finding two young men like you so soon. I've come to talk about the education programme we're setting up here and I'm sure you're interested. There'll. . . .'

They looked at each other ever so briefly.

'Well, yes,' the first man said, 'we are interested, but the truth is, as far as I'm concerned, I really only want to learn one thing. Ancient Hebrew. I'm not really interested in anything else.'

'And me,' said his friend. 'I want to learn Sumerian.'

'I can hardly believe my ears,' I said in wonder. 'Hebrew. Sumerian. I never dreamed I'd be so lucky. I knew as soon as I saw you I'd picked the right people. You're on Monday's schedule, aren't you? Well. I studied both Hebrew and Sumerian. Yes. Isn't it amazing? So on Monday morning stay back after the others and we'll start your class. I can't tell you how thrilled I am.' And with that I got out quick.

I went straight to the library and finally got a children's encyclopedia and turned to the language bit. From it I wrote a short history of the Hebrews and one of the Sumerians where writing began, adding that I felt sure they would want to read the greatest books each language had to offer – the Bible in the original Hebrew and the early tablets on book-keeping the Sumerians made so long ago.

I drew an ancient Sumerian tablet with bookkeeping records and also made a table of signs that stood for words, a table of numbers and a table of signs that showed the beginning of cuniform writing. I also, in case I needed more material, showed in picture form how the word developed from a picture to a cuniform mark.

The Hebrews, I said, did not use vowels. To get my student used to this I wrote a passage in English without vowels to be written out in full. I also drew some Hebrew characters to be copied.

On Monday morning I gave them a special smile which must have curled them up inside. I had won my battle with the stove but only at the cost of an hour's sleep. After the BW and P talk was over I called the two men out and took them across the camp to two rooms I'd already prepared and made as comfortable as possible. I put one in each room and gave each the history I'd prepared, then went between rooms, talking about the Hebrews/Sumerians and testing the work they'd done hitherto. I'd arranged with a nearby admin. sergeant to provide coffee, 9 o'clockish, and very glad I was to see it.

'You may as well have your coffee together,' I said, 'when you can talk over this morning's efforts and I'll be in the other room preparing the work for the next session.'

'How . . . er . . . how long does it go on for?' one man said.

'Well, really,' I said, 'it should last for five and a half hours, that is six hours less half an hour for BW and P. But to begin with we'll spend a lot less time on the subject till you've really got the hang of things, so there's a tilly coming at 10.00 hours to take you to the depot.'

When I got back with burning zeal and enthusiasm lighting my eyes like a beacon, the spokesman said, 'Er . . . er. We've . . . er . . . been thinking. We've enjoyed the lesson, but though . . . it's . . . er . . . interesting . . . Hebrew isn't very useful is it? Nobody bothers with it now. What other classes can we come to?'

'Woodwork,' I said. 'Cookery, leatherwork, maths, French, or really anything else you fancy.'

'Woodwork would be nice,' they said.

'Right. Next Monday, woodwork it is.'

The following morning when I went to the mess for my stewed tea and bread the cook came out. 'What'll it be?' he said. 'Fried eggs, tomatoes, a little bit of bacon, eh? And fresh tea or coffee?'

The following day the half-hour early rising was cancelled. The infant education programme was getting shakily to its feet.

After consultation with those in authority, it was decided that one-fifth of the camp would stand down every morning. Classes would begin 07.30 hours and go on till midday when 3-tonners would take them all back to the depot. It wasn't six hours a week but it was a lot better than nothing.

About two months later we had an inspection. By this time we had classes in cookery, dressmaking, English, maths, French, leatherwork, hairdressing, woodwork, economics, art and musical appreciation. Finally, the Brass Hat got to us and I joined in at the tail end of his entourage. At the first class, hairdressing, he asked a question. The CO passed it on to the education officer who passed it on to me, and I sent the answer back through the same channels, in reverse. At the next stop the Brass Hat said, 'I think we'll let the Sergeant speak for herself,' and I told him, as we went round, how the timetable worked out, how many we had taking each course, who the teacher was etc.

Two days later I was sent for and informed I'd been made up to warrant officer. Still in a daze I packed and was taken in a tilly to HQ where, after I'd been shown to my quarters and had my kit dumped, I met up with the junior commander i/c education.

'It'll cut out a lot of time,' she said, 'if we get on first-name terms straight away. My name's Mary. And yours?'

'Linda,' I managed to articulate.

'Now I'll show you the fount of education itself before we go on a wider tour of inspection,' she said and led the way to a construction whereon was writ the inscription

W.O. M.L. Summers
Education

and, with what sacrilege I can scarce describe, she went forward and pushed her way in as if she were going through a common door made of mean wood into a mediocre room of no architectural significance whatsoever, instead of reverently pausing before an inscription enshrined in letters of gold upon a portal made of the finest cedarwood into a chamber hung with rich tapestries and purest silks with a floor of rare marble leading up to a desk fashioned from fragrant sandalwood inlaid with gold and precious stones – silver not being thought worthy under the circumstances.

'And now,' Mary went on while I struggled to gain composure, 'we'll leave this seat of learning behind for the day and go to town where I'll take you to a place that serves coffee – real coffee. Out of this world! Altogether out of this world.'

Sorrows, they say, never come singly. Neither do joys it seems. At the same time I had two letters, one offering me a place in university, the other offering a place in teachers' training college.

I wanted to go home. I wanted to share this marvellous news with my family. I also wanted to visit the Co-op, for I was still an employee of theirs and I had a loyalty towards them.

I had another decision to make. Peter, my boyfriend, was due for demobilization shortly and he wanted us to settle down. Also, I had been offered a place at Co-operative College, not so many years ago the height of my ambition. So I had several boats waiting to take me further on my journey. Some of them would have to be burned, but which?

Two days later, I travelled up to Newcastle overnight, arriving in Central Station at about 6 a.m. I bought an early morning paper and went to one of the big hotels.

'I'm breaking my journey,' I said to the night porter. 'I'd like tea now, the use of a bathroom and breakfast at about a 7.45.'

At 9 o'clock, bathed, wearing clean linen and fed, I boarded the bus for Ashington, the one that would take me to the bus station.

As the bus drew into the station, I got off slowly to savour the sweetness of the moment and, as I stepped down, I almost bumped into a woman I knew. She stood stock still and stared at me in surprise.

'What!' she said, 'Are you still here? How long leave do you get? Our Mary hardly ever gets home, she works that hard. Mind but she's doing well is our Mary. But she always had more about her than most. They just never understood her at that school. Her officer thinks the world of her. Thinks the world of her he does. If it had been left to her officers she would have been a sergeant by now. But it's a hard lot she's in with. Have ye got yourself a lad yet?'

'Well, no, not really . . . I. . . .'

'No? Surely with all them lads coming back there's one that has a bit fancy for you. No? Well, mind. Don't leave it too late or you'll be left with the cleft stick. Our Mary has a lad. What a nice lad he is! We couldn't have wished forra nicer. He cames off a good family. Well, I'll have to get away. Nice to have seen ye and had your crack. Aa'll tell Mary when I write. When did ye say ye were goin' back?'

'Tonight.'

'Well, at least you've had a good holiday. My some folks has all the luck. Still, I suppose your mother was pleased to see ye. Tarra well. Look after yourself.'

I nodded and smiled and made my way to the Arcade, to the general office, there to ask if I might see the secretary. He was busy and I had to wait a while. When he was able to see me I went to his office and acquainted him with the fact that I had several choices before me regarding my future career. If it was possible, I said, I would like to serve the society in some way. I was, after all, still their employee. I wondered if there was any future in the society for me in the field of Education.

He said there wasn't but if anything cropped up he would let me know. In the meantime would I write to the society resigning my position if I didn't intend to return, as he had been given to understand such was the case. I said I would and left.

At Arrowsmiths I stopped and looked at the people now going about their business in the street. Like everywhere else, Ashington, after nearly six years of war, was beginning to look shabby, but, in spite of that, there was a buoyancy, a sense of well-being and prosperity in the air.

I, too, had changed. The dreams and ambitions, conflicts and confusions were still there but they had taken on a different aspect. I thought hard enough, but not always constructively. After my interview with Mr Reilly, I had been liberated. Life in any enclosed community allows for flowering only within prescribed bounds – I had to accept the doctrine and way of life handed down. It was from this I thought I'd been liberated. Yet, I belonged here and I had no desire whatever to estrange myself from my family and the friends of my childhood and adolescence. Northumberland with all its beauty had always been my home. But a returning would now be a personal choice. I had no obligations to settle in Ashington or anywhere else.

I wanted to teach. I wanted to be part of this new Education Act as soon as possible. And I wanted to teach here in the north-east. Also, I wanted a degree. But if I went to university it would take three years at least. At training college it would take much less time and I could carry on with what I was doing (I had already done inter arts) and get my degree that way through a correspondence course. Also, I wouldn't marry. Not yet at any rate.

Perhaps the thing that influenced me most in the university/college debate was the factor I did not consciously acknowledge, namely, I was over 21. By the time I had finished my course at university I would be in my late twenties. And that for a girl was 'old', too old.

So perhaps I was not nearly as liberated as I thought. I still acknowledged the 21 deadline and the possibility of being left 'on the shelf'.

For many years I was to speculate on whether or not I made a wise decision that day. Wise or not, my mind was made up. I went home.

17. *Valete*

The rest is sunshine with only a few shadows, and those fleeting.

There is no drama in happiness. It rarely makes the headlines. The things that go wrong, the things people do that we don't approve of, make the interesting reading. Even in love stories the fact that the lovers are clasped in each other's arms and are going to live happily ever after is left to the very last sentence. After that there's no more to be said. There's not a great deal of interest where there's no trouble.

What, then, made this period such a happy one for me? The happiness existed almost entirely in the work aspect of my life. For many reasons, work-wise, this was the best part of a long and varied working life.

What made it so? First of all, I suppose, there was the set-up. I was in charge of a fair area of units and an education centre. Over me were two officers, the first of whom was the nominal officer in the unit where I was officially stationed. All officers are given nominal charge of specific areas such as entertainment and education. The officer, in this case Mary, became a friend and we were on first-name terms. She really had no specific qualifications in this field. The other officer whom I shall call Junior Commander Brown, had. She was in the Army Education Corps (still not Royal). She was in overall charge of all those in the AEC but, that aside, my position was autonomous. I was responsible for helping to set up units similar to the one I'd set up when I first qualified for entry into the AEC and, thereafter, to help in improving the running thereof.

Also, now that education for the troops was becoming established, those who attended the courses had actually come to learn. There was a fairly wide choice of subjects so that a wide variety of tastes was catered for. And we had begun to prepare students for external examinations. I did not myself take classes on a regular basis but I was often asked to be a guest lecturer both on sites or units, and outside to civilian groups such as rural institutes and even schools. The things I enjoyed doing most and for which I was in constant demand, were discussions. These were always over subscribed and it was a case of first come, first served. The titles of some discussion subjects still survive.

A man's attitude to life is reflected in his attitude to women.

The army obscures the individual.

The army does things the hard way regardless.

Be good, sweet maid.

The modern miss is the future mistress.

The recipe for success.

Should ATS be sent over to Germany at the end of the war so that our soldiers do not fraternize with the frauleins?

Another adjunct to my well-being as far as work was concerned at this time was I had no other responsibilities. I did not have to prepare food or look after my room or have any form of domestic responsibility. I came and went as I pleased or the requirements of my job dictated. There was no one to tell me I must go to bed at such and such an hour and rise at another hour; no one to insist when the light went out and when it might be put on again. If, for some reason, I wished to work undisturbed even till the early hours of the morning, then this I could do as long as my health stood up to it.

Added to all this, the AEC authorities where I was pursued a policy which I thought excellent in the extreme. Once a month all AEC personnel in the area met in Nottingham for a day at least, but it could be extended to a weekend. In my case it always was. The most important day was Saturday when we met for coffee and talked about our various experiences, difficulties and triumphs during the preceding month. After lunch, one of us gave a short talk on some aspect of education. We did this on a rota system.

As well as these monthly meetings we had periodical sessions lasting a week at the extra mural departments of one or other of the universities. What a catharsis these occasions proved to be! Guest speakers were engaged, discussions were legion, visits to the theatre and to concerts (music) were arranged. I, at least, left these occasions refreshed and invigorated. They were a sort of health farm for educationalists.

And, overall, was the wonder that never left me – that I had actually achieved my goal. There had been times when I thought I was destined to be part of the flotsam of army life, rising and falling with the tide, helpless to do other, so that the getting there was even more wonderful. In fact I had gone further than I had thought possible and the result was sweet to my taste.

And yet, I was still the same person, growing into the job before me as I had earlier grown into becoming a grocer, and, later, a number one. What changed was not me so much as the attitude of others towards me, or rather, towards the office I held. Only a few months previously I had been an all-purpose lance-corporal with diminishing prospects and no fixed abode. Now I was addressed as ma'am.

Work apart, it was a carefree time. Parties, spontaneous and otherwise were the order of the day. One had freedom to carry out whims – a sudden desire on a Sunday afternoon to take a portable gramophone to some nearby green spot and lie back gazing up at the blue overhead and the puffy, fluffy white cottonwool clouds that occasionally floated by, heightening the lazy, hazy day with its background of music.

And there were the demob. parties. One such party was a grand fancy-dress ball held at one of the camps. I went as Prince Charming in a black velvet hat with trailing white feathers, frilly white blouse, black velvet brief pants, black silk tights, black high heeled shoes and long black cane with silver top. I got first prize. A friend dressed as Princess Charming also got a prize. She was one of those for whom the party had been arranged, she and her boyfriend, a captain. Everyone knew about their romance but it had been kept 'secret' because, had it come out into the open, they would have been fraternizing and Jane would have been posted.

Now, not only could they declare their love, they announced their engagement. We clapped and cheered them, danced round them as they stood flushed with happiness in the centre of the ring and sang 'For They are Jolly Good Fellows' after which, hand-in-hand they left the party and the army. I must confess that, as I watched them go in the aura of their love for each other, a shadow passed over me and I thought, 'Why not me?' But it passed. I had so much jam I could not complain if sometimes I found the bread a little thick.

Then my summons came. In less than a month I would be a student at a college in Newcastle. I began to clear my desk.

My demob party gathered momentum throughout my penultimate day of service career and went on through the night. At 06.00 hours we separated to make our toilets, and change and reassemble for breakfast. After breakfast they went with me to the station. I hung out of the window and as the train gave its first jerking, movement forward, the crowd that had come to see me off started to sing,

> 'Will ye no come back again?
> Will ye no come back again?
> Better loved ye canna be.
> Will ye no come back again?'

Tears streamed down my cheeks. In spite of that, the story had a happy ending.